Linda
Campbell
(5388)

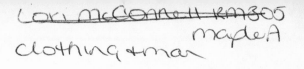

2820

Essentials of Textiles

Essentials of Textiles

Marjory L. Joseph
California State University, Northridge

Holt, Rinehart and Winston
New York   Chicago   San Francisco   Atlanta
Dallas   Montreal   Toronto   London   Sydney

To W.D.J. and N.J.J.

Editor   Rita Gilbert
Picture editor   Joan Curtis
Senior project editor   Lester A. Sheinis
Project editor   Kristin Camitta
Production manager   Sandra Baker
Designer   Marlene Rothkin Vine

Library of Congress Cataloging in Publication Data

Joseph, Marjory L.
Essentials of textiles.

1. Textile industry.   2. Textile fabrics.
3. Textile fibers.   I. Title.
TS1445.J63   677   75-33710

ISBN: 0-03-086297-3

Preface

Essentials of Textiles is designed for students and for general readers who wish to have a fundamental understanding of textiles—their nature, selection, use, and care. While based on *Introductory Textile Science* (Holt, Rinehart and Winston, 2d edition, 1972), this new text has been written specifically for students who do not intend to make textiles their major subject of study, as well as for those readers who have little or no background in the sciences. To that end I have avoided the more advanced chemical aspects of textile science, concentrating instead on the kinds of information that will help the reader to become an intelligent consumer of textile products.

My primary goals in writing *Essentials of Textiles* were:
- To stimulate the reader's desire to recognize and appreciate textile fabrics and products.
- To establish guides that will help the student in the selection, use, and care of textile products.
- To facilitate an understanding of the interrelationships among fibers, yarns, fabric structures, finishes, and coloring agents; and to indicate the complexity of these relationships in terms of the selection, use, care, and appreciation of textile products.

Essentials of Textiles has been organized sequentially, so that the student can better visualize the complete fiber-to-product cycle. The text begins with a general introduction to fiber theory and classification, as well as methods for identifying specific fibers. Part II discusses the various natural and man-made fibers individually, with attention given to their production, properties, and major applications. Part III addresses the structure of yarns; Part IV, the different means of fabric construction. Types of finishes and methods of color introduction—so vital to an understanding of textile performance—form the subject of Part V. Part VI concludes the text with a summary of factors to consider in the selection and care of textiles. Conversion tables following the text provide a ready reference for metric equivalents.

Illustrations of textile products and processes are very important to an understanding of the field, particularly for those who are unable to visit manufacturing plants. Consequently, the text is supported by more than three hundred photographs and line drawings that show every aspect of textiles, from fiber production to end-use. A series of 22 full-color plates demonstrates those aspects associated with dyeing and printing.

The textile industry is one of the most dynamic in the world, with new fibers, processes, and refinements being introduced constantly. In *Essentials of Textiles* I have attempted to offer the reader the most up-to-date information regarding textile fibers and their modifications—on yarn manufacture, fabric construction, textile finishes and colors. Equally important from the consumer's point of view is an awareness of laws and regulations that affect the textile industry. It is to be hoped that, armed with this knowledge, the consumer will be better able to choose and care for the myriad textile products that form an integral part of contemporary life.

Granada Hills, California   M.L.J.
December 1975

Contents

Introduction 1

Textile fibers and their use predate recorded history. Archeological evidence indicates that textiles of fine quality were made thousands of years before written records cite their existence. The early history of textile fibers and fabrics has been determined by such archeological finds as spinning whorls, distaff and loom weights, and fragments of fabrics found in such locations as the Swiss lake regions and Egyptian tombs. Tales told by parents to children from generation to generation, designs and evidence of fabrics used in planning or constructing some pottery wares, and, eventually, written records further testify to the early importance of fabrics. Many readers may remember looms in the homes of grandparents, in museums, or in historic houses. Moreover, the current interest in all the fiber crafts has led to the introduction of construction devices—from the simple frame to the complicated floor loom—in many contemporary homes. Some individuals weave as a hobby or for relaxation, but a growing number have attained a professional level of competence.

The history of textiles is an integral part of the history of civilization. The legendary fig leaf of the Garden of Eden was supplanted by textile body coverings, and textiles also assumed a place of importance in the home. Early civilizations possessed both ingenuity and a desire to enhance

Figure 1.1 Tapestry-woven rug with lotus pattern, from the tomb of Kha, Thebes. 18th Dynasty (c. 14th century B.C.). Linen. (*Museo Egizio, Turin*)

appearance and environment. These factors contributed, over the centuries, to the development of complicated fabrics and ultimately to enormous technological expansion.

All early fibers derived from plant or animal life. Wool, flax (linen), cotton, and silk were the most important. Sometime in the early history of textiles, asbestos, a mineral matter, was introduced. While asbestos never attained the popularity of the other fibers, it has remained valuable for selected applications. Historical records indicate that, in remote ages, plant and animal fibers were used with a minimum amount of processing. Most early fabrics probably were made by a simple plain weave (one-up-one-down) interlacing of groups of fibers and yarns or by knotting or plaiting groups of fibers, grasses, or other raw materials.

Spinning and weaving seem to have emerged during the Stone Ages. Stone Age peoples wrapped animal furs around themselves as body covering, but whether this was for warmth, modesty, prestige, status, decoration, or combinations of these factors remains a topic of conjecture. Nonetheless, as techniques for fastening these skins together became more sophisticated, clothing was created; and, as people began to appreciate the resultant warmth and decoration—as well as, perhaps, prestige and status—the integration of fabrics with daily life gained impetus. Evidence suggests that weaving developed as part of the process of interlacing branches and leaves in the construction of shelters. Eventually, primitive peoples learned to spin yarn from the available fibers and to weave, or interlace, these yarns to form cloth.

The Industrial Revolution of the 18th and 19th centuries transferred the processing of fibers and manufacture of fabrics from the home and small cottage shop to the factory. Mechanization gained importance, and gradually the textile industry expanded. As processing equipment and techniques were developed and as machine power replaced hand power, the use of cotton, wool, linen, and silk increased. Cotton and wool were especially affected; their growth and production became the concerns of governments throughout the world. Tariffs were levied, wars fought, and regimes toppled because of the political, social, and economic pressures that accompanied industrial advances in the production, marketing, and application of textiles.

Until the 20th century, the textile industry depended upon the sources and forces of nature for all fibers. Rayon, the first manufactured fiber, was developed, marketed, and made into a practical reality in the early 1900s, followed in the 1920s by cellulose acetate. Since the late 1930s—and especially since the second World War—scientists have produced dozens of new fibers, with many variants of each type. Developments in fibers, fabrics, finishes, and other textile processing techniques have made greater advances in the past fifty years than in the prior five thousand years of recorded history.

The decades of the sixties and seventies have brought major changes in manufacturing processes and equipment involved with the production of yarns and fabrics. Second-, third-, and even fourth-generation developments in man-made fibers have altered behavior, processing, appearance,

Figure 1.2 Sumerian statue of a priest, from Khafaje. Early Dynastic Period (c. 3000–2340 B.C.). (*University Museum, Philadelphia*)

Figure 1.3 Early spinning mill, 1835. (*Radio Times Hulton Picture Library*)

use, and care of these products. Research in chemical finishing of fibers and fabrics, as well as in color choice, application, and durability, are providing the consumer with products that meet actual and felt needs.

Textile fibers have served for many things, and new applications for these "building blocks" are being found continually. Clothing, home furnishing materials, and domestics represent the most common applications, but fibers are also important in the building trades; are chosen for insulation in appliances; provide industry with such products as filter cloths, pulley belts, and conveyor belts; appear in all forms of transportation; in fact touch upon nearly every type of activity or situation conceivable, including the conquest of space and exploration on the moon.

The word *textile* comes from the Latin *textilis* and from the verb *texere,* which means "to weave." Today, a *textile* is freely defined as *any product made from fibers,* and the name is applied to nonwoven fabrics, knitted fabrics, and all special fabric constructions in addition to woven goods. The term *textile fiber* refers to *any product capable of being woven or otherwise made into fabrics.*

The textile industry is one of the largest in the world. If all facets of this vast economic and industrial giant are considered, it probably involves more people and more money than any other industry. Even if we limit its scope to the growth, production, manufacture, and processing of fibers to fabrics, the textile industry still ranks among those at the top in terms of both workers and dollar value.

Production and consumption of fibers in the United States and in the world have increased at a tremendous rate. Table 1.1 cites the per-capita consumption of fibers in pounds for several years. While per-capita consumption was higher in 1968 than in 1969, and higher in 1973 than in 1974, the change is relatively small, and the overall pattern for the

Table 1.1 United States Civilian Per-Capita Consumption of Fibers in Pounds[a]

Year	Man-Made Fibers	Cotton	Wool	Total
1950	9.5	29.3	4.5	43.3
1955	11.0	25.4	3.3	39.7
1960	10.0	23.3	3.4	36.7
1962	12.7	22.9	3.4	39.0
1964	16.2	22.5	3.0	41.7
1966	20.2	25.1	2.9	48.2
1968	26.6	22.0	2.6	51.2
1969	27.8	20.6	2.3	50.7
1970	27.7	19.8	1.7	49.2
1971	33.0	20.5	1.3	54.8
1972	37.7	20.0	1.3	59.0
1973	42.0	18.5	1.0	61.5
1974	36.2	16.1	0.7	53.0

[a]Adapted from *Textile Organon.*

sixties and seventies indicates a gradual increase in the unit or individual consumption of fibers. This growth has occurred despite the trend to lighter fibers that produce more yardage at less weight per yard than older fibers such as cotton, wool, linen, and rayon.

Total consumption of fibers in the United States, as well as total production and consumption of fibers in the world (Table 1.2), has increased in part as a result of higher per-capita consumption and in part because of the population explosion in the late 1960s. These figures should indicate clearly the significance of textile fibers and products to both the national and the international economy.

In addition to the economic factors, textile fibers and fabrics are important for their aesthetic properties. The constant search for new and different fabrics reflects an innate desire in most people for attractive surroundings and colorful, decorative apparel. Fabrics must be fashioned in innovative ways to form the many textile products found in the environment.

The modern consumer also wants fabrics to be comfortable and to require a minimum amount of care. New fibers, combinations of fibers, techniques of fabric structure, and chemical finishing methods aid in providing the consumer with easy-care textiles.

Why is a knowledge of textiles of value to all consumers? There is no brief answer to such a question, and some may argue that not everyone will find it of value. However, every individual normally is exposed to textile products in various forms and should be concerned with their selection, use, and maintenance. This book will attempt to provide the reader with basic information that should make decision-making about

Table 1.2   World Production of Man-Made Fibers, Cotton, Wool, and Silk[a]
Data in millions of pounds. Percentage of total in parentheses.

Year	Man-Made Fibers		Cotton	Raw Wool	Silk	Grand Total
	Rayon and Acetate	Noncellulosic				
1950	3553 (17)	153 (*)	14,654 (71)	2330 (11)	42 (*)	20,732
1955	5030 (17)	587 (02)	20,926 (71)	2789 (10)	64 (*)	29,389
1960	5749 (17)	1548 (05)	22,295 (68)	3225 (10)	68 (*)	32,885
1962	6315 (18)	2381 (07)	23,052 (66)	3257 (09)	73 (*)	35,078
1964	7245 (18)	3728 (10)	24,930 (64)	3263 (08)	72 (*)	39,238
1966	7370 (19)	5473 (14)	23,274 (59)	3387 (09)	78 (*)	39,580
1968	7776 (17)	8336 (18)	25,629 (56)	3537 (08)	83 (*)	45,372
1969	7837 (17)	9683 (21)	24,820 (54)	3548 (08)	84 (*)	45,972
1970	7573 (16)	10,871 (23)	24,947 (53)	3499 (08)	83 (*)	46,973
1971	7590 (14)	12,352 (24)	28,201 (53)	3433 (08)	90 (*)	51,666
1972	7837 (14)	14,041 (25)	29,493 (53)	3206 (07)	93 (*)	54,670
1973	8061 (14)	16,805 (29)	29,972 (51)	3129 (06)	97 (*)	58,064
1974	7734 (13)	16,435 (28)	29,972 (52)	3259 (07)	99 (*)	57,499

[a] Adapted from *Textile Organon*.
*Less than 1%.

the selection, use, and care of textiles an easy, enjoyable, and satisfying task.

Textile products are characterized by properties, components, or definitive parts. These include:

fiber or fibers, type and properties
fiber arrangement and/or yarn structure
fabric structure
color—type and method of application
finish—type, durability, method of application
product assembly—how the fabric is formed into an end-use product

All fabrics are composed of fibers, some type of fiber arrangement, and some type of fabric structure. Many have the fibers arranged into yarn structure, and most provide for some type of color application and/or finishing processes. Whenever textiles are formed into end-use products, the concept of product fabrication becomes part of the overall process. End-use manufacture involves additional characteristics that are not included specifically in this text. The remaining fabric properties—fiber, fiber arrangement or yarn structure, fabric structure, color, and finish—receive detailed treatment, with the emphasis placed on the ways in which various textile characteristics influence the consumer's decisions about selection, use, and care.

Part I of this book discusses general information related to textile fibers. The remainder has been arranged in the normal order of manufacturing steps involved in production of usable textile fabrics. Part II is devoted to a discussion of specific textile fibers with emphasis placed on properties important to consumers. It includes a brief look at the history of natural fibers and the background of man-made fibers. Part III deals with yarn structure, Part IV with fabric structure. Part V explains finishing procedures and color application. A final chapter is aimed at the end-use of fabrics and includes information that should be helpful to the concerned consumer.

Fiber Theory and Classification

As the textile industry has grown, a science has evolved—one that, like any other discipline, has its own language, terminology, and methods of categorization. The scope of textile knowledge and technology has expanded at a fantastic rate in this century, so it has been necessary to refine the established definitions and classes, to sharpen the tools of the trade, so to speak. The next three chapters explain many of the descriptive terms that are used in textile science and outline a basic system of classification that will help the consumer cope with the myriad textile fibers available today.

Fiber Theory

Fibers are the building blocks with which textile yarns and fabrics are created. Textile fibers appear in natural sources such as seed pods (cotton), animal hair (wool), or plant stems (linen). They can be manufactured from natural fibrous materials such as wood pulp (rayon), or synthesized from chemicals with no resemblance to fibrous forms (nylon, polyester).

Fiber Properties

In order to qualify for use as a textile fiber, a material must possess certain essential properties or characteristics. These primary properties include *high length-to-breadth (width) ratio, tenacity* or adequate strength, *flexibility* or pliability, cohesiveness or *spinning quality,* and *uniformity.* Secondary properties are those that are desirable but not essential. Often, their major role consists of increasing consumer satisfaction with the ultimate fabric. Characteristics in this group include *physical shape, specific gravity, luster, moisture regain, elastic recovery, elongation, resilience, thermal behavior, resist-*

ance to biological organisms, and *resistance to chemicals* and other environmental conditions. The following discussion includes definitions and brief descriptions of these properties.

Primary Fiber Properties

High Length-to-Width Ratio   Fibers must be considerably longer than they are wide to permit processing into yarns and fabrics. This quality is referred to as a high *length-to-width* or *length-to-breadth ratio.* Since the property is essential for fabrication, we can assume that all fibers on the market automatically possess an adequate length-to-width ratio.

Tenacity   While strength varies among different kinds of fibers, it must always be sufficient to withstand chemical and machine processing of the fibers as well as to provide durability in the end-product. Weak fibers, unless there are compensating properties, will result in textile products that break apart at an early stage of service.

Flexibility   Fibers must be bendable, pliable, or flexible if they are to be made into yarns and fabrics that can be creased, that have the quality of drapability and the capacity to move with the body, that "give" when walked or sat upon, and that permit freedom of movement. Many substances in nature resemble fibrous forms, but because they are stiff or brittle, they do not make practical textile fibers.

It is generally accepted that a fiber must flex repeatedly in order to be classified as pliable. Fibers of different types vary in their degree of pliability. Relative pliability determines the ease with which fibers, yarns, fabrics, and end-use items will bend or give; it is important in fabric durability and, therefore, in end-use choice.

Spinning Quality or Cohesiveness   Cohesiveness can best be described as the ability of fibers to stick together during fiber arranging or yarn manufacturing processes. The cohesiveness of fibers may be due to the longitudinal contour or the cross-section shape that enables them to fit together and adhere to each other, or it may result from the surface or skin structure of the fibers, which causes them to stick together. When fiber shape and surface are inappropriate, the cohesive quality can be achieved by using filament fibers, which twist easily into yarn. Fiber length is then considered the equivalent of cohesiveness. Texturizing—a recent development—builds coils, zigzags, or other surface shaping and contributes to cohesiveness. In this technique the term *spinning quality* is used as a substitute for cohesiveness.

The spinning quality of a fiber may be seen in such characteristics as yarn fineness, fabric thickness, snagging or roughening of surface texture, appearance, and durability. Without cohesiveness or spinning quality, fibers would not hold together properly, and consumers would become unhappy with their purchase.

Uniformity   For the processing of yarns it is important that fibers be similar in length and width, in spinning quality, and in flexibility. Uniformity will produce even yarns and, ultimately, provide fabrics of uniform appearance that give relatively consistent service.

Consumers may not be as aware of primary properties as they are of secondary ones, because the latter produce a wider variation in product characteristics. Since primary properties are essential, products lacking them in an adequate degree cannot be converted into commercially important textiles. Nevertheless, the consumer should be familiar and concerned with these basic properties inasmuch as they determine product behavior.

Secondary Properties

Secondary characteristics vary among different fiber types and among modifications within the types. They provide a basis for describing and classifying fibers and are important to the consumer as determinants of end-product quality. It must be noted that finishing processes can affect secondary properties in some fibers. When desirable characteristics are absent or of a low level, finishing techniques can introduce or improve them. Manufacturers can also modify, alter, or eliminate undesirable properties.

Physical Shape   In addition to the high length-to-breadth ratio, the shape of a fiber includes such factors as average length, surface contour, surface irregularities, and cross section. These properties serve as the basis for a description of both the macroscopic (low magnification) and microscopic (high magnification) appearance of a fiber. They are responsible for certain differences in yarn and fabric properties important to consumers and will be discussed in later sections.

Specific Gravity   The specific gravity of a fiber indicates the *density* relative to that of water. Density measurements for comparison are made at 4°C (39°F). The density of water at that temperature is 1.

The differences among fibers in terms of specific gravity are reflected in such characteristics as fabric weight for identically constructed fabrics. Fabrics composed of fibers such as nylon or acrylic (with low density) will be lighter than fabrics of cotton or rayon (with high density), provided all other factors are identical.

It is interesting to note that fibers with a specific gravity of less than 1 will float on water. For these products special consideration may be required in the choice of laundering techniques.

Luster   Luster refers to the gloss or shine that a fiber possesses. It depends upon the amount of light reflected by a fiber and determines the fiber's natural brightness or dullness. Among natural fibers, silk inherently has a high luster, cotton a low luster. In manufactured fibers it is possible to control the degree of luster, either raising it or reducing it by means of added pigments or other modifying processes. The development of fabrics with varying degrees of luster is a highly desirable improvement for consumers, since it provides wider aesthetic choices.

Moisture Regain and Moisture Absorption Most textile fibers have a certain amount of water as an integral part of their structure. This water is called *moisture regain* and is expressed as a percentage of the weight of the moisture-free fiber.

The terms moisture regain and moisture absorption are sometimes used synonymously. However, *moisture absorption* frequently indicates the moisture absorbed at the saturation point.

Fibers with good moisture regain will accept dyes and finishes more readily than fibers with low regain. A few fibers have no regain at all, and this creates many problems in processing. The relation of fiber strength to moisture content is another important consideration in evaluating fiber behavior. Some fibers are stronger wet than dry, others are weaker when wet, and still others exhibit no change. Therefore, the care of textile products will be influenced by the strength-regain relationship. For example, a fiber with low wet strength, such as rayon, requires careful treatment during laundering to prevent undue stress on the wet fiber. Cotton, which has greater strength wet than dry, can be laundered with ease. Fibers with little or no regain will wash and dry quickly. Moisture regain also influences comfort. For fuller discussion of this factor, see Chapter 32.

Elastic Recovery and Elongation The amount of stretch or extension that a fiber will accept is referred to as elongation. *Breaking elongation* is the amount of stretch a fiber undergoes to the point where it breaks.

Elastic recovery indicates the percent of return from elongation to the original length. If a fiber returns to its original length from a specified (x) amount of attenuation or stretch, it is said to have 100 percent elastic recovery at x-percent elongation.

The amount of elongation is an important factor in evaluating elastic recovery. Some fibers with low elongation have excellent elastic recovery; however, this property is of little value because of the insignificant elongation. Thus, it becomes obvious that elongation and elasticity must be considered together in fiber evaluation. A fiber with extremely high elongation but medium to low elastic recovery might be undesirable, because the product would not return to size after extension. The effect of stretch and recovery, then, becomes highly important to consumers in that it governs shape retention, appearance, and comfort of textile products.

Resiliency The ability of a fiber to return to shape after compression, bending, creasing, or similar deformation is called resiliency. It helps to determine a fabric's crease recovery or smooth-surface retention. Resiliency is evaluated on a comparative basis from excellent to poor. Elastic recovery is a significant factor in the resiliency of a fiber or fabric, and, usually, good elastic recovery indicates good resiliency.

Flammability and Other Thermal Reactions   The chapters concerning specific fiber groups include sections devoted to thermal reactions. These sections are primarily descriptive and indicate the behavior of individual fibers at various temperatures.

Burning characteristics of fibers are of special concern to consumers. With the news media and testing groups, in effect, acting as consumer advocates, government agencies have begun to consider the safety of textiles. Federal legislation on flammability of textiles has been amended and is discussed in some detail later in this book (see page 231). Some state legislation actually exceeds federal specifications. Methods of testing are still a topic of controversy, and the care of flame-treated fabrics is creating major problems for consumers as well as for the textile industry. But flammability of textile products should be considered as one factor in any purchase by the consumer, and, of course, fibers with a low incidence of burning will be safer than fibers that burn quickly.

Other thermal characteristics of textiles are important in their use and care. These factors influence temperatures for laundering (both washing and drying), for ironing, and for dry cleaning.

Secondary properties and characteristics of fibers will be discussed in greater detail in specific fiber chapters. The importance of each characteristic and its influence upon selection, use, comfort, appearance, durability, and maintenance will be pinpointed. Discussion will include fiber reaction to chemicals, to environmental and climatic conditions, to microorganisms such as bacteria and fungi, and to insects.

A factor that plays a major part in the success or failure of a fiber is cost. The production and processing of a fiber must be sufficiently economical so that the final price of goods does not exceed the consumer's willingness or ability to pay. This does not prevent the expenditure of vast sums for research and development of new fibers, but it does tend to rule out the mass production of costly fibers. The same economic reality holds true for natural fibers. Wherever growth and processing costs result in exorbitantly expensive products, the competitive market will not support a successful sale.

Molecular Arrangement

Fiber molecules are polymers—large molecules produced by linking together many monomers, or small molecular units—and the molecules have a high length-to-width ratio just as does the fiber itself. One source describes a fiber molecule in comparative terms by stating that if a typical fiber molecule were $\frac{1}{8}$ inch in diameter, it would be 40 feet long.[1] Actually,

[1] "The Solid State of Polyethylene," *Scientific American,* Vol. 211, 5 (November 1964), p. 81.

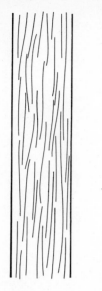

Figure 2.1 Schematic diagram illustrating highly oriented molecules within a fiber.

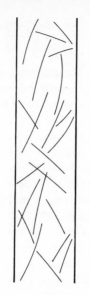

Figure 2.2 Schematic diagram illustrating molecules in a random or amorphous arrangement, with low orientation.

Figure 2.3 Schematic diagram illustrating molecules in a crystalline arrangement but not oriented with fiber axis.

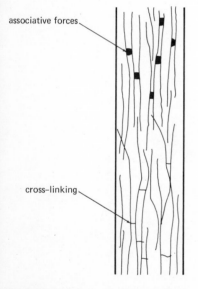

Figure 2.4 Schematic diagram illustrating associative forces and cross-linking between molecules.

of course, the fiber molecule is ultramicroscopic, but this example suggests the relation of length to width.

The arrangement of molecules within the fiber varies widely. They may be *highly oriented,* which means that they are parallel to each other and to the longitudinal axis of the fiber. Or the molecules may exhibit *low orientation,* which means that they lie in random arrangements. High orientation is associated with good fiber strength and low elongation, while low orientation tends to produce the opposite—low strength and high elongation. Other characteristics that are altered by the degree of orientation include absorbency, moisture regain, and flexibility. In the case of absorbency in particular, various problems encountered during dyeing and finishing are directly related to the orientation of the fibers.

Fiber
Classification

3

Systems of classification have been in use for hundreds of years. In the early stages of scientific development it became obvious that placing like items together made for increased understanding. When the study of textile fibers was new, a simple type of classification served—one based on a systematic arrangement of fibers into the categories of animal, vegetable, and mineral matter.

With the development of man-made fibers this classification became obsolete, and new systems had to be devised. It was apparent to those studying textiles that soon it would be practically impossible to remember all the properties and characteristics of each individual fiber. Thus, scientists reasoned that if fibers could be classified into like groups, a person could become acquainted with the general properties of each group and would then need to know only the special properties of individual fibers in order to select, use, and care for textile products intelligently.

Over the years, many systems of classification have been recommended. Some are no longer sufficiently discerning for the innumerable fibers on the market at the present time. Several older systems are still helpful for major divisions, but due to the complexity of the current fiber situation, it is now necessary to add selected subclassifications.

In 1960 the Textile Fiber Products Identification Act (TFPIA) became effective. This legislation requires that most textile products sold at retail have labels stating the textile fiber content. To reduce consumer confusion, the legislation established sixteen *generic,* or family, names for the grouping of all manufactured fibers of anticipated commercial value. A seventeenth term was designated that could be used for one fiber with special properties. Since then, four generic classifications have been added. In general, the fibers within a specific group possess the same basic properties and require the same care. Therefore, an up-to-date system of fiber classification should include these generic terms at least as a partial basis for fiber categorization.

Tables 3.1 and 3.2 present a workable system for classifying natural and man-made fibers. In Table 3.2 all generic terms are indicated with an asterisk and with initial lower-case letters. Most generic groups also include fibers that have trademark names under which special products are advertised. These trade names are capitalized.

The use of the terms *animal, vegetable,* and *mineral* in fiber classification has been challenged because there are differences between the behavior of vegetable cellulose and vegetable protein, both of which are employed in the manufacture of some man-made fibers. Furthermore, criticism has been directed at the fairly common division of natural and manufactured fibers as the only basis for classification.

The use of the terms *thermoplastic* and *nonthermoplastic*—meaning the ability or lack of ability of a substance to become soft upon application of

Table 3.1 Natural Fibers

A. cellulosic fibers
  1. seed hairs
    a. cotton
    b. kapok
  2. bast fibers
    a. flax
    b. ramie
    c. hemp
    d. jute
  3. leaf fibers
    a. abaca
    b. pineapple
    c. agave (sisal)
  4. nut husk fibers
    a. coir (coconut)
B. protein fibers
  1. animal-hair fibers

    a. wool
    b. specialty hair
      1. alpaca
      2. camel
      3. cashmere
      4. mohair
      5. vicuña
    c. fur fibers
      1. Angora rabbit
  2. animal secretion
    a. silk
      1. cultivated silk
      2. wild silk
    b. spider silk
C. mineral fiber
  1. asbestos
D. natural rubber

Table 3.2   Man-Made or Manufactured Fibers

A. man-made cellulosic fibers
  1. rayon*
    a. cuprammonium rayon
        Bemberg (currently
          not manufactured)
    b. viscose rayon
      1. regular and high
          tenacity rayon
        Avisco
        Coloray
        Enka
      2. high-wet-modulus
          rayon
        Avril
        Zantrel
B. man-made modified cellulosic
   fibers
  1. acetate*
    a. secondary acetate
        Celanese
        Celaperm (solution
          dyed)
        Chromspun (solution
          dyed)
        DuPont
        Estron
    b. triacetate**
        Arnel
C. man-made protein fibers
  1. azlon*
      Merinova
      Fibro
D. man-made noncellulosic fibers
  1. condensation polymer fibers
    a. nylon*
      1. type 6,6
        Antron
        Astroturf
        Blue "C"
        Cadon
        Cumuloft
        501
      2. type 6
        Caprolan
        Enka
        Touch (bicomponent)

  3. type 6T
  4. type 11
      Rilsan
  5. type 6,10
      Nylex
      Quill
  6. type not identified
      Qiana
      PACM
      Cantrece (bicompo-
        nent)
    b. aramid*
    c. polyester*
      Avlin
      Blue "C"
      Dacron
      Encron
      Fortrel
      Kodel
      Quintess
      Trevira
  2. addition polymer fibers
    a. anidex*
      ANIM 8
    b. acrylic*
      Acrilan
      Creslan
      Nomelle
      Orlon
      Sayelle
      Wintuk
      Zefran
    c. modacrylic*
      Dynel
      Verel (no longer in pro-
        duction)
      Kanekalon
    d. nytril*
      none currently manufac-
        tured in the U.S.
    e. olefin*
      1. polyethylene
        Tyvek

Table 3.2 Man-Made or Manufactured Fibers—*continued*

2. addition polymer fibers—
   continued
       2. polypropylene
         Herculon
         Marvess
         Polyloom
         Typar
         Vectra
     f. saran*
     g. vinal*
       Kuralon
       PVA
     h. vinyon*
       Rhovyl
     i. novoloid*
       Kynol
   3. elastomers
     a. spandex*
       Lycra
       Numa
       Unel
     b. rubber*
     c. lastrile**
E. man-made mineral fibers
   1. glass*
     Beta
     Fiberglas
     PPG

    2. metallic*
       Brunsmet
       Chromel R
       Lurex
F. other man-made fibers
   1. Alginate
   2. inorganic
     Avceram (carbon silica)
     Fiberfax (alumina silica)
     Lexan (polycarbonate)
     quartz fibers
     Thornel (graphite)
     Boron
     Sapphire
   3. unclassified
     A-Tell (polyethylene oxy-
       benzoate)
     PBI (polybenzimidazole)
     Raycelon (biconstituent;
       rayon + nylon)
     Source (biconstituent;
       nylon + polyester)
     Tricelon (biconstituent;
       nylon + acetate)
     Arnel-plus (biconstituent;
       nylon + triacetate)
     Teflon (tetrafluoroethylene)
     Monvelle (biconstituent;
       nylon + spandex)

*Generic terms as identified in the Textile Fiber Product Identification Act.
**Those terms that may be used as generic names when the fiber meets special requirements as cited in the TFPIA.

heat—has some merit in fiber classification, but since these terms fundamentally describe the properties of certain fibers, this distinction, too, may cause confusion and misinterpretation.

The system for classification used in this text is based upon the following:

1. The principal origin of the fiber. Fibers either occur as fibrous forms in nature or they are manufactured; thus, a scientific breakdown to indicate origin produces two groups: namely, the natural fibers (Table 3.1) and the man-made fibers (Table 3.2).
2. The general chemical type. Fibers are protein, cellulosic, mineral, or noncellulosic.

3. The generic term. The generic term, or family name, as specified in the Textile Fiber Products Identification Act, provides scientifically cogent bases for grouping like fibers.
4. The inclusion of common names or trade names of fibers. Many people are familiar with common names and trade names for fibers; therefore, examples of these should be included in any classification as a means of identifying the group name to the reader.

The examples below will clarify the classification method used and the way it meets the previously stated concepts related to fiber grouping:

		example	
1. the major origin of the fiber	natural	man-made
2. the general chemical type	cellulosic	man-made cellulosic
3. the general type or generic grouping	seed hair	rayon
4. specific fiber name	cotton	Avisco rayon

In using the classification charts, it is important to remember that specificity needs may vary with different groups of consumers. The list of fibers under each category is not complete. For example, there are many more bast fibers than those listed in Table 3.1. Specific fibers included are those that are considered commercially important, easily recognizable, and useful to consumers. Students wishing to study some of the less familiar fibers in greater detail will find additional data in references listed in the bibliography.

It should be noted that the TFPIA legislation used in the fiber classification of this text does not provide new names for natural fibers. Except for hair fibers, natural fibers are identified by their common name in labeling textile products. Legislation, as cited in the Wool Products Labeling Act, provides that all hair fibers may be labeled as "wool." However, the name of the actual animal, such as vicuña, has sufficient selling power so that products of this type usually are labeled by animal name or by a special name given to the fiber, such as mohair.

Due to the tremendous number of trademarked fibers available on the market, this part of the table is incomplete. Where the generic name is familiar, such as "rayon," the list of trademark names is sketchy. More complete listings will be found in standard reference works.[1]

There is and always will be some disagreement between fiber manufacturers and the Federal Trade Commission (FTC) regarding the group to which a fiber is assigned. This is especially true as new fibers are developed that might not fit into existing categories or that have sufficient variations so that the manufacturer would like a new generic group.

---

[1] Adeline A. Dembeck, *Guidebook to Man-Made Textile Fibers and Textured Yarns of the World,* 3d ed. (New York: United Piece Dye Works, 1967).

The original TFPIA provided for adding new generic classes when necessary. Four have been added in recent years: lastrile, anidex, aramid, and novoloid.

While the TFPIA requires that most textile products be labeled only with the generic name of the fiber, trademark names usually accompany the generic term as advertising for the manufacturer and as an attraction to the consumer. The required legislation is helpful, but it does not take the place of sound scientific knowledge. The consumer who can recognize fiber names and identify, classify, and evaluate fibers is qualified to make intelligent selection of fibers and fabrics and the proper decision concerning use and care of the textile product. The informed consumer has the advantage of understanding why fibers react as they do to physical, chemical, and biological stimuli. This, in turn, provides the foundation for intelligent selection, use, and care.

Fiber Identification 4

Qualitative identification of a fiber is difficult and may require several tests. It is not the intent of this book to list all possible tests nor even to include the common laboratory tests, but rather to discuss the methods used in determining general fiber categories, along with specific data on the use and care of fibers.

Much of the information presented here is in chart form. The discussion indicates general procedures for identification and suggests interpretation. Additional reactions and properties are cited in sections concerning specific fibers.

Consumers should find the ability to identify fibers extremely valuable. It may help in verifying label content, providing information for product care, and recognizing legitimate complaints about performance of a textile product.

Tests for Fiber Identification

The Burning Test

While the burning test is a good preliminary test, it does not identify fibers specifically. It does offer valuable data regarding appropriate care, however, and it indicates general fiber groupings. Problems arise when yarns or fabrics composed of two or more fibers are tested. The test will usually give the reaction of the fiber that burns most easily. But if a thermoplastic heat-sensitive fiber is involved, it might melt or withdraw from the flame and pull other fibers with it.

Although the procedure for the burning test is simple, care must be taken when working with open flames to prevent injury to people or damage to property. The following steps will provide guidance:

1. Select one or two yarns from the warp (lengthwise threads) of the fabric if woven; for knitted fabrics, unravel a few inches of yarn or cut a narrow sliver of fabric.
2. Untwist yarns so the fibers are in a loose mass.
3. Hold the loosened fibers in forceps (small tweezers), and move them toward the flame from the side.
4. Observe the reaction as they approach the flame.
5. Move them into the flame for one or two seconds and then pull them out, observing behavior all the while.
6. Notice any odor given off by the fiber during the burning or charring.
7. Observe ash or residue formed.
8. Repeat for the filling yarn (crosswise threads) if fabric is woven.

If fabric does not have a yarn structure or if it is impossible to remove yarns, a small sliver of the fabric can be used; but if more than one fiber is involved, the result may be misleading.

A caution about the burning test: Dyes and finishes may alter the flammability and the burning characteristics of a textile product. See Table 4.1 for typical reactions of common fibers to flame.

Microscopic Evaluation

It is possible to be quite specific in identification of some fibers through microscopic observations. For this test fibers should be mounted to obtain views of lengthwise dimensions or cross sections. Unfortunately, several of the man-made fibers are so similar that additional analysis may be required for positive identification.

Since most consumers will not have microscopes available, the technique has little value outside the laboratory. Also, this facet of fiber data does not play a part in use and care. It is, therefore, not discussed in depth in this book. However, the table of microscopic characteristics is included for reference (Table 4.2).

Table 4.1 Chart of Burning Characteristics of Fibers

Fiber	Approaching Flame	In Flame	Removed from Flame	Odor	Residue
natural cellulose					
cotton and flax	does not shrink away; ignites upon contact	burns quickly	continues burning; afterglow	similar to burning paper	light, feathery; light to charcoal gray in color
man-made cellulose					
rayon	does not shrink away; ignites upon contact	burns quickly	continues burning; afterglow	similar to burning paper	light, fluffy residue; very small amount
man-made modified cellulose					
acetate	fuses and melts away from flame; ignites quickly	burns quickly	continues to burn rapidly	acrid (hot vinegar)	irregular-shaped, hard, black bead
natural protein					
wool	curls away from flame	burns slowly	self-extinguishing	similar to burning hair	brittle, small black bead
silk	curls away from flame	burns slowly and sputters	usually self-extinguishing	similar to burning hair	beadlike, crushable, black
weighted silk	curls away from flame	burns slowly and sputters	usually self-extinguishing	similar to burning hair	the shape of fiber or fabric
man-made protein					
azlons	curls away from flame	burns slowly	self-extinguishing	similar to burning hair	brittle, small black bead
natural mineral					
asbestos	does not melt (safe fiber)	glows red if heat is sufficient	returns to original form	none	same as original
man-made mineral					
glass	will not burn	softens, glows red to orange	hardens; may change shape	none	hard, white bead
metallic	*pure* metal no reaction	glows red	hardens	none	skeleton outline
	coated metal melts, fuses and shrinks	burns according to behavior of coating		none	hard, black bead

Table 4.1   Chart of Burning Characteristics of Fibers—*continued*

Fiber	Approaching Flame	In Flame	Removed from Flame	Odor	Residue
man-made synthesized					
acrylic	fuses away from flame; melts; ignites readily	burns rapidly with hot flame and sputtering; melts	continues to burn and melt; hot molten polymer will drop off while burning	acrid	hard, black, irregular bead
modacrylic	fuses away from flame; melts (considered safe)	burns slowly if at all; does not feed a flame; melts	self-extinguishing	acrid, chemical odor	irregular, hard black bead
nylon	melts away from flame; shrinks, fuses	burns slowly with melting	self-extinguishing	celery	hard, tough, gray or tan bead
polyester	fuses; melts and shrinks away from flame	burns slowly and continues to melt	self-extinguishing	chemical odor	hard, tough, black or brown bead
olefin	fuses; shrinks, and curls away from flame	melts and burns	continues to burn and melt; gives off black sooty smoke	chemical odor	hard, tough, tan bead
saran	fuses, melts, and shrinks away from flame	melts; yellow flame	self-extinguishing	chemical odor	irregular, crisp black bead
vinal	fuses, shrinks, curls away from flame	burns with melting	continues to burn with melting	chemical odor	hard, tough, tan bead
vinyon	fuses and melts away from flame	burns slowly with melting	self-extinguishing	acrid	hard, black, irregular bead
elastomeric					
spandex	fuses but does not shrink away from flame	burns with melting	continues to burn with melting	chemical odor	soft, sticky, and gummy
rubber	shrinks away from flame	burns rapidly and melts	continues burning	sulfur or chemical odor	tacky, soft black residue

Table 4.2 Microscopic Appearance of Textile Fibers

Fiber	Longitudinal Appearance	Cross-Sectional Shape
man-made		
acetate Arnel	distinct lengthwise striations; no cross markings	irregular shape with crenulated or serrated outline
acrylic		
Acrilan, Courtelle, Creslan, Zefran	rodlike with smooth surface and profile	nearly round or bean shape
Orlon	broad and often indistinct lengthwise striation; no cross markings	dog bone
bicomponent Orlon	lengthwise striations; no cross markings	irregular mushroom or acorn
modacrylic		
Dynel	lengthwise striations; no cross markings	irregular worm or ribbonlike
Verel	broad and often indistinct lengthwise striation; no cross markings	dog bone
nylon		
nylon 6, nylon 6,6 regular	rodlike with smooth surface and profile	round or nearly round
Antron, "501," and Cadon	broad, sometimes indistinct lengthwise striations; no cross markings	trilobal
olefin		
polyethylene, polypropylene	rodlike with smooth surface and profile	round or nearly round
polyester		
Dacron, Fortrel, Kodel, and Vycron	rodlike with smooth surface and profile	round or nearly round
Dacron type 62	broad, sometimes indistinct lengthwise striations; no cross markings	trilobal
rayon		
viscose, regular	distinct lengthwise striations; no cross markings	irregular shape with crenulated or serrated outline
high-tenacity viscose	rodlike with smooth surface; indistinct striations or none	slightly irregular shape with few serrations
high-wet-modulus viscose Avril, Lirelle, Zantrel	rodlike, smooth surface	round or oval shaped
Cuprammonium, Fabelta Z-54	rodlike with smooth surface and profile	round or nearly round
saran Saran	rodlike with smooth surface and profile	round or nearly round
spandex Lycra	broad, often indistinct lengthwise striation; no cross markings	dog bone
natural		
cotton, mercerized and not mercerized	ribbonlike convolutions (twists) sometimes change direction, and are less frequent in mercerized fibers; no significant lengthwise striations, but lumen may appear as striations in some fibers	tubular shape with tubes usually collapsed, and irregular in size

Table 4.2   Microscopic Appearance of Textile Fibers—*continued*

Fiber	Longitudinal Appearance	Cross-Sectional Shape
natural—*continued*		
flax, bleached	bamboolike, pronounced cross-marking nodes; no significant lengthwise striations	very irregular in size as well as shape; round and oval are most prevalent
silk, boiled off	smooth surface and profile, but may contain nodes; no significant length-wise striations	mostly triangular with point of triangle usually rounded off; irregular in size and shape
wool, cashmere, mohair and regular (Merino)	rough surface, cross markings due to surface scales; medulla or central fiber core sometimes apparent in coarse grades	round or nearly round; medulla may appear shaded

Solubility

The behavior of a fiber in specific chemical reagents is frequently cited as a definite means of identification. This is especially true when solubility data are combined with other test results. Knowledge of the chemical reactions of fibers is of value to the consumer in the processes of stain removal, cleaning, and laundering (Table 4.3).

Acetone, which dissolves acetate and Arnel triacetate, is found in fingernail polish and polish removers; accidental spillage would cause initial stiffening of fabric, followed by disintegration.

Table 4.3   Scheme for Identification by Fiber Solubility
Use the same sample of yarns or fabric until the total substrate has been destroyed. Rinse the residue thoroughly after each test. Observe the behavior of the substance at each step. It may be of value to observe the residue under the microscope. The sample should remain in the solution for five minutes before moving to the next step.

Chemical	Removes
1. glacial acetic acid, 25°C (75°F)	acetate, triacetate
2. hydrochloric acid 1 : 1, 25°C (75°F)	nylon 6, and 6,6
3. sodium hypochlorite, 25°C (75°F) 5 percent available chlorine	silk, wool
4. dioxane, 100°C (212°F)	saran
5. meta Xylene, at boil	olefins
6. ammonium thiocyanate, at boil, 70 percent by weight	acrylics
7. butyrolactone, 25°C (75°F)	modacrylics and nytriles
8. dimethyl formamide, 95°C (200°F)—not always effective	spandex
9. sulfuric acid, 75 percent by weight, 25°C (75°F)	cellulosics
10. meta Cresol, 95°C (200°F)	polyesters

Vinegar, a 5- to 6-percent acetic acid, will not destroy fibers that would be dissolved by concentrated, *glacial* acetic acid. It could weaken the fibers, however.

Sodium hypochlorite with 5 percent available chlorine is standard undiluted bleach such as Clorox® and similar products. Chlorine bleaches dissolve wool and silk and may weaken other fibers. Thus, bleaches must be used with caution.

Cresol, a component part of Lysol, can damage or destroy nylons, acetate, spandex, and polyesters.

Other chemical reagents used in fiber identification are seldom encountered in home care procedures.

Textile Fibers

Most people have little difficulty in understanding natural fibers. It is easy enough to relate the hair on a sheep or some other animal to the loose wool fibers in a sweater, for example. In both visual and tactile properties, the raw material and finished product resemble each other.

On the other hand, man-made fibers pose a somewhat greater challenge. Even in this technological age, many individuals—particularly those with no training in chemistry—cannot readily grasp the process by which a chemical solution is transformed into fibers that ultimately make cloth. To eliminate this problem we present here a brief introduction to the manufacture of fibers. The chapters that follow give more detail about specific processes as they relate to the fibers in question.

Man-made fibers are formed by passing a chemical substance through a *spinnerette.* This device consists of a series of tiny holes. As the fiber substance emerges from the spinnerette—or is *extruded* from the spinnerette—it hardens or coagulates into a fine filament. The size of the filament depends on the size of the openings in the spinnerette, plus the stretching and other processing that follows.

The chemical substance from which the filaments are to be formed is converted into a fluid state either by dissolving the material in a solvent of some type or by melting the substance. If the fiber polymer cannot be dissolved or melted, it must be converted into a soluble substance by chemical action and then reconverted to the fiber polymer after the filament has been formed. The change back to the fiber polymer form occurs, usually, by chemical action in a spinning bath or by evaporation. There are three basic types of spinning procedures used in the manufacture of fibers.

The *wet spinning* process requires that the fiber solution, forced through the spinnerette, emerge from the spinnerette into a liquid that causes coagulation and filament formation. This process frequently involves conversion of the fiber material into a soluble derivative; the extrusion in the coagulating bath results in reconversion or reconstitution of the fiber through reactions between the soluble fiber derivative and the chemicals in the spinning bath.

The *dry spinning* process occurs when the fiber solution emerges into a warm air chamber. The warm air causes the solvent to evaporate so that the fiber filaments form and harden. This technique may also involve the formation of a soluble derivative of the fiber that is forced through the spinnerette. As the solvent evaporates, the fiber is reconstituted and returns to its standard chemical form.

In *melt spinning,* the fiber chemical is melted and the molten solution is forced through the spinnerette into an environment that causes the solution to harden into the filament form. Melt spinning does not require any chemical change in the fiber material for the spinning operation.

Other terms applied to man-made fiber manufacture that are basic to an understanding of processes involved are:

Delustering   When man-made fibers are formulated, the basic combination of chemicals frequently produces a filament with a high degree of luster. Overlustrous fibers are not desirable in most cases, so to make fibers that do meet the needs of consumers, manufacturers deluster them during processing.

Texturizing   To yield products with a desirable degree of bulk and/or stretch characteristics, man-made fibers are frequently texturized. The processes undertaken to achieve this are discussed in Chapter 19.

Stretching and Orientation   After the filaments have been formed, they are stretched to reduce the fiber diameter, to arrange the fiber molecules in an orderly manner, to provide the fiber with adequate strength, and to enhance the ability to resist dimensional change.

Man-made fibers take several forms:

Monofilament Yarn   A man-made fiber yarn can be composed of a single filament extruded to the diameter desired for the yarn. These yarns are stiffer than multifilament yarns.

Multifilament Yarns   Often, a number of individual filaments will be combined to make a yarn, these filaments being held together by twist or some other means. Twist is the usual method. Multifilament yarns are more flexible and preferred for fabrics to be used for apparel items and home furnishing fabrics where drape is necessary.

Staple   Man-made staple fibers are short fibers cut to the length required for the processing equipment, the typical length of either cotton fibers or wool fibers. Staple fibers are cut from filaments extruded in large bundles called *tow*.

Natural Cellulosic Fibers 5

Fibrous materials are found in nearly all plant life, but some plants in particular have proved to be important sources of textile fibers for the manufacture of yarn, cord, and fabrics. These plant fibers consist largely of cellulose and therefore are classified as *natural cellulosic* or *vegetable* fibers. The term natural cellulosic is preferred, for it indicates the simple chemistry of the substances and provides a scientific method for comparing natural cellulose with man-made cellulose fibers. The natural cellulose fibers commonly encountered in consumer goods include cotton and linen (flax), as well as jute, ramie, and hemp. Many of these fibers are used to some degree in all parts of the world, depending on availability, cost, appearance, and comfort.

Cotton

Historical Review

The origin of cotton is unknown. Archeologists have contributed valuable information concerning the fiber's early use, but there is a dearth of evidence to indicate when or where cotton first grew. Data suggesting that cotton was grown in Egypt about 12,000 B.C. remain inconclusive; however, most authorities agree that cotton was produced in India about 3000 B.C. and that India was the principal country in which cotton was widely utilized before 2500 B.C.

For centuries it was variously thought that cotton was a product of the Old World; that it was brought to the shores of the Americas by early explorers; that it spread to both the Eastern and Western Hemispheres from a long-lost land in the Pacific; that it was carried from the Old World to the New World by way of a land route across the Bering Straits. Reliable data now indicate that cotton was indigenous to the lands comprising Asia, Africa, and North and South America. Carbon 14 tests have produced evidence that cotton was grown and made into fabrics in Peru as early as 2500 B.C. Thus, it would seem that cotton culture developed simultaneously in several areas of the world. This supposition is further upheld by the fact that botanical differences are evident between Eastern and Western cotton plants.

The word "cotton" derives from the Arabic word *quoton* or *qutun*, which means a plant found in conquered lands. *Muslin* is also taken from the Arabic language and was applied to cottons woven in Mosel. Ancient writers described this cloth as being "so sheer that it was invisible when spread over the ground and saturated with dew."

Figure 5.1 Cotton fabric, woven and twined. Huaca Prieta, Chicama Valley, Peru. Pre-Ceramic Period (c. 2300 B.C.). (*American Museum of Natural History, New York*)

Cotton culture in what is now the United States dates back about 2500 years, having originated in the area of Utah, Texas, and Arizona. Fragments of cotton fabrics have been found in dry caves and burial sites of the American Indians who inhabited the Southwest centuries ago, and anthropologists interpret this fact as indicating the importance of fabrics to early Indian cultures. The fragments are believed to antedate the Christian era by five hundred years. It is known also that the Pueblo Indians—Hopi, Zuni, and others—have used cotton since the first century A.D.

The earliest recorded planting of cotton on the East Coast occurred in Florida in 1536. However, the primary purpose of this crop was not the fiber but simply enjoyment of the blossom. Cultivation of the plant for fiber use and as a profit-making venture occurred in Virginia, where cotton was abundant, between 1607 and 1620. Records show that cotton was cultivated throughout the Carolinas about 1665; by 1700 the cotton grown there furnished clothing to one-fifth of the population of those states.

Most early cotton was of the Sea Island variety, because the Churka or roller gin imported from India could separate seeds and fiber in this type only. However, as cotton culture moved inland, it was found that Sea Island cotton would not thrive, and Upland varieties were adopted. These were impossible to gin on the Churka, so hand separation of seed and fiber was required. After the invention of the saw-type gin by Eli Whitney in 1793, production of Upland cotton increased rapidly. The cash value of the cotton crop jumped from $150,000 in 1793 to over $8 million in a ten-year period.

The economic effects of the invention of the cotton gin were revolutionary. Increase in cotton production and the subsequent development of low-cost textiles led directly to the industrialization of both Europe and America, as well as to the massive export-import business between the two continents. Indirectly, the effects were equally overwhelming, but far from beneficial. Slavery, which had been dying out, was stimulated anew on a huge scale. It became the adjunct of Southern cotton culture, subject of the political controversies of the early 19th century. With slavery as its focus, the ideological split in the United States ultimately resulted in the American Civil War.

Cotton also provided an early example of environmental mishandling. Plantations were established without proper care of the soil. Then, as the earth became depleted of necessary nutrients, the plantation owners simply moved West, plundering more soil and leaving a trail of valueless land.

Originally, the factories for manufacturing and processing cotton into yarns and fabrics were located mostly in the New England states because of an abundance of water power and human power. Samuel Slater, a textile machinist from England, had opened the first spinning mill in the United States in 1791. By 1810 there were 226 mills in the New England area. But after the Civil War, a vastly changed economy dictated a movement of cotton manufacturing to the source of its fiber supply in the South. Not only did the move South reduce transportation costs and taxes, but it provided manufacturing plants with plentiful and cheap labor. It also, incidentally, brought social change to a hitherto agrarian society. For example, electricity was first used as a source of power in a cotton weaving plant in South Carolina. Since the beginning of the 20th century, most cotton manufactured in the United States has been processed in Southern mills.

All the while, the production of cotton fiber increased through improved farming procedures. By 1900, the United States was producing over ten million bales of cotton fiber per year. At that time the total world production was only fourteen million bales. By 1926, U.S. production had increased to more than eighteen million bales, and although there was a drop during the Great Depression, it had climbed to a record high of over 18.5 million bales per year by the late thirties. Cotton did not go into a decline until the middle part of this century, when man-made fibers became accepted and—eventually—preferred. For the past decade cotton production has been between 9 and 12 million bales per year.

The export of cotton fiber has fluctuated with the popularity of its use worldwide. At the turn of the century the United States exported approximately seven million bales of cotton. By 1926, exports had climbed to nearly eleven million bales. Since then, however, there has been a decline to the current 2.8 million bales.

For a time the United States also imported some cotton—mostly long staple fibers—from Egypt and other Near East areas. But with the development of long staple cotton production in states of the American Southwest, import of this fiber ceased.

Figure 5.2 The original cotton gin invented by Eli Whitney. (*Bettmann Archive*)

In recent years considerable time, energy, and money have been spent in attempts to improve the fiber properties and processing methods of cotton to keep it competitive with man-made fibers. Nevertheless, in many end-use applications formerly considered the province of cotton, man-made fibers are now dominant. Consumption figures (see Table 1.2) clearly indicate the change. Consumption of cotton in the United States dropped to approximately 29 percent in 1973 and 28 percent in 1974. In the world market, however, cotton still accounts for slightly more than 50 percent of all fibers used.

Growth and Production

The cotton plant is a member of the *Malvacae* family. In appearance cotton blossoms resemble hibiscus or hollyhocks. The plant is cultivated most satisfactorily in warm climates, both humid and dry, where irrigation can supply the water needed.

The cotton blossom, which appears about one hundred days after planting, is beautiful. Creamy white or light yellow the first day, it changes to pink, lavender, or red on the second day. But the petals drop off after about 48 hours, leaving the boll or seed pod in which the fibers form. Fifty to eighty days later the pod bursts open, and the fleecy cotton fibers are ready for picking. The flowers appear over a long period of time, and, thus, the harvest period of mature cotton is of similar duration.

Before picking, especially if mechanical pickers are used, the plants are sprayed with defoliants, which cause the leaves to shrivel and fall off. As the cotton bolls mature and open, the fleecy fibers cascade out of the boll in the form of "locks" of fiber.

left: Figure 5.3 Cotton plant with fiber locks. Long staple.

right: Figure 5.4 A single cotton boll, Upland variety. Fibers are in a loose fluffy mass.

Cotton can be picked by hand, by mechanical picking machines, or by stripping devices. Hand picking results in more uniform and better-quality cotton, because the pickers can select the mature fibers only, and they can repick the fields as many times as it is profitable. However, labor for this type of picking is scarce, and wages are high, so it is becoming economically unprofitable to use hand pickers except in small fields.

Picking machines are of two types: the picker and the stripper. The picker pulls the fibers from the open bolls, while the stripper pulls the entire boll from the plant. Both machines are important. Pickers work best on fields with lush growth and high fiber yield; they are designed to pick one or two rows and can go over the fields several times each season. Strippers are most effective on the fields of low yield and low-growing plants; they always pull from two rows simultaneously in a "once-over" operation.

left: Figure 5.5   A mechanical picker. This unit picks a field twice if production warrants it. (*National Cotton Council of America*)

right: Figure 5.6   A cotton stripper. The machine makes one pass over the field. (*National Cotton Council of America*)

Processing

After the cotton has been picked, it is taken to the gin, where the fiber, called *cotton lint* by the trade, is separated from the seed. The gin used today is much the same as the first saw-gin designed by Eli Whitney. In addition to separating lint from seed, the modern gin will remove some foreign matter, such as dirt, twigs, leaves, and parts of the bolls. The seeds are a valuable by-product of the cotton industry and produce cattle feed and cottonseed oil. The fibers or cotton lint are packed into large bales at the gin. Each bale weighs about 500 pounds gross.

Samples of fibers are removed from the bales for determining the class. Factors in this classification include the staple length, the grade, and the

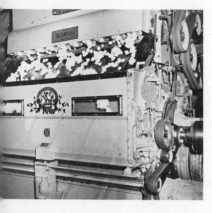

Figure 5.7 A modern cotton gin in operation. (*National Cotton Council of America*)

character of the cotton. *Staple length* refers to the length of the lint and is determined to some degree by the variety of cotton.

Fiber grade depends on color, amount of foreign matter present, and ginning preparation. The color can vary from white to gray or yellow. Cotton may be spotted or tinged, bright or dull. The spotted and tinged cotton is a frequent result of "one-time" picking, in which bolls that have been opened for some time are mixed with newly opened bolls.

Foreign matter with the fiber includes leaves, twigs, broken bracts (parts of the boll or seed pod), dust, dirt, and sand. Hand-picked cotton usually has a low amount of foreign matter, while mechanically picked fibers can have much or little, depending on picking conditions. Fibers pulled off the ground have additional dirt and soil embedded in them.

The quality of the ginning influences the grade of cotton. Poor ginning results in irregular cotton, which reduces the grade. The system for grading cotton is controlled by the U.S. Department of Agriculture (USDA).

In addition to classification on the basis of staple length, micronaire fineness, color, and foreign matter present, cotton is also rated in terms of its character. This includes such properties as fiber strength, uniformity, cohesiveness, pliability, elastic recovery, fineness, and resiliency. These properties are determined generally on a "bundle" of fibers rather than on individual ones. When all this information has been tabulated, the final quality of the cotton is assessed in establishing fiber price.

After ginning and classification are complete, the cotton bales are shipped to manufacturers, where yarns and fabrics are made. These construction procedures are discussed in Parts III and IV.

Fiber Properties

Microscopic Properties

Cotton fibers are composed of an outer cuticle (skin) and primary wall, a secondary wall, and a central core or *lumen*. Immature fibers exhibit thin wall structures and large lumen, while mature fibers have thick walls and small lumen that may not be continuous, because the wall closes the lumen in some sections.

Figure 5.8 Cotton bales weighing approximately 500 pounds are wrapped in burlap and secured with metal straps for shipment to the yarn manufacturer. Before being placed in the opening room, the metal straps are cut and the burlap wrapping removed. (*Springs Mills*)

The longitudinal view of the fiber shows a ribbonlike shape with twist (convolutions) at irregular intervals (Fig. 5.9). The diameter of the fiber narrows at the tip. The lumen may appear as a shaded area or as striations; this is more obvious in immature fibers.

Fibers that have been swollen, as in mercerization, do not show the twist as clearly as untreated ones. Compared to the latter, swollen fibers appear smooth and round. Immature fibers also have few convolutions.

The cross section of the fiber usually shows three areas: the outer skin, the secondary wall, and the lumen (Fig. 5.10). The contour varies considerably: some fibers are nearly circular, some are elliptical, and some are kidney-shaped. Immature fibers are generally more irregular in contour than mature fibers.

Physical Properties

Among the distinguishing qualities of cotton fibers are shape, luster, strength, elastic recovery and elongation, resiliency, specific gravity, moisture absorption, and dimensional stability. These properties are evaluated in Table 5.1.

Fiber length and width help to identify common varietal strains. Upland cotton, the major strain produced in the United States, has a diameter of approximately 18 microns and a length of less than $1\frac{1}{8}$ inches. The American Upland variety includes such types as Acala, Deltapine, Crocker, Delfos, Empire, and Stoneville.

Sea Island and American-Egyptian cotton are long-staple varieties. They are fine in width—usually less than 15 microns—and more than $1\frac{1}{8}$ inches in length. Sea Island was grown primarily on the islands off the Georgia coast, but since the 1950s there has been almost no production of this strain. American-Egyptian cotton is raised in Arizona, California, and New Mexico, and sold under such names as Pima and Supima. The amount of long-staple cotton produced is small because it is costly to cultivate and process, but it can be made into fine-quality and beautiful fabrics.

Compared to other fibers, cotton has moderate to above-average strength. It tends to get stronger when wet—which means it is easy to care for.

Since the resiliency and elastic recovery of cotton are low, and elongation is comparatively low also, fabrics wrinkle easily and do not recover from creasing. Therefore, modern cotton fabrics require finishes. Finishing may cause side effects such as reduced strength, for example, but consumers will accept them in order to have easy care, smooth surface retention, and other functional properties.

An important aspect of cotton and cotton-blend fabrics is their ability to absorb moisture. This is a comfort factor; materials that pick up body moisture are much more comfortable than those that have a clammy feel.

Cotton fibers are relatively stable and do not stretch or shrink. Cotton *fabrics,* however, do tend to shrink as a result of tensions encountered

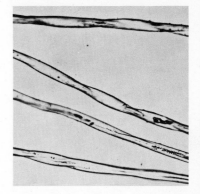

Figure 5.9 Photomicrograph of regular cotton, longitudinal view. (*E. I. DuPont de Nemours & Company*)

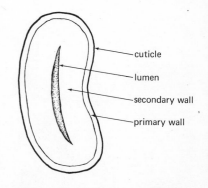

Figure 5.10 Cross section of a cotton fiber.

Table 5.1   Physical Properties of Cotton Fibers

Property	Evaluation
shape	fairly uniform in width, 12–20 microns length variable from $\frac{1}{2}$ to $2\frac{1}{2}$ inches; most fibers $\frac{7}{8}$ to $1\frac{1}{4}$ inch width and length aid in distinguishing varieties
luster	low
strength	3.0 to 5.0 grams per denier, medium strength wet strength 110–120% of dry
elastic recovery and elongation	low elasticity; elongation 3–7%
resiliency	low
specific gravity	1.54
moisture absorption	8.5% at standard conditions, 15–25% at saturation
dimensional stability of fiber	considered relatively stable

during yarn and fabric construction. Consequently, the fabrics require treatment to render them less susceptible to shrinkage.

Thermal Properties

Cotton burns readily and quickly with the smell of burning paper. It leaves a small amount of fluffy gray ash. Long exposure to dry heat above 149°C (300°F) will cause the fiber to decompose gradually and temperatures greater than 246°C (475°F) will result in rapid deterioration. Normal exposure to heat encountered in routine care and processing will not damage cotton, but fabrics will scorch if ironed with too-high temperatures. Finishes, such as starch or durable press, increase the tendency to scorch.

Chemical Properties

Cotton is highly resistant to alkalies; in fact, they are used in finishing and processing the fiber. Most detergents and laundry aids are alkaline, so cotton can be laundered in these solutions with no fiber damage.

Strong acids destroy cotton, and hot dilute acids will cause disintegration. Cold dilute acids cause gradual fiber weakening, but the process is slow and may not be immediately evident.

Cotton is highly resistant to most organic solvents and to all those used in normal care and stain removal.

Prolonged exposure to sunlight will cause the cotton fiber to become yellow and will gradually result in loss of strength. This damage is accentuated in the presence of moisture, some vat dyes, and some sulfur dyes. If properly stored in dry and dark areas, cotton will retain most of its strength and appearance.

Biological Properties

Cotton is damaged by various microorganisms. Mildew will produce a disagreeable odor and will result in rotting and loss of strength. Certain bacteria encountered in hot, moist, and dry conditions will cause decay.

Moths and beetles that damage some fibers will not usually attack cotton. But silverfish do eat cotton cellulose, especially if it is sized.

Cotton in Use

Cotton is the most universally used fiber, and it is excellent for a multitude of purposes. Fabrics of cotton are available in a wide price range. They are usually inexpensive because the fiber is comparatively low in price. When they are expensive, it may be the result of factors such as costly finishing

Figure 5.11 Chintz draperies of cotton and Dacron polyester blend. (*E. I. DuPont de Nemours & Company*)

procedures or added fashion characteristics. Cotton and cotton blends have virtually universal consumer acceptance. They provide not only durability but also easy care.

Cotton fibers produce fabrics that are characterized by comfort, excellent launderability, high absorbency, good color fastness if proper dyes are used, easy dyeability and a high degree of pliability, flexibility, heat resistance, and durability. Finishing processes must be applied to make cotton fabrics water repellent, stain resistant, flame retardant, shrink-proof, or durable press.

Flax

Historical Review

Flax is considered by many authorities to be the oldest fiber used in the Western world. Fragments of flax (linen) fabrics have been found in excavations at the prehistoric lake regions of Switzerland, which date back to about 10,000 B.C.

The use of linen in Egypt before 3000 B.C. has been verified. The fiber was made into mummy wrappings until the practice of mummification declined and also probably used for ceremonial robes and decorative costumes. These early linen fabrics were of a fineness that has never been duplicated—even with sophisticated modern machinery. Examples have been found that were spun so fine that more than 360 single threads joined together formed one warp thread. Other fabrics were made with more than 500 yarns per inch.[1]

The use of flax spread from the Mediterranean region to parts of Europe. Belgium became one of the important centers for growing flax because of the chemicals in the water of the River Lys.[2] This water was found to be exceptional in retting flax and it produced high-quality fibers. The town of Courtrai, located on the Lys, became a major center for the flax industry and has remained so to this day.

Linen fabric was introduced in Great Britain from Egypt about 1000 B.C., but actual use of the flax, which was wild in England, probably did not occur until the 1st century A.D. At that time, it is likely that Britons used flax fiber for coarse yarns and fabrics. However, at the same time, Ireland was beginning to process flax into fine linen fabrics, and by A.D. 500 Irish linen was held in high esteem by the rulers of Europe. During the 17th century the British government, in an attempt to maintain control of the wool industry in England, encouraged the Irish to develop their linen industry while limiting their production of wool.

Flax seed was brought to America by early settlers. Many colonists grew their own flax, spun their own yarns, and made their own fabric. A common fabric of that period was a combination of linen and wool, called "linsey-woolsey." The Industrial Revolution and development of the

[1] *CIBA Review,* No. 49, p. 1766.
[2] *CIBA Review,* No. 49, p. 1775.

factory system took textile production out of the home, and since machinery most suitable for processing flax was developed in Europe, flax production for textile use in America came to a virtual halt.

Today, the Soviet Union grows most of the flax for fiber. Other producers include New Zealand, Belgium, Ireland, and the nations of Eastern Europe. The United States grows flax for seed and for the resulting by-product, linseed oil, but imports almost all of the flax fiber for textiles, usually in the form of finished linen fabrics.

Growth and Production

Flax is a bast fiber. It is obtained from the stalk or stem of the *Linum usitatissimum*. The flax plant needs a temperate climate with generally cloudy skies and adequate moisture. It must have a slightly acid soil to obtain the considerable nutritive value it requires. Soils containing silicate and clay are preferred for flax growth. A crop rotation program of about five years tends to produce the best fiber.

Flax seed is planted by hand in April or May. When the crop is to be used for the production of fiber, the seeds are sown close together, so plants will have slim stems with foliage and seeds at the top only. The flax plant reaches a height of 2 to 4 feet. Its blossoms are a delicate pale blue or white. If the flax is meant for fiber, it is pulled before the seeds are ripe.

Processing

Pulling and Rippling

Flax for fiber is pulled by hand or by mechanical pullers to keep the roots intact, for the fibers extend below ground surface. If flax is cut, the fibers become permanently discolored.

left: Figure 5.12 Flax seed is planted in the spring and grows to about 3 feet in height. Large machines harvest the plants by pulling. The plants are never cut. The stalks are bundled. The threshing machines remove the seeds used for linseed oil. (*Belgian Linen Association*)

right: Figure 5.13 Bundles of flax are loaded into retting tanks. The soaking action combined with chemicals or bacteria loosens the flax fibers from the woody portion of the stalk. (*Belgian Linen Association*)

Harvesting occurs in late August when the plant is a rich golden brown color. After drying, the flax is *rippled;* that is, it is pulled through special threshing machines that remove the seed pods or bolls.

Retting

To obtain the fibers from the stalk, the outer woody portion must be removed. This process, known as *retting,* can be accomplished by several procedures.

Dew retting involves the spreading of flax on the ground, where it is exposed to the action of dew and sunlight. This natural method of retting gives uneven results but provides the strongest and most durable linen. Unfortunately, it requires a comparatively long period of time; the average exposure is from four to six weeks.

Pool retting is a process whereby the flax is packed in sheaves and immersed in pools of stagnant water. Bacteria develop in the water and rot away the stalk covering. When retting is complete, the water is drained

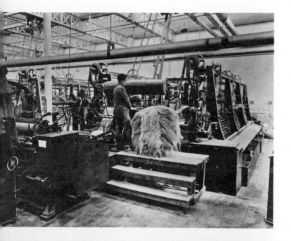

left: Figure 5.14 The flax is pulled over a series of teeth, graduated in size, to separate the fibers from waste and to clean and straighten them. The hackled flax, in piles, is fed into the drawing machines that form the flax fibers into a wide, continuous sliver. (*Belgian Linen Association*)

below left: Figure 5.15 Long wisps of combed flax emerge from the combing machine. (*Belgian Linen Association*)

below: Figure 5.16 Combed flax passes through a drawing machine. It emerges in a continuous ribbon or drawn sliver ready for final spinning operations. (*Belgian Linen Association*)

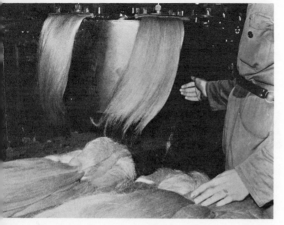

away, and the flax is dried preparatory to the next step. Pool retting requires from two to four weeks.

Tank retting, similar to pool retting, utilizes large tanks in which the flax is stacked. The tank is filled with water that increases the speed of the bacterial action. Retting is then accomplished in a few days.

Both pool and tank retting give good-quality flax that is light in color, uniform in size and strength.

Stream retting, practiced in some areas, calls for the flax to be stacked along the banks of slow-moving streams. The constantly moving water slows down the retting procedure considerably, but it reduces the unpleasant smell associated with dew and pool retting and produces good-quality flax. A long time is needed for this retting technique; it frequently takes as long as dew retting.

Chemical retting is accomplished by stacking the flax in tanks, filling the tanks with water, and adding chemicals such as sodium hydroxide, sodium carbonate, or dilute sulphuric acid. Chemical retting can be accomplished in a matter of hours instead of days or weeks. However, it must be carefully controlled in order to prevent damage to the fiber.

Breaking and Scutching

After retting is complete, the flax is passed between fluted rollers that break the outer woody covering into small particles. The fiber is then subjected to the scutching process, which separates the outer covering from the spinnable fiber. Since the early 19th century this has been done by a mechanical device.

Hackling

After scutching, the flax fibers are *hackled* or combed. This separates the short fibers, called *tow,* from long fibers, called *line.* It is accomplished by drawing the fibers between several sets of pins, each successive set finer than the preceding.

Spinning

The flax fibers are drawn out into yarn, and twist is imparted. Flax fibers are spun either dry or wet, but wet spinning is considered to give the best-quality yarn. Basically, the final yarn processing is similar to that used for other staple fibers.

Fiber Properties

Microscopic Properties

Flax fiber consists of fibrils or bundles of fiber cells held together by bonding or by a gummy substance. Under the microscope the longi-

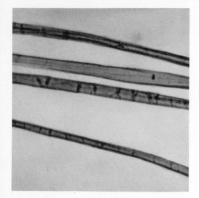

Figure 5.17 Photomicrograph of flax fiber, longitudinal view. (*E. I. DuPont de Nemours & Company*)

tudinal view of the fiber shows the width to be quite irregular. The central canal or lumen casts a shadow, giving a slightly darker effect down the center. There are no convolutions as in cotton, but longitudinal lines or striations can be seen. The points at which the fiber width changes are marked by swellings and irregular joint formations called *nodes*. These resemble the joints on bamboo.

The cross section view clearly shows the lumen, the thick outer wall, and a somewhat polygonal shape. Immature flax may be oval in shape and usually has a larger lumen than mature fiber.

Physical Properties

Flax fibers are not so fine as cotton because cells are held together in bundles. Line fibers are quite long—usually more than 12 inches and frequently from 18 to 22 inches—while tow fibers are less than 12 inches long and can be as short as a fraction of an inch.

The natural color of flax varies from light ivory to dark tan or gray. Choice fibers from Belgium and the other Low Countries are a pale sandy color and require little bleaching.

Flax possesses a high natural luster that produces attractive yarns and fabrics.

It is a strong fiber, which usually has a tenacity of 5.5 to 6.5 grams per denier. Occasionally, a fiber of inferior quality may have a tenacity as low as 2.5 grams per denier.

Most linen fabrics used in apparel are treated with resin finishes to improve appearance. However, this process reduces fabric strength. Without resin finishes linen is strong, durable, and easy to maintain.

Flax is naturally stiff and resists bending. The fiber has little elasticity, elongation, and resiliency. Thus, linen fabrics are prone to crease and wrinkle badly. Finishes must be applied to offset these disadvantages.

Flax has a standard moisture regain of 12 percent. The saturation regain is comparable to that of other cellulosic fibers. This quality makes for a comfortable apparel fabric.

While flax fibers do not stretch or shrink to any marked degree, treated linen fabrics may do so as a result of the finishing processes.

Thermal Properties

Flax burns like any other cellulosic fiber. It will withstand temperatures to 149°C (300°F) for long periods of time with little change. Above 149°C prolonged exposure will result in gradual discoloration and degradation. Safe ironing temperatures may go as high as 260°C (500°F) as long as the fabric is not held at the high temperature for any length of time.

Chemical Properties

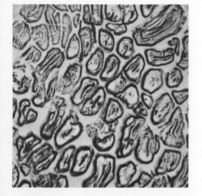

Figure 5.18 Photomicrograph of flax fiber, cross section. (*E. I. DuPont de Nemours & Company*)

Flax is highly resistant to alkaline solutions, cool dilute acids, and dry cleaning solvents, but it is damaged by hot dilute acids and concentrated

Figure 5.19 Draperies and upholstery on chair and hassock of linen and cotton blend. (*Schumacher*)

acids. There is a gradual loss of strength when linen fabrics are exposed to sunlight. This is not serious—especially when the light is filtered through window glass. Linen, therefore, makes a good choice for curtain and drapery fabrics. Properly stored, flax will age remarkably well.

Biological Properties

Dry linen has excellent resistance to mildew. In a moist or humid atmosphere, however, mildew will grow rapidly and damage the fiber. Flax is generally resistant to household pests and insects.

Linen in Use

Flax has relatively high strength and can be made into fine yarns and sheer fabrics that are both strong and cool. Comfort is further enhanced by the wicking properties of linen. Fabrics composed of flax are popular for wearing apparel because, in addition to being cool, they maintain their clean appearance and are easily laundered.

Linen is used for table coverings because it wears well, it looks attractive and elegant, and the yarns lie flat after a beetling finish has been applied. *Beetling* involves beating the cloth with large wooden blocks to flatten the yarns. This also gives the fabric a gloss. A high-speed beetling machine has been developed that utilizes metallic hammers, which can be controlled in various ways to give light or heavy blows to the fabric and produce a desirable product.

Linen fabrics may be smooth and sheer, coarse, homespun in effect, or highly patterned by means of the Jacquard weave. They are used for apparel and for a wide variety of domestic fabrics. There is considerable prestige associated with linen; it has a high heritage and sentiment value.

The resistance of flax to chemicals and laundering as well as to deterioration from age and sunlight, plus the strength of the fiber, combine to produce fabrics with long life. Linen fabrics respond satisfactorily to laundering, the preferred method of cleaning. Because of the structure of the fiber, it does not soil quickly, and unless stained, it does not require bleaching.

Jute

Jute is also a bast fiber. Like flax, it has been used since the dawn of civilization; however, it attained economic importance only during the latter part of the 18th century. In fabric form jute is frequently called *burlap;* it is the "sackcloth" referred to in the Bible.

Today, jute is one of the most widely used fibers and appeals particularly to developing countries because of its low cost. It recently enjoyed limited success as a fashion fabric for wearing apparel. However, jute is a weak fiber so it is normally limited to products in which durability is not important.

Natural jute has a yellow to brown or gray color, with a silky luster. It is difficult to bleach completely; thus, many fabrics are dark, natural tan or brown in color.

Jute has only moderate strength, low elongation of less than 2 percent, and poor elastic recovery. It reacts to chemicals in the same way as cotton and flax.

Jute shows good resistance to microorganisms and insects. Moisture increases the speed of deterioration, but dry jute will last for a very long time. The fabric works well for bagging, because it does not stretch. It is rough and coarse, which tends to keep stacks of bags in position and resist slippage. Jute also serves as backing in the manufacture of linoleum and carpets.

Ramie

Frequently called *China Grass,* ramie is a bast fiber that has been cultivated for hundreds of years in China and Formosa. Some evidence indicates that ramie was grown in the Mediterranean civilizations as early as flax; however, its use in China was of much greater importance. The history of ramie's development centers in the Orient, and only in comparatively recent centuries has the fiber become important in Western civilizations. At the present time, ramie is grown commercially in China, Japan, Egypt, France, Italy, Indonesia, Russia, and the United States.

The ramie plant, a member of the nettle family, is a perennial shrub that can be cut several times a season after the necessary preliminary growth. It can be started from seeds, which necessitates a developmental

Figure 5.20   Ramie plants during early growth. (*R. V. Allison, Belle Glade Experimental Station, Florida*)

period of three years before fibers are formed; or it can be grown from root cuttings, which mature within two to three years.

After cutting, the ramie stalks are decorticated by either hand or machine. *Decortication* consists of peeling away or beating off the bark to free the bast fibers. Fibers are dried in the sun for bleaching. Then they are degummed in caustic soda to remove pectins and waxes. Finally, they are washed and dried.

Ramie fibers are long—more than 18 inches—and very fine. They are white and lustrous, almost silklike in appearance. Ramie is strong in terms of resistance to pull. However, the fibers are too stiff and brittle for good pliability. Elastic recovery and elongation are poor.

Ramie reacts chemically in the same manner as other cellulosic fibers, except that it is not easily damaged by cold concentrated mineral acids. The high degree of molecular crystallinity and low molecular accessibility reduces the rate of acid penetration and thus the rate of damage. Of special interest is the fact that ramie is highly resistant to microorganisms, insects, and rotting.

Ramie fabrics sometimes resemble fine linen, or they can be heavy and coarse like canvas. Some historians believe that ramie, not linen, was used for mummy wrappings in ancient Egypt. In foreign markets today, fine ramie fabrics are made into shirts, table coverings and napkins.

Hemp

Hemp is a bast fiber that was probably used first in Asia. Records indicate it was cultivated in China before 2300 B.C. Sometime during the Early Christian era, hemp was carried into Gaul and became an important fiber throughout Europe.

Today, hemp is grown on every continent and in nearly every country. A tough plant, it will grow at altitudes to 8000 feet and in climates where

Figure 5.21   Ramie stalks with decorticated and degummed fibers. (*R. V. Allison, Belle Glade Experimental Station, Florida*)

Figure 5.22   Cutting hemp by hand. (*Ciba Review*)

temperatures are warm or hot. Hemp can be replanted in the same fields more frequently than flax.

The processing of hemp is very similar to that of flax. The fiber requires retting to loosen the outer covering, followed by stripping or scutching to obtain the usable fibers. Hackling, or drawing and spinning of the fibers into yarns, is the final step before fabric manufacture. The fiber is dark tan or brown and is difficult to bleach, but it can be dyed bright and dark colors.

The hemp fibers vary widely in length, depending on their ultimate use. Industrial fibers may be several inches long, while fibers meant for domestic textiles are about $\frac{3}{4}$ inch to 1 inch long. The specific gravity of hemp is 1.48 grams per denier. It exhibits low elongation and poor elasticity. Standard moisture regain is 12 percent, and hemp can absorb moisture up to 30 percent of its weight.

Hot concentrated alkalies will destroy hemp, but hot or cold dilute or cold concentrated alkalies will not damage it. With the exception of cool weak acids, mineral acids will reduce the strength and eventually destroy the fiber completely. Organic solvents used in cleaning and bleaches, if handled properly, will not damage hemp.

The thermal reactions of hemp and the effect of sunlight are the same as for cotton. Hemp is moth resistant, but mildew will attack it.

Coarse hemp fibers and yarns are made into cordage, rope, sacking, and heavy-duty tarpaulins. In Italy, fine hemp fibers serve for interior design and apparel fabrics.

left: Figure 5.23   Retting hemp. The fibers are laid in rafts and submerged by stone weights. (*Ciba Review*)

right: Figure 5.24   Stacking hemp to dry after retting. (*Ciba Review*)

Miscellaneous Plant Fibers

Other plant fibers discussed in this text include those that have limited use in the United States for specific products and those with topical interest to the textile student.

Sisal, one of a group of fibers obtained from plant leaves, comes from a plant that belongs to the *Agave* family and is raised in Mexico, especially in the Yucatán Peninsula. The fiber is also cultivated in Africa, Java, and some areas of Central and South America. The leaves, which grow in a rosette from a short trunk, are cut when they are about four years old. Processing of the fibers involves separating them from the fleshy part of the leaf and removing pectins, chlorophyll, and other noncellulosic substances. Sisal can be dyed bright colors. It is important in the manufacture of such items as matting, rough totes and handbags, ropes and cordage, and native-style hats. The tourist is likely to encounter sisal in brightly colored shopping bags with patterned designs, varicolored place mats, and novelty items.

Abaca derives from a plant that belongs to the banana family. In appearance it is often mistaken for the edible banana tree. The plant grows mainly in the Philippines, and most of the textile fiber is processed there. Abaca is cultivated for its appearance in the southwestern United States, especially in California, in parts of Mexico, and occasionally in Florida. The leaf stalk from which the fiber is taken may reach a length of 25 feet. The fibers, therefore, are generally long; usable strands of abaca fiber may be up to 15 feet in length. Good-quality abaca has a natural luster and is an off-white color. Poor grades are dark gray or brown. The fiber is strong and flexible and therefore exceptionally good for making rope and cordage, place mats for outdoor or indoor use, and clothing. The fabric is delicate, lightweight, yet strong.

Figure 5.25 Carpet tiles of sisal fiber woven with an inch-thick cut pile, in stripes and solid color. (*Jack Lenor Larsen, Inc.*)

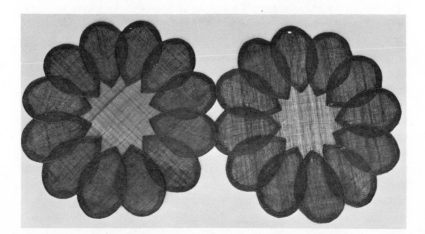

Figure 5.26 Place mats of abaca fiber.

Figure 5.27 Evening bag of embroidered piña fiber.

Piña fiber, from the leaves of the pineapple plant, is also produced in the Philippines. It is a white or light ivory colored fiber about 2 to 4 inches in length. The fiber is fine, lustrous, soft, flexible, and strong, as well as highly resistant to water. Fabrics of piña may be either soft and delicate or crisp. Considerable fiber goes into making "peasant" type clothing and table coverings with elaborate embroidery. The fabrics are easily cleaned and will retain their appearance for long periods of time. Substances with a high-acid content or strong enzymes, such as cranberry juice, will cause rapid fiber degradation, however, and they must be rinsed out quickly.

Coir, a fiber from a seed source, appears often in matting and cordage. Obtained from the coconut, it is the fibrous mass between the outer shell and the actual nut. The natural color of coir is a rich cinnamon brown, and the fiber is frequently left undyed for floor mats and outdoor carpets or patio coverings. Because of a high degree of stiffness, coir is wrinkle resistant, strong, and impervious to abrasive wear. In addition, it can stand exposure to weather, especially water, so it proves to be a very practical fiber for mats and similar products. The fiber can be dyed dark colors, but it is difficult to bleach it sufficiently to produce pale hues.

Kapok, a seed hair fiber, comes from the Java kapok or "silk cotton" tree. The huge tree grows in tropical regions and rises to a height of 50 feet or more. The seed pods, 3 to 6 inches in length, resemble the cotton boll. Ginning is not necessary, since the fibers can be dried, after which the seeds will shake away easily. Kapok is extremely light, buoyant, and soft. The fiber is difficult to spin into yarns, so its major use is for padding and stuffing, particularly in upholstered furniture and mattresses. Because it is nonallergenic, it makes an excellent filling for pillows. The best-known use for kapok is in life preservers. Kapok-filled preservers will support up to thirty times the weight of the preserver and will not become waterlogged.

Man-Made Cellulosic Fibers: Rayon

6

Historical Review

The first written comment concerning the potential of creating man-made fibers is found in Robert Hooke's *Micrographia,* published in 1664. Hooke predicted that eventually there would be a way to duplicate the excrement of the silkworm. However, not until the 19th century did scientists actually make artificial fibers. In 1855 George Audemars made filaments from a solution of mulberry twigs in nitric acid. In 1857 E. J. Hughes created fibers from a solution of starch, glue, resins, and tannins.

The major breakthrough in the production of man-made fibers occurred in 1862, when Ozanam invented the spinning jet or spinnerette. This remarkable little device is the basis for all manufactured fiber production (Fig. 6.1).

In 1883 J. W. Swan produced filaments by forcing a solution of cellulose nitrate in glacial acetic acid through a spinning jet. However, credit for the invention of rayon is generally given to Count Hilaire Chardonnet, who produced a cellulose nitrate that he dissolved in alcohol. This solution was forced through the spinnerette into water or warm air.

Figure 6.1 Spinnerettes used in the formation of man-made fibers.

The filaments hardened, were stretched to orient the molecules and introduce sufficient strength, and finally were denitrated and purified to reduce flammability. By 1889 Chardonnet had exhibited fabric samples, and by 1895 his company, the Société Anonyme pour la Fabrication de la Soie de Chardonnet, was paying dividends.

The viscose process was discovered in 1891 by the English scientists, C. F. Cross and E. J. Bevan. Since that time, the operation has been greatly modified and improved. The first American rayon operation, called the American Viscose Company, was opened in 1910. Today, this organization is a division of the FMC Corporation and is a major force in the rayon industry.

An important part of the mechanical development of rayon manu-facturing was the invention of the spinning box by C. F. Topham in 1905. This box caught the fibers and imparted sufficient twist to hold the filaments in place.

Between 1916 and 1930 companies such as DuPont, Industrial Rayon, Celanese, and American Enka joined the ranks of manufacturers of viscose rayon. In 1926, American Bemberg, now Beaunit Mills, introduced the cuprammonium process for manufacturing fibers.

Rayon received its name in 1924. Before that it had been called *artificial silk,* and because of the general dislike for things "artificial," many potential consumers avoided it. The fiber also had another draw-back: it was an inferior product. After it became identified as *rayon,* and following numerous modifications to improve its properties, the fiber gained public acceptance.

Rayon was first employed in tire cord in 1937. To increase the practicability of rayon for automobile tires, a group of manufacturers developed a unique high-strength rayon filament. Identified by the term *Tyrex,* this fiber is still in use today.

The decade of the fifties saw many improvements in existing rayon fibers, as well as the development of high-strength rayon, special carpet rayon, and high-wet-modulus rayon. However, during the same period factories began closing because of increased use of other fibers. While a considerable share of the rayon produced is still utilized for clothing, an important market for rayon is the field of home-furnishing fabrics.

The Textile Fiber Products Identification Act defines *rayon* as

> a manufactured fiber composed of regenerated cellulose, as well as manu-factured fibers composed of regenerated cellulose in which substituents have replaced not more than 15 percent of the hydrogens of the hydroxyl groups.

Manufacturing Processes

Viscose Rayon

The principal raw material for viscose rayon is wood pulp. *Cotton linters*— the cotton fibers that are too short for yarn or fabric manufacturing—are also used. The wood pulp and linters are processed, and pure cellulose is extracted and formed into thin sheets about 2 feet square (Fig. 6.2). These sheets are steeped in an alkali solution until the cellulose is converted to soda cellulose. The alkali pulp is then shredded into a crumb form, which is aged for a specific time. After aging, the cellulose crumb must be treated with carbon disulfide (Fig. 6.3). This process changes its color from white to bright orange and results chemically in a product called sodium cellulose xanthate.

The xanthate is dissolved in dilute sodium hydroxide, whereupon it becomes a honey-colored liquid. This solution is aged until it reaches the correct viscosity, or thickness, to form fibers. The viscous solution is pumped to the spinning tanks, delivered to the spinning machines, and forced by pump through a spinnerette into a dilute acid bath. The acid reacts with the solution, causing pure cellulose to coagulate into filament fibers. The filaments are thoroughly washed to remove any residual color and impurities that might adhere to the fibers. This method of making fibers is called *wet spinning*.

Eventually, the filaments are collected and either combined directly into yarns or cut into short lengths for spinning into yarns by one of the methods used for cotton or wool fibers (see p. 134).

The orifices in the spinnerette vary in size and number. Small holes produce fine filaments, and the number of openings determines the number of filaments in the finished yarn. When staple fibers are cut for spun yarns, a large spinnerette is used with approximately three thousand openings. These filaments are collected into a group called *tow* before they are cut into the desired length for yarn construction.

Viscose fibers are bright and shiny if not treated. To reduce the luster a chemical, usually titanium dioxide, is added to the solution before spinning. This delustering agent breaks up the light rays and reduces the shine. The degree of dullness can be controlled by the amount of chemical added.

Solution-dyed viscose can be manufactured through the addition of color pigment to the spinning solution before extrusion. This technique improves colorfastness properties. Several manufacturers have solution-dyed viscose on the market: American Enka (Kolorbon), American Viscose (Avicolor), Courtauld (Coloray), and IRC Fibers (Dy-Lok).

To make high-quality spun yarns manufacturers add crimp to staple fibers. The crimp causes the fibers to hold together with ease and gives body to the yarn.

Special Viscose Fibers

Most leading manufacturers of viscose rayon produce it in different tenacities. Regular-, medium-, and high-tenacity viscose rayons differ primarily in strength and to some degree in elongation properties. In addition to standard viscose fibers, some manufacturers are producing modified fibers that have properties considered desirable for selected

Figure 6.2 Cellulose in sheet form being packed into steeping tanks. (*Celanese Corporation*)

Figure 6.3 Cellulose crumbs treated with carbon disulfide become orange-colored cellulose xanthate. (*FMC Corporation*)

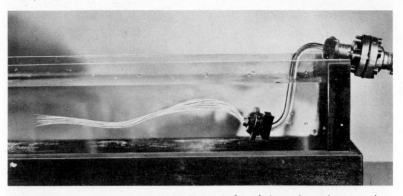

Figure 6.4 Wet spinning. Viscose solution is forced through a spinnerette into a coagulating bath to form filaments. (*FMC Corporation*)

end-use requirements. The most important modification available is high-wet-modulus viscose rayon, achieved by changing the proportion of chemicals used in the coagulating bath and by a variation in the aging time. This special rayon includes such trademarks as Avril, Nupron, Zantrel, and Xena. Its fibers are more like cotton than other rayons in their mechanical, physical, and chemical properties. They have better dimensional stability.

High-wet-modulus rayons are excellent in durable press products blended with polyesters. They accept "minimum-care" finishes somewhat better than regular rayons. Other desirable properties of high-wet-modulus fibers include: good stability to laundering and easy care; ability to be

Figure 6.5 Flow chart showing processes in viscose rayon manufacture.

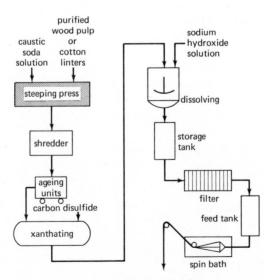

mercerized; and a crisp, lofty hand. (*Hand* relates to the "feel" of a fabric—the qualities that can be ascertained by touching it.)

Cuprammonium Rayon

E. Schweitzer, in 1857, discovered that cellulose would dissolve in a solution of ammonia and copper oxide. This reaction was not applied to the manufacture of fibers until 1891, when Max Fremery and Johann Urban made cupra rayon in Germany. However, it was not a successful venture until 1901, when Edmund Thiele, working for J. P. Bemberg Company, devised the stretch spinning process that made practical fibers of good strength and fineness. The fiber was eventually marketed as fine-quality cuprammonium rayon.

In the cuprammonium process, cellulose from cotton linters or wood pulp is purified and bleached to a pure white, then dissolved in a solution of ammonia, copper sulfate, and caustic soda. The resultant clear blue liquid requires no aging before spinning and is not damaged if extended storage is required. Any undissolved cellulose and other impurities are filtered out of the liquid mixture before fibers are formed.

The spinning solution is pumped through the spinnerette into a funnel through which soft water is running. The movement of the water stretches the newly formed filaments and introduces a small amount of molecular orientation. The fibers then move to the spinning machines, where they are washed, put through a mild acid bath to remove any adhering solution, rinsed, and twisted into yarns.

Saponified Cellulose Rayon

The Celanese Corporation makes a saponified cellulose rayon—Fortisan—that is processed differently from other rayons. The first step in the

Figure 6.6 Flow chart showing processes in cuprammonium manufacture.

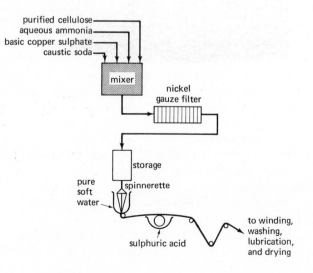

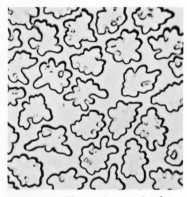

manufacture of this product is formation of cellulose acetate fibers. The acetate is then converted to pure cellulose in a chemical process called *saponification.* Only limited amounts of this fiber are produced and most of that is used by the Government.

Fiber Properties

Microscopic Properties

Since rayon is a manufactured fiber, the maker can control its size and shape to a great extent, and different types of rayon fibers, thus, can vary considerably in appearance.

The length or longitudinal appearance of regular viscose rayon exhibits uniform diameter and interior parallel lines called *striations*. These striations are the result of light reflection by the irregular surface contour (Fig. 6.7). If the fiber has been delustered, it will have a grainy, pitted appearance; bright fiber is relatively transparent. The cross section of the fiber shows highly irregular or serrated edges (Fig. 6.8). Here, too, the presence of delusterants is indicated by a spotted effect, while bright fiber appears crystal clear.

High-tenacity viscose is similar to regular viscose, except that it may have a less irregular contour and therefore show fewer striations in the longitudinal view. It may appear almost round in cross section. The same holds true for high-wet-modulus rayon.

In the longitudinal view cuprammonium rayon is uniform in width; it is smooth surfaced and has no markings or striations (Fig. 6.9). The cross section is round or oval and relatively clear (Fig. 6.10).

Physical Properties

The length, width (diameter), and luster of rayon fibers can be controlled and may be determined by end-use application.

The strength of most rayons is relatively low and is further decreased when fibers are wet, which means that rayon fabrics require careful handling in laundering. High-tenacity and high-wet-modulus viscose fibers are considerably stronger, with dry and wet strength equal to or better than cotton. They can, therefore, be laundered like cotton.

Elastic recovery and resiliency of regular viscose and cuprammonium rayons are low, while elongation for both fibers is high. These fabrics tend to wrinkle and stretch easily—weaknesses that can be corrected by finishes. High-wet-modulus rayon is less subject to stretching and wrinkling, but even these products are better when properly finished.

Rayon fibers have good moisture absorbency, which makes them accept dyes well. The same property also contributes to the high degree of comfort in rayon apparel fabrics.

While regular rayons are subject to stretching in yarn and fabric manufacture, followed by relaxation shrinkage after laundering, the new high-wet-modulus viscose rayon fibers do not stretch easily, and thus are less likely to suffer relaxation shrinkage.

Fabric construction as well as fiber characteristics contribute to the degree of relaxation shrinkage. Tightly woven fabrics will exhibit less size change because of the compact arrangement of yarns and fibers. Finishes are used on most rayon fabrics to control the dimensional stability.

Thermal Properties

Rayon is cellulose, so it burns rapidly with a yellow flame, leaving a small amount of light gray residue. When the flame is extinguished, there may be an *afterglow*.

Hot water and iron temperatures from 149°C (300°F) to 177°C (350°F) can be used safely, but exposure to high temperatures for an extended period of time results in fiber degradation.

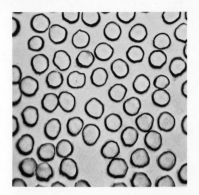

Figure 6.10 Photomicrograph of cuprammonium rayon, cross section. (*E. I. DuPont de Nemours & Company*)

Chemical Properties

Since rayon is chemically identical to cotton, it responds in much the same manner to chemical stimuli. Minor differences stem from the reduced degree of polymerization that accompanies manufacturing.

Table 6.1   Physical Properties of Rayon Fibers

Property	Viscose				Cuprammonium
	Regular	Medium	High	High-Wet-Modulus	
shape	Can be controlled by the manufacturer. Therefore uniform in appearance. Length and denier determined by manufacturer for end-use. Filament and staple.				
luster	controlled by manufacturer ⟶				
strength-gpd					
dry	1.5–2.4	2.4–3.2	3.0–5.0	3.4–5.5	1.7–2.3
wet	0.7–1.4	1.2–1.9	1.9–4.3	2.7–4.0	0.95–1.35
% elastic recovery— 2% extension	82	97	to 100	95	75
% elongation					
dry	15–30	15–20	9–26	6.5–18	10–17
wet	20–40	17–30	14–34	7.0–33	17–33
resiliency	low	low	low	low–medium	low
specific gravity	1.46–1.54 ⟶				
moisture absorption 20°C (70°F) 65% R.H.	11.5–16 ⟶				12.5
saturation	25–27 ⟶				27.0

Strong alkali solutions cause rayon fibers to swell and eventually produce a loss of strength; weak alkalies do not damage them. Like cotton and other natural cellulose fibers, the high-wet-modulus fibers can be mercerized by the application of caustic soda solutions.

Hot and cold concentrated acids cause rayons to disintegrate. Hot dilute acids result in fiber deterioration, but cold dilute acids have little or no effect. Resistance to dry-cleaning solvents and stain-removal agents is good. Bleaches will generally not harm most fabrics, but some finished materials may react very unfavorably to them. It is essential that any bleach be properly diluted and used according to directions.

Regular rayon fibers will deteriorate from extended exposure to the sun, whereas high-wet-modulus rayon will withstand it well enough to give adequate service in drapery fabrics and other interior design uses.

Biological Properties

Rayons resist all insects except silverfish, which are injurious to fibers unprotected by special finishes. Mildew will destroy rayons of all types, and soil increases the ease with which mildew forms, thus accelerating the damage. Rayon fibers are subject to harm by rot-producing bacteria. However, the high-wet-modulus viscose is fairly resistant to these bacteria, and special finishes increase the resistance of other rayons.

Rayon Fibers in Use

Rayon is used extensively in apparel and home furnishing fabrics (Fig. 6.11). High-tenacity fibers, including Tyrex and Fortisan, are employed in automobile tires and various industrial applications. Because it can be produced in either filament or staple form, rayon offers more variety in fabric and yarn construction than do cotton and other natural cellulose fibers. Through control of fiber size, yarn number, fabric construction techniques, and finishes, fabrics can be produced that are sheer, heavy, soft, firm, stiff, or limp; yarns can be simple, complex, or textured (see Parts III and IV).

Blends or combination fabrics now available include polyester and rayon, acrylic and rayon, nylon and rayon, acetate and rayon, cotton and rayon, and linen and rayon. Rayon contributes absorbency, comfort, and softness when blended with polyesters, acrylics, and nylons. With cotton, rayon enhances the appearance of the fabric.

High-wet-modulus rayon fibers have gained wide consumer acceptance. They compare favorably with cotton in strength, and they accept durable-press finishes easily.

Regular viscose rayon tends to stretch when wet. As it dries the fibers may shrink. This poses care problems for the consumer. It is important to handle regular rayons carefully during laundering to reduce size distortion. Finishes can be applied that increase the stability of rayon during use and care. Fabrics composed of improved rayon fibers can be laundered easily

Figure 6.11 Women's suit of rayon. (*FMC Corporation*)

and safely. While the laundry treatment and handling depends upon yarn and fabric construction, finish and color application, and fiber content, rayon will not be damaged by detergents and other laundry aids such as starches, fabric softeners, and water softeners. When essential for appearance, rayons can be bleached with hypochlorite or peroxide bleaches, as long as these are properly diluted to prevent fiber damage.

Rayon can be ironed at medium to high temperatures, although fiber finishes may require medium to medium-low temperatures. In fact, since rayon is cellulose, it can tolerate the same general care given to cotton fabrics of the same type and with the same finishing and color application.

For many years the term rayon encompassed cellulose fibers made by viscose, cuprammonium, and other processes, as well as modified cellulose fibers such as cellulose acetate. In 1951, the Federal Trade Commission ruled that, if named on labels, *rayon* was to indicate man-made cellulosic fibers and *acetate* was to indicate fibers composed of cellulose acetate. The Labeling Law of 1960 made such labeling mandatory as part of the total fiber-labeling legislation. However, confusion still exists, and the phrases "acetate rayon" or "rayon acetate" are still heard. Both are incorrect and misleading. Blends or combinations of the two fibers should indicate the percent of each fiber present, and labels should inform the consumer that the fabric is composed of both rayon and acetate.

Manufacturers of several rayon fibers, such as Nupron, Xena, Avril, and Zantrel, have established quality certification programs that permit the use of the trademark only when the fabric meets certain specifications established by the company producing the fiber. These programs assure the consumer that the fabric meets established performance characteristics as stated on attached labels.

Figure 6.12 Men's apparel of rayon. (*FMC Corporation*)

7 Modified Cellulose Fibers: Acetate and Triacetate

Historical Review

Cellulose acetate, an ester of cellulose and acetic acid, was first made in 1869 by Paul Schutzenberger. However, not until 35 years later was a practical, safe, and relatively inexpensive technique for producing cellulose acetate discovered by Henri and Camille Dreyfus. For several years the Dreyfus brothers manufactured their product in the form of lacquers, plastic film, and "dope" for use on early airplane fabrics. In 1913 they made filaments of the substance, but World War I interrupted their work, and successful commercial production of acetate fibers was postponed.

The Dreyfus firm produced acetate fibers in England in 1921, and in 1924 an allied organization started production of the fiber in the United States. Since that time several companies have established factories for the manufacture of acetate fibers. American companies now producing acetate include Celanese Corporation (the first commercially successful manufacturer), DuPont, the fiber division of FMC Corporation, and Tennessee Eastman Company.

Triacetate fibers were developed along with regular secondary acetate. However, manufacture of triacetate was delayed until the middle of the

20th century, when satisfactory and relatively safe solvents became available in sufficient quantity to make the production economically profitable. Since then much work has gone into the perfection of appropriate coloring processes for triacetate.

Arnel, the triacetate fiber made in the United States by Celanese Corporation, was introduced in 1952, and large-scale commercial production began in 1955. Both acetate and triacetate are respected fibers for today's fabrics.

Acetate is defined by the 1960 Labeling Law as

> a manufactured fiber in which the fiber-forming substance is cellulose acetate. Where not less than 92 percent of the hydroxyl groups are acetylated, the term triacetate may be used as a generic description of the fiber.

Manufacture of Acetate (Secondary or Regular)

The raw materials for manufacturing acetate include cellulose, acetic acid, and acetic anhydride, plus sulfuric acid as a catalyst. Cellulose is obtained from either wood pulp or cotton linters, then purified, bleached, and shredded. Fed into pre-treatment tanks, the shredded cellulose is thoroughly mixed with glacial acetic acid and held for a specified length of time. The pretreated pulp is transferred to kneading machines called *acetylators,* where acetic anhydride is added. During this step the cellulose assumes liquid form as a new chemical compound, cellulose acetate. The clear liquid is called *acid dope.* It is aged or ripened in special storage tanks, with water added as needed to reduce the acid concentration. Hydrolysis occurs during the ripening and results in the formation of acetate. When this secondary acetate solution is mixed with water, it precipitates out in the form of small flakes. The flakes are washed thoroughly and dried. During the precipitation and washing process the excess acetic acid and the sulfuric acid are recovered for reuse.

The cellulose acetate flakes are dissolved in acetone to form *spinning dope.* This spinning solution is forced, first, through filters to remove any undissolved acetate and impurities and, then, through the spinnerette into a warm-air chamber. Here the acetone evaporates and is recovered for reuse while the acetate coagulates as it falls through the chamber. The filaments traveling downward are twisted together to form yarn. This method of fiber manufacture is called *dry spinning* (Fig. 7.4).

Manufacture of Triacetate (Arnel)

Triacetate is manufactured from the same raw materials as secondary acetate, but the ripening stage, in which hydrolysis of the acetate occurs, is omitted in triacetate production. To produce the spinning solution, the dried triacetate flake is dissolved in methylene chloride and dry spun into a warm-air chamber.

Fiber Properties

Microscopic Properties

When viewed longitudinally, acetate is uniform in width with several lines parallel to the length (Fig. 7.5). These striations are farther apart than in viscose rayon. Bright acetate is clear while dull or pigmented acetate appears speckled or pitted. The cross section of acetate is lobed with irregular curves but no sharp serrations like those found in viscose (Fig. 7.6).

Triacetate is very similar in microscopic appearance to acetate (Fig. 7.7). It may have clearer striations, and the cross section is both lobed and somewhat serrated (Fig. 7.8). Positive distinction between triacetate and secondary acetate by microscopy is not successful.

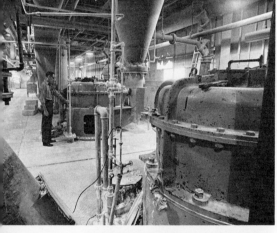

left: Figure 7.1 Mixing tanks for preparing cellulose acetate; top level. Tanks are two stories high. (*Celanese Corporation*)

below left: Figure 7.2 Cellulose acetate flake. (*Celanese Corporation*)

below: Figure 7.3 Cellulose acetate solution is tested frequently to determine when it is ready for spinning. (*Celanese Corporation*)

Physical Properties

The length, diameter, and luster of acetate and triacetate depend upon end-use, with manufacturers producing a wide variety of fibers. The makers of spinning jets have developed jets with orifices of different shapes that can turn out modified fibers, such as flat filaments—for example, *crystal acetate.*

Both acetate and triacetate have low strength, so they require careful handling in laundering or cleaning. But the desirable properties of hand, drape, and appearance make the fabrics attractive to designers and consumers.

Acetate's low elastic recovery coupled with its low resiliency causes fabrics to become easily wrinkled and permanently deformed. Triacetate has somewhat better elastic recovery, and its resiliency is good. It holds its shape and appearance; wrinkles hang out; laundering is relatively simple.

Figure 7.4 Acetate fibers are dry spun. The solution is forced through the spinnerette into an air chamber where the fibers are formed as the solvent evaporates in a heated environment. (*Celanese Corporation*)

Figure 7.5 Photomicrograph of acetate fiber, longitudinal view. (*E. I. DuPont de Nemours & Company*)

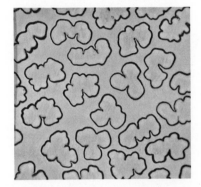

Figure 7.6 Photomicrograph of acetate fiber, cross section. (*E. I. DuPont de Nemours & Company*)

Figure 7.7 Photomicrograph of triacetate, longitudinal view. (*E. I. DuPont de Nemours & Company*)

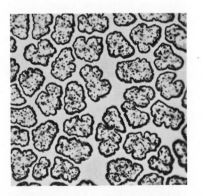

Figure 7.8 Photomicrograph of triacetate fiber, cross section. (*E. I. DuPont de Nemours & Company*)

Table 7.1 Physical Properties of Acetate

Property	Acetate	Triacetate
shape	Can be controlled by the manufacturer. Therefore, uniform in observed appearance. Length and denier determined by manufacturer for end-use. Filament and staple.	
luster	controlled	controlled
strength–gpd		
dry	1.2–1.5	1.2–1.4
wet	0.9–1.0	0.8–1.0
% elastic recovery		
	100 @ 1% extension	90–100 @ 1–2% extension
	48–65 @ 4% extension	80–84 @ 4% extension
% elongation		
dry	23–45	25–40
wet	35–45	30–40
resiliency	low	good
density	1.32	1.30
% moisture absorption 20°C (70°F) 65% R.H.	6.5	3.2–3.5
saturation	14.0	9.0

The moisture regain of acetate is slightly less than cotton, that of triacetate fairly low. Generally, it is adequate for comfort in fabrics. But the lower moisture regain coupled with the molecular arrangement makes dyeing of both fibers difficult and requires special dyes.

Acetate and triacetate fibers are comparatively resistant to stretch or shrinkage unless fabric relaxation occurs. The fibers may shrink if exposed to high temperatures.

Thermal Properties

Acetate and triacetate are thermoplastic fibers and are easily softened by high temperatures. The fibers melt and burn evenly, forming a hard, black bead ash. They give off an odor similar to that of hot vinegar. Because of their sensitivity to high temperatures, acetate fabrics should be ironed at low to medium settings with steam. Triacetate (Arnel) can be "heat treated" to withstand higher temperatures without damage. The same treatment also permits setting permanent pleats and creases in Arnel triacetate fabrics.

Chemical Properties

Dilute alkalies have little effect on acetate or triacetate. Concentrated alkalies cause saponification of both and eventually a loss in fiber weight and a reduction in the soft hand of fabrics.

Concentrated acids weaken the fibers drastically and in most instances cause complete disintegration. Dilute hot acids may cause decomposition or, at least, a loss of strength. Cold dilute acids weaken the fiber if exposure is prolonged.

Petroleum products used in dry cleaning do not damage acetate or triacetate. However, such solvents as acetone, phenol, and chloroform will destroy the fibers. One should be cautious using fingernail polish remover, paint removers, and the like, for they often contain acetone.

Sunlight causes a loss of strength in acetate fiber but has little effect on triacetate. In storage, too, acetate fibers become weaker while Arnel triacetate has excellent stability to aging.

All acetates develop static charges, especially when dry, because they are poor conductors of electricity.

Biological Properties

Fungi such as mildew and bacteria may discolor acetate fibers. Some weakening of acetate may occur, but triacetate retains its strength.

Moths and other household pests do not damage acetates and triacetates. However, silverfish may attack heavily sized fibers in order to eat the sizing. Naturally, this will damage the fiber and alter its hand and appearance.

Acetates in Use

Regular acetate is preferred by many designers for its outstanding drapability and desirable hand. It can be made into fabrics of varying weight, thickness, and degree of softness or stiffness. Because of the thermoplastic property, acetate should be either dry cleaned or laundered and ironed at warm, not hot, temperatures. The relatively low moisture regain of acetate renders fibers resistant to damage by staining and to size change from shrinkage or stretch. Acetate fabrics should not be wrung or twisted when wet, for they retain creases. The fiber accepts special dyestuffs satisfactorily, and white acetate retains its whiteness, if properly laundered, with a minimum of bleaching. In many instances, no bleaching is required. In addition to a wide variety of apparel applications, acetate finds considerable use in household fabrics, such as drapery and upholstery materials.

Triacetate has the versatility and desirable properties of regular acetate, plus additional characteristics that influence its care and use. It accepts permanent pleats and creases that will withstand wear and maintenance. The fabric is dimensionally stable and can be processed and maintained at temperatures slightly higher than regular acetate. It has a somewhat crisper hand than acetate (Fig. 7.10).

Figure 7.9 Chiffon caftan of Celanese acetate. (*Celanese Corporation*)

Figure 7.10 Informal summer evening wear of 100 percent Arnel triacetate. (*Celanese Corporation*)

Arnel triacetate appears in blends, where it imparts stability and wrinkle resistance. Both acetate and triacetate are used in knitted fabric construction, but triacetate knits especially will hold their shape, retain permanent pleats, and pack beautifully. The manufacturers of Arnel maintain a quality certification program. Products labeled with the trademark Arnel have met specifications that are considered desirable by the fiber producer.

Arnel triacetate is more expensive than regular acetate, and both fibers are higher in price than viscose rayon or cotton, but they cost less than many noncellulosic polymer fibers.

When acetate is solution-dyed—that is, when color is added to the chemical solution before the fibers are formed—it may acquire a special trade name. The most common solution-dyed acetate fibers are Chromspun and Celaperm.

Natural Protein Fibers 8

Natural protein fibers are obtained from animal sources. Most fibers in this group are the hair covering from animals; the rest are animal secretions.

Hair fibers include coverings from such animals as sheep, mohair goat, cashmere goat, camel, llama, alpaca, and vicuña; fur fibers come from animals more often valued for their pelts, such as mink, rabbit, beaver, and muskrat. Secretions are obtained from the larva or worm stage of the silkworm, *Bombyx mori,* from various wild silkworm species of the types *Antheraea* and *Attacus,* and from the spider that spins fine fibers in making its web. Hair and fur fibers have many properties in common with secretion fibers, but some characteristics are quite different.

Fibers in this group have excellent moisture absorbency. Their standard moisture regain is high, and they absorb additional moisture at the saturation point. Protein fibers tend to be warmer than natural cellulose fibers. The low degree of electrical conductance contributes to a buildup of static charge, so the resulting yarns and fabrics tend to release much static electricity, although this problem is reduced in the presence of moisture.

Natural protein fibers have poor resistance to alkalies and can be dissolved in a 5-percent solution of sodium hydroxide at the boiling point. Most fibers in this group show good resistance to acids, the exception being silk, which is damaged or completely destroyed by concentrated mineral acids. Protein fibers are harmed by many oxidizing agents, particularly chlorine-type oxidizing bleaches. However, hydrogen peroxide, also an oxidizing agent, is used safely and successfully to bleach wool and silk. Sunlight causes white fabrics of the natural protein fibers to discolor slowly and turn yellow.

Fibers in this group have good resiliency and elastic recovery. All protein fibers except silk are comparatively weak, so care must be exercised in cleaning.

In recent years the status of protein fibers has been threatened by the increasing use of man-made fibers, but their popularity has continued because of the many outstanding properties they possess.

Wool

Historical Review

The early history of wool is lost in antiquity. Sheepskin, including the hair, was probably used long before the discovery that the fibers could be spun into yarns or even felted into fabric. There is no evidence to support the theory that wool was the first fiber to be processed into fabric, but it seems certain that, as a part of the skin, wool was used for covering and protection by prehistoric people.

Today, sheep are raised in every state of the contiguous United States and in most countries located in the temperate zones of both the Northern and Southern Hemispheres. The center for sheep raising in the United States is in the West.

Although large areas in the United States are suitable for wool production, much wool is imported. A relatively large proportion of the import comes from Australia, where fine-quality wool is produced.

Growth and Production

To provide the finest-quality wool for the present-day consumer, manufacturers control production carefully and scientifically. Sheep are inoculated against disease, dipped in chemicals to protect them against insects, and fed nutritionally balanced diets to produce healthy animals. Sheep in small herds live in sanitary, fenced-in shelters, and are allowed to graze in clean pastures. Large herds in the western states are usually permitted to

Figure 8.1 Shearing sheep to obtain wool fibers. (*United States Department of Agriculture*)

roam in open range land, but, even in these large areas there is always a sheepherder to watch the animals and keep them under control.

Wool can be sheared from the living animal or pulled from the hide after the animal has been slaughtered for its meat. The sheared wool is called *fleece* or *clip wool*. Wool taken from the slaughtered animal hide is called *pulled wool* and is frequently of inferior quality.

Shearing takes place once a year in most states (Fig. 8.1); occasionally in the southern states wool may be sheared twice in order to keep the animal more comfortable and to eliminate extra long, coarse fibers. The sheep is sheared in early spring and the fleece removed in one piece by expert shearers. It is then rolled, packed into bags, and shipped to the nearest processing plant.

Pulled wool is removed from the hide by one of two methods. It may be treated with a depilatory that loosens the fibers and permits it to be pulled away from the skin without damaging the hide, or it can be loosened by the action of bacteria on the root end of the fiber. Pulled wool is usually mixed with fleece wool by manufacturers.

Preliminary grading of wool fibers occurs while the fibers are still in the fleece, because this step is important in determining cost. Fleeces are then shipped to the mill, where they are prepared for processing.

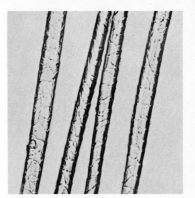

Figure 8.2 Photomicrograph of wool fiber, longitudinal view. (*E. I. DuPont de Nemours & Company*)

Fiber Properties

Microscopic Properties

Under microscopic observation, the length of the wool fiber clearly shows a scalelike structure (Fig. 8.2). The size of the scale varies from very small to comparatively broad and large. Fine wool does not have as clear and distinct scales as coarse wool, but they can be identified under magnification as low as 100 power.

A cross section of wool shows three distinct parts of the fiber (Fig. 8.3). The outer layer is called the *epidermis* and is composed of the scales. The major portion of the fiber is the *cortex,* which accounts for about 90 percent of the fiber mass. In the center is the *medulla.* This is the area through which food reaches the fiber during growth. It contains the pigment that gives color to the fibers.

Physical Properties

Wool fibers vary in length from about $1\frac{1}{2}$ inches to 15 inches. Fine wools are usually from $1\frac{1}{2}$ to 5 inches long, medium wools from $2\frac{1}{2}$ to 6 inches, and coarse wools from 5 to 15 inches. The width of wool also varies considerably. Fine fibers such as Merino have an average diameter of about 15 to 17 microns, medium wools from 24 to 34 microns, and coarse wools about 40 microns. Some wool fibers are exceptionally stiff and coarse. These are called *kemp*.

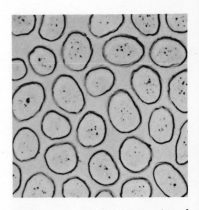

Figure 8.3 Photomicrograph of wool fiber, cross section. (*E. I. DuPont de Nemours & Company*)

Table 8.1   Physical Properties of Wool

shape	length—1$\frac{1}{2}$ inches–15 inches width—15–70 microns natural crimp or waviness
luster	medium
strength–gpd dry wet	 1.0–1.7 0.8–1.6
% elastic recovery	99 at 2% extension
% elongation dry wet	 20–40 20–70+
resiliency	excellent
density	1.30–1.32
moisture absorption 20° (70°F) 65% R.H. saturation	 13.6–16.0 29+

Wool fibers have a natural crimp, a built-in waviness (Fig. 8.4). This crimp increases the elasticity and elongation properties of the fiber and also aids in yarn manufacturing. It is three-dimensional in character and moves not only above and below a central axis but also to the right and left of it.

Wool varies in degree of luster. Fine fibers and some that are medium have enough luster to appear silky. The color of the natural wool fiber depends upon the breed of sheep. Most wool, after scouring, is a yellowish-white or ivory color. It also may be gray, black, tan, or brown.

Compared to many other fibers, wool is weak. This weakness restricts the kinds of yarn and fabric constructions that can be used satisfactorily. However, other properties such as resiliency, elongation, and elastic

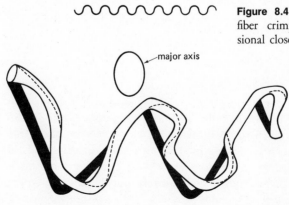

Figure 8.4 Diagram of wool fiber crimp and three-dimensional close-up of the fiber.

major axis

recovery compensate for the low strength; they allow for production of wool yarns and fabrics that are durable.

The elongation of wool is good, elastic recovery very good, and resiliency exceptionally good. As a result, wool fabrics will readily spring back into shape after crushing or creasing. Through the application of heat, moisture, and pressure, durable creases or pleats can be put into wool fabrics. The excellent resilience of wool fiber also gives it loft, which produces open, porous fabrics with good covering power, or thick, warm fabrics that are light in weight.

Wool will absorb moisture to a high degree—approximately 30 percent of its weight. This ability is responsible for the comfort of wool in humid, cold atmospheres. As part of the moisture absorption function, wool produces or liberates heat.

The same property also permits it to accept color easily. However, in spite of the ability to absorb, the fiber has a hydrophobic surface and tends to shed liquid.

When wool yarns and fabrics are subjected to mechanical action, such as agitation or abrasion combined with heat and moisture, they tend to become entangled and matted. This causes yarns to decrease in length and increase in diameter, which, in turn, results in fabrics that are dimensionally smaller in length and width but thicker than the original. This is called *felting shrinkage* and is used to advantage in making more compact, fuller, and more attractive fabrics. Obviously, improper control of this process would result in highly unsatisfactory products.

Wool fabrics are quite likely to shrink after weaving or knitting as a result of yarn and fabric relaxation. This is called *relaxation shrinkage.* The elasticity and elongation of wool means that it will be extended during yarn manufacture. Sometimes fibers and yarns are held in a partially extended state after yarns and fabrics have been made. Moisture tends to release the tension of yarns, and they will return to their original length, causing the fabric or product to shrink.

Thermal Properties

Wool burns slowly in the presence of flame with a slight sputtering. It is self-extinguishing; that is, it stops burning when removed from the source of fire. A crisp, brittle, black, bead-shaped residue is formed as wool burns, and the odor given off may be compared to the smell of burning hair, meat, or feathers.

Wool should be ironed at temperatures below 140°C (300°F). Steam or a damp press cloth should always be used.

Chemical Properties

Wool protein is particularly susceptible to damage by alkaline substances. Solutions of 5 percent sodium hydroxide will dissolve the fiber. Strong detergents or soap should be avoided.

Wool is considered resistant to action by mild or dilute acids, but strong concentrated mineral acids will bring about its decomposition.

Solvents used in cleaning and stain removal for wool fabrics have no deleterious effects; however, chlorine bleaches damage the fiber and in concentrated form will dissolve it.

After prolonged exposure to direct sunlight wool deteriorates. But if the fabric is properly protected and stored, there is no destructive effect.

Biological Properties

Wool has good resistance to bacteria and mildew. However, both organisms may attack stains on the fabric, particularly food stains. If wool is stored in an atmosphere where moisture is present, mildew will form, and eventually it will destroy the fiber. Rot-producing bacteria will bring about the destruction of wool that has been subjected to moisture and soil for long periods of time.

Because wool is a protein and may be considered a modified food product, it becomes an appetizing meal for several types of insects. The larvae of the clothes moth and of the carpet beetle are the most common predators on wool as a source of food. Various treatments suggested to prevent this damage include

1. Spraying the fabric with chemicals that will kill the insects. These finishes need frequent renewing since dry cleaning removes them.

2. Applying chemicals that react with the wool molecule and make the fiber unpalatable to the moth. This process is durable to laundering or dry cleaning and is the most successful.

3. Using substances in close proximity to wool that give off odors that are noxious to the insects.

Wool in Use

Woolen and worsted fabrics are widely used throughout the world, and they have special acceptance in the United States for their many desirable properties. They are naturally crease resistant, flexible and elastic, absorbent, warm, and comfortable. Wool fabrics tailor well, press easily, and can be shaped to conform to the body.

In terms of care wool is rather demanding. A major problem with the fabric is its tendency for shrinkage. It can be dry cleaned and pressed easily, but laundering is difficult because wool cannot tolerate agitation or temperature change. If handling is kept to a minimum, if the wool is not hand-wrung or agitated, and if warm or cool water is used throughout both washing and rinsing, wool can be laundered without damage. Some wools on the market today have been processed with special finishes or blended with a stabilizing fiber. These fabrics can be laundered relatively easily, and they generally retain their original size and appearance.

Chlorine bleaches cannot be used on wool. When bleaching is required, it must be done with hydrogen peroxide or similar bleaching

Figure 8.5 Men's and women's apparel of wool. Woman's dress is of wool voile. (*Wool Bureau, Inc.*)

compounds. Mild soaps and detergents are recommended for laundering wool fabrics.

Wool is easily dyed and has good colorfastness when proper dyestuffs are used.

After wear, woven wool garments should be placed on hangers and brushed carefully. This removes surface dust and soil and permits wrinkles to hang out. Knitted garments, especially loose knits such as sweaters and stoles, should be aired and then folded and stored in drawers to prevent sagging and misshaping from hangers. Frequent cleaning reduces insect damage and increases the life of wool products.

Newer man-made fibers have replaced wool in many end-uses. The per-capita consumption of wool in the United States has continued to decline and now accounts for only slightly more than 5 percent of the fibers used. However, many people enjoy its pleasant hand, and wool is still a desirable choice for warm fabrics and for durable apparel and home furnishings.

Wool Products Labeling Act

The Wool Products Labeling Act was passed by Congress in 1939. The purpose of the law is

> to protect producers, manufacturers, distributors and consumers from the unrevealed presence of substitutes and mixtures in spun, woven, knit, felted, or otherwise manufactured wool products.

This legislation requires that any product containing wool (except upholstery and floor coverings) have a label affixed that specifies the wool as new, reprocessed, or reused. The term *wool* is defined by the act as fiber of animal origin grown naturally as the coat of a living animal. The definition does not specify the sheep as the fiber's source. However, the vast majority of products labeled as wool are composed of fibers from sheep. The term *wool* also indicates fiber that is being used for the first time in the complete manufacture of a wool product. Fibers processed as far as the yarn state, recovered (pulled apart into fiber form), and reconstructed in new yarns may be labeled as wool. *Virgin wool* denotes new fiber that has been made into yarns and fabrics for the first time. *Lamb's wool* means that it has been clipped from sheep less than eight months old. *Reprocessed wool* refers to fibers reclaimed from scraps of fabrics that were never used. These come from cutting rooms, fabric samples, and similar sources. The fabrics are converted or *garnetted* (shredded) back into a fibrous state before being made into new yarns and fabrics. *Reused wool* refers to fibers reclaimed from fabrics that have been worn or used, with old rags and clothing comprising the major source. Reused wool is sometimes called *shoddy*.

The quality of both reused and reprocessed wool is usually lower than that of new fibers. During the garnetting process the fibers are frequently damaged by tearing and breaking. However, the warmth property is maintained, and fabrics of reused wool are satisfactory for interlining fabrics, inexpensive blankets, and similar products. Reprocessed wool has warmth, some resiliency, and good durability. In fact, new wool of poor quality may give less wear than reprocessed or reused wool of high original quality.

All products containing wool must be labeled with the fiber content and the percentages of the various types of wool. The Wool Products Labeling Act is a protection to the consumer against the purchase of fabrics designed to imitate wool in appearance but that would not possess the desirable qualities of a true wool product. In the case of blends, where one of the fibers is wool, this act covers identification for the woolen part, while the Textile Fiber Products Identification Act of 1960 provides for the labeling of the other fibers in the blend.

Specialty and Fur Fibers

Fibers from such animals as the goat, camel, alpaca, and llama are referred to as *specialty fibers*. They are available in limited quantities and are desired for special characteristics. Although these fibers may also be identified as wool, this is seldom done because the salespower of the specialty fibers is enhanced by the specific fiber or animal name.

Mohair

Mohair is the fiber of the Angora goat (Fig. 8.6). (It is not to be confused with the fur fiber obtained from the Angora rabbit.) Angora goats usually are sheared twice a year, in which case the fibers are fine and silky in appearance and measure 4 to 6 inches in length. Occasionally, the goats are sheared once a year to make the fibers longer—from 9 to 12 inches.

Figure 8.6 Angora goat, source of mohair fibers. (*United States Department of Agriculture*)

Mohair resembles wool in both physical and chemical properties. Its major advantages include remarkable resistance to wear and abrasion, a high degree of luster, excellent resiliency, and adaptability to complex yarns and textured fabrics. Suiting and sportswear fabrics, upholstery, rugs, and draperies may be of mohair or of a blend including mohair fibers.

Cashmere

Cashmere is the fiber of the cashmere (Kashmir) goat, which is raised in Asia. Tibet, India, Persia, and parts of China are major sources. The fiber is combed from the animal, and the yield per goat averages about 4 ounces of good fiber. The short fibers—1 to $3\frac{1}{2}$ inches—are very soft and fine; longer fibers—2 to 5 inches—are somewhat coarse and stiff.

Since the yearly production of true cashmere is very small, the fiber is expensive. Cashmere fabrics are considered luxury items, but the consumers who want very soft, warm, comfortable, and attractive products will pay the price.

The cashmere fiber is highly adaptable. It can produce either fine or thick yarns, which, in turn, can be constructed into thick, medium, or rather lightweight fabrics, appropriate to both warm and cool climates.

Cashmere is similar to wool in most properties, except for the fact that it is more easily damaged by alkalies. If properly maintained, it will give good service.

Camel Hair

The Bactrian, or two-humped camel, is the source of camel-hair fiber. This breed serves as a means of transportation in Asia in the desert regions of China, Tibet, and Mongolia. The animal sheds about 5 pounds of fiber each year, which is used in textile products. The outer camel fibers are coarse and utilized only in low-quality merchandise, but the fine, short underhairs are as soft and fine as top-quality wool. In addition, camel hair possesses thermal properties similar to those of wool that keep the wearer warm in extremely cold weather.

Fine camel-hair products require the same careful handling as cashmere and mohair. Camel hair is used in coating fabrics, sportswear, and knitted products. The natural tan to reddish brown color is very attractive and is retained for many choice fabrics.

Coarse camel-hair fibers are used in industry for special belting and in artists' brushes. Natives make blankets out of the coarse fibers.

Alpaca

The alpaca is a member of the camel family native to South America. It thrives in the Andes Mountain regions of Peru, Bolivia, Ecuador, and Argentina. The fiber is sheared from the animal once every two years. The fine fibers, which are separated from the coarse guard hairs, are used in fabric manufacturing.

Like camel hair, alpaca offers excellent warmth and insulation. The fibers are strong and glossy and make fabrics similar in appearance to mohair. Alpaca fabrics appear in suits, dresses, plush upholstery, and linings. The natural fiber color ranges from white to brown and black, and a variety of attractive fabrics can be created without additional dyestuffs.

Llama

Also a member of the camel family, the llama produces fibers similar to those of the alpaca and is found in the same geographical area. The fibers, sheared once a year, are soft, strong, and relatively uniform in length and diameter but somewhat weaker than alpaca or camel hair.

South American Indians weave most of the pure llama fabrics. Some fiber is sold to wool manufacturers for blending with sheep's wool, other specialty fibers, or man-made fibers.

Vicuña

The most valuable and most prized hair fiber is that taken from the vicuña. This small animal (about the size of a large dog) is found in the Andes Mountains at elevations of approximately 16,000 feet. It is a member of the llama family and thus of the South American camel family. The vicuña is extremely wild, and attempts to domesticate it have been relatively unsuccessful so far, but efforts by ranchers to raise the animal in captivity are continuing.

Vicuña is one of the softest fibers in the world. It is fine and lustrous, has a lovely cinnamon brown or light tan color, and is strong enough to make very desirable fabrics. It is also very light in weight and very warm. Choice uses of the fiber are for coats, suit fabrics, and soft shawls or capes.

As yet, the fiber can be obtained only by killing the animal, and the Peruvian government limits the yearly kill. Each animal yields about 4 ounces of fine fiber plus 10 to 12 ounces of shorter, less choice fiber. The total yearly production is just a few thousand pounds, so garments and fabrics of vicuña compare in price with good fur coats.

Fur Fibers

Fibers often blended in small amounts with wool or man-made fibers are obtained from several animals more frequently used for fur pelts. These include mink, beaver, fox, chinchilla, muskrat, nutria, raccoon, and rabbit. They are added to fabrics primarily for softness, color interest, and prestige value.

The angora fiber from the Angora rabbit appears frequently in knitting yarns and in knitted fabrics, because it gives a fluffy, white, silky appearance to products. The Angora rabbit is raised in France, Italy, Japan, and the United States. The fur is combed and clipped every three months. Fibers are smooth, lustrous, fine, and resilient.

Most specialty and fur fibers require careful handling. They are luxury items and should be treated with considerable respect. The recommended care for these fibers is dry cleaning.

Silk

Historical Review

The history of silk combines fact and myth, and it is difficult to separate truth from fiction. However, the legends concerning silk are romantic and interesting.

Emperor Huang-Ti, who ruled China sometime between 2700 and 2600 B.C., assigned his Empress, Hsi-Ling-Shi, the task of studying a blight that was damaging the Imperial mulberry grove. Tiny white worms were devouring the leaves, then crawling from leaf to stem to spin shining, pale (almost white) cocoons. Hsi-Ling-Shi gathered a handful of cocoons and carried them into her apartment, where she accidentally dropped one into a basin of hot water.

The empress noticed that the cocoon separated into a delicate cobweb-like tangle from which she could draw a slender, tiny filament into the air. She further observed the filament was continuous, and the more she unwound, the smaller the cocoon became. Thus, one legend (probably a combination of fact and fiction) records the discovery of silk fibers.

Throughout the development of the silk industry, this fiber has maintained a position of great prestige and is still considered a luxury item. Silk is often called the "queen of fibers," a title well deserved by virtue of its association with royalty, the care required in its culture, and the properties and characteristics with which it has been endowed.

Sericulture (Growth and Production)

Silk is produced by the larvae of several moths, but the *Bombyx mori* is the only one raised under controlled conditions. These larvae live on mulberry leaves only, and each tiny larva consumes an extremely large number of leaves. Raising these insects is a skilled occupation and requires countless hours of labor. The present-day industry is carefully controlled in relation to disease prevention, and modern silk "factories" are as clean and frequently as sterile as hospital operating rooms.

The female *Bombyx mori* lays eggs once a month. She may lay as many as seven hundred. Each egg is about the size of a pinhead, and each has a small dot on one end that is soft and permits the larva to hatch easily. The eggs are carefully screened and tested to ensure freedom from disease. They can be kept for long periods of time in cold storage without damage. When a supply of fresh young mulberry leaves is ready, the eggs are warmed slightly, and three to seven days later the worm hatches and begins to feed on the tender leaves. The new larvae are about $\frac{1}{4}$ inch long. Although the larvae of the *Bombyx mori* are called silkworms, they are technically caterpillars.

During the growth cycle of the larva, it moults (sheds its outer skin) four times. Each time it grows a new skin to fit its larger size. After the fourth moulting, it eats for about ten days, making a total eating period of about 35 days. At the end of the growing period the caterpillar has increased about 10,000 times over the weight of the newly hatched larva. It is more than 3 inches long and from $\frac{1}{4}$ to $\frac{1}{2}$ inch in diameter. In this state it is ready to spin its chrysalis case or cocoon.

The larva attaches itself to a specially constructed straw frame, rears its head, and begins to spew the silk liquid, which hardens on contact with air. The larva spins by moving its head in a figure-eight motion and constructs the cocoon from the outside in (Fig. 8.7). As it spins, the larva decreases in size, and upon completion of the cocoon it changes into the dormant *chrysalis*. Except for those to be used for breeding, the cocoons are subjected to heat, which kills the chrysalis. These cocoons can then be stored until they are unreeled in preparation for yarn manufacturing.

The silkworm extrudes the liquid fiber from two tiny orifices or *spinnerettes* in its head. As the liquid emerges into the air, it solidifies into silk filaments (Fig. 8.8). The fibers, coated with a gummy substance called *sericin,* are extruded by two glands in close proximity to the cocoon.

Raising of silkworms is a highly scientific art. The process must be carefully controlled in order to maintain healthy larvae and moths that will produce a supply of high-quality fiber.

In addition to the sericulture of *Bombyx mori,* several other moths produce larvae that spin cocoons composed of usable silk fiber. Probably the most important in this group are the moths responsible for tussah silk. These larvae feed on oak leaves and grow wild.

left: Figure 8.7 Silkworms and cocoons. (*International Silk Association*)

right: Figure 8.8 Silk filaments and cocoons.

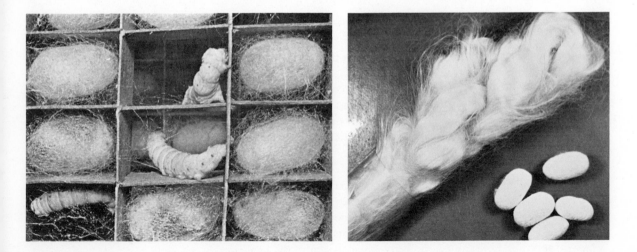

Processing

Reeling

Silk filaments are unwound from the cocoons in a manufacturing plant called a *filature*. Several cocoons are placed in hot water to soften the gum, and the surfaces are brushed lightly to find the ends of the filaments. These ends are collected, threaded through a guide, and wound onto a wheel called a reel, hence the name *reeling*.

Reeling requires extremely skillful operators (Fig. 8.9). The fibers are narrower at the beginnings and ends, and experienced workers can join cocoons so the diameter of reeled yarn remains constant. Only uniform reeled silk will sell for premium prices.

Throwing

As the fibers are combined and pulled onto the reel, twist can be inserted to hold the filaments together. This is called *throwing,* and the resulting yarn is *thrown yarn.* Fibers may be thrown in a separate operation.

Spinning

Short ends of silk fibers from the outer and inner edges of the cocoons and from broken cocoons are spun into yarns in a manner similar to that used for cotton.

Degumming

Sericin remains on the fibers during reeling and throwing. Frequently it is left on through the fabric construction processes. Before finishing the

Figure 8.9 Silk reeling in present-day factory in China. (*Eastfoto*)

Figure 8.10 Photomicrograph of silk fiber, longitudinal view. (*E. I. DuPont de Nemours & Company*)

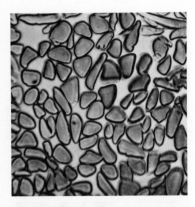

Figure 8.11 Photomicrograph of silk fiber, cross section. (*E. I. DuPont de Nemours & Company*)

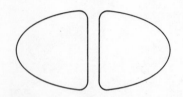

Figure 8.12 Diagram of silk filaments or brins as formed by silkworm.

gum is removed by boiling the fabric in soap and water. If stiffness is desired in the completed fabric, some of the sericin may be replaced, but this is seldom desirable, since the presence of gum or sericin increases the tendency for silk to waterspot.

Fiber Properties

Silk is a natural protein fiber. The actual fiber protein, called *fibroin,* is composed of about fifteen amino acids hooked together in long molecular chains. *Sericin,* the gum that holds the filaments together, is also a protein substance.

Microscopic Properties

Cultivated degummed silk, viewed longitudinally under a microscope, resembles a smooth, transparent rod (Fig. 8.10). If gum is still present, fiber surfaces are rough and irregular. Wild silk tends to be uneven and darker. It may have longitudinal striations.

Cross-sectional views of silk show triangular fibers with no markings (Fig. 8.11). Two filaments usually lie with their flat sides together. This can be explained by the fact that two filaments are extruded simultaneously by each silkworm, and they come together as indicated in Figure 8.12. The two filaments are called *brins.*

Physical Properties

Silk filaments are very fine and long. They usually measure about 1000 to 1300 yards and can be as long as 3000 yards. The width of silk is from 9 to 11 microns. The fibers are quite smooth, have a high natural luster or sheen, and are off-white to cream in color. Wild silk is uneven, has slightly less luster, and is tan to light brown in color.

Silk is one of the stronger fibers used in making fabrics. Dry silk has good elastic recovery and moderate elongation. When it is wet, fiber strength is slightly reduced and elongation increases considerably.

Silk has medium resiliency. Creases will hang out relatively well but not as quickly or as completely as in wool.

The moisture regain of silk is relatively high. At saturation the regain is about 30 percent. The absorption property of silk helps in the application of dyes and finishes, but, unlike many fibers, silk will absorb impurities in liquids such as metal salts. These contaminants tend to damage silk by weakening the fiber or sometimes even causing ruptures to occur.

Silk filaments, yarns, and fabrics have good resistance to stretch or shrinkage when laundered or dry cleaned. Crepe fabrics will shrink when wet but can be steamed back to size easily.

Table 8.2 Physical Properties of Silk

shape and appearance	fine, 9–11 microns in diameter
	1000–1300 yards long
	smooth, even, white to cream color
	wild silk is uneven and dark in color
luster	high
strength–gpd	
dry	2.4–5.1
wet	2.0–4.3
% elastic recovery	92 at 2% extension
% elongation	
dry	10–25
wet	33–35
resiliency	medium
density	1.25–1.34
moisture absorption	
20°C (70°F) 65% R.H.	11.0
saturation	25–35

Thermal Properties

Silk will burn when directly in the path of flame. After removal from the flame it will sputter and eventually extinguish itself. It leaves a crisp, brittle ash and gives off an odor like that of burning hair or feathers.

Silk scorches easily if ironed with temperatures above 149°C (300°F), and white silk will turn yellow if pressed with a hot iron. The use of steam or a press cloth is recommended.

Chemical Properties

Silk is damaged by strong alkalies and will dissolve in heated caustic soda. Weak alkalies such as soap, borax, and ammonia cause little damage to silk unless they remain in contact with the fabric for a long time.

While mineral acids can dissolve silk and cause fiber contraction and shrinkage, organic acids do no damage and are used in finishing processes. In fact, some authorities maintain that the *scroop* of silk—the characteristic rustling or crunching sound—is developed by exposure to organic acids.

Cleaning solvents and spot-removing agents do not damage silk, but chlorine bleaches cause fiber disintegration. Hydrogen peroxide and perborate bleaches can be used safely.

Sunlight tends to accelerate the breakdown of silk, as does the oxygen in the atmosphere. Therefore, unless it is stored in sealed containers, the fiber will lose strength and eventually be destroyed.

Figure 8.13 Silk fabric in brocade pattern.

Silk is a poor conductor of electricity, which results in the buildup of static charges. Like other protein fibers, it has a lower thermal or heat conductivity than cellulosic fibers. This factor, coupled with general compactness of construction, creates fabrics that tend to be warmer than comparable fabrics of cellulosic fibers.

Biological Properties

Silk resists attack by mildew and most other bacteria and fungi. It has good resistance to the clothes moth, but carpet beetles will eat it. Destruction attributed to moths has usually been caused by carpet beetles.

Silk in Use

Silk has been the "queen of fibers" for centuries. As in the past, it is still used for luxury fabrics and for high-fashion items. At the same time, its durability makes it practical for modern-day usage (Fig. 8.13).

Dry cleaning is the preferred method of care for silk fabrics. However, if handled carefully, some silk products can be hand laundered. A mild soap or synthetic detergent in warm, not hot, water should be used for silk, and it should receive minimal handling. Thorough rinsing is required, and the best method for extracting the water is to roll the garment in a towel and then hang it in a cool place, out of the sun, to dry. Silk should be ironed or pressed with medium to low ironing temperatures, and steam is acceptable.

If silk requires bleaching, hydrogen peroxide or perborate bleach, not chlorine types, must be used for chlorine is destructive to silk. One problem with silk fabrics is that body perspiration tends to weaken the fibers and frequently will alter the color. Many deodorants and antiperspirants contain aluminum chloride, which is damaging to silk. It is advisable to wear protective dress shields.

Silk offers an incredible variety in fabric and yarn structure as well as in colors since it dyes easily and well. It is versatile and can be used in sportswear; men's and women's suits; lingerie; dress, blouse, and shirt fabrics; and decorator fabrics for homes or offices.

Because of its strength, silk is durable, and with proper care it will withstand years of wear. Except for extremely hot days, silk fabrics are comfortable and maintain a neat and attractive appearance.

Many silk fabrics cost more than similar fabrics of man-made fibers. However, the consumer who has formed an attachment to silk will pay high prices. Silk combines strength, flexibility, good moisture absorption, softness, warmth, luxurious appearance, and durability, so it creates choice products for the discerning consumer.

Man-Made Protein Fibers: Azlons

The generic name assigned to man-made protein fibers by the Textile Fiber Products Identification Act is azlon. The act defines *azlon* as

> a manufactured fiber in which the fiber-forming substance is composed of any regenerated naturally occurring protein.

There are no azlon fibers currently in production in the United States, but a few are still being manufactured in other countries. Despite the present inactivity, the fibers have sufficient importance to merit brief discussion.

Production

The steps in manufacturing protein fibers are similar for all varieties. Protein is extracted from its original source by various techniques and then processed into a spinning solution that can be extruded through the spinnerette. After extrusion, the fiber is coagulated in a chemical bath. To produce sufficient strength for use in fabrics, protein fibers are stretched slightly to improve molecular orientation. Nonetheless, molecular arrangement remains highly amorphous compared to that of most other fibers. Finally, protein fibers are treated by a hardening bath to impart dimensional stability and chemical resistance.

Fiber Properties

Since man-made protein fibers attract limited interest, the following discussion is restricted to two fibers produced in Europe that may appear in consumer goods in the United States.

Fibrolane

A casein fiber manufactured in England, Fibrolane is characterized by exceptional softness and warmth, high moisture regain, and good resistance to sunlight and insect damage.

Merinova

Merinova, a product of Italy, has the same general properties as Fibrolane. It is frequently blended with rayon fibers to make a soft fabric that drapes well, gives a good appearance, and is characterized by warmth.

Man-Made Protein Fibers in Use

Protein fibers on the current market, as well as those that have been discontinued, resemble wool in many respects. Azlon fibers do not felt as wool fibers do, so fabrics composed of blends of azlon and a normally washable fiber can be considered launderable. Blends of azlon and wool fibers should receive the same care recommended for wool. All azlon fibers are weak and require gentle handling. Unlike wool, however, these fabrics do not shrink.

The major use for the azlons is in blends with stronger fibers. They will add softness, warmth, loftiness, and resilience to fabrics. Of considerable importance is the fact that although man-made protein fibers have properties similar to wool, their cost is much lower.

Polyamide Fibers: Nylon and Aramid

Nylon

Historical Review

The history of nylon is a story of scientific research and development. In 1927 the DuPont Company gave a small group of scientists unrestricted funds for basic research in the hope that new scientific information would ultimately lead to chemical advancement. A year later the research team, headed by Wallace Carothers, a brilliant young organic chemist, began to study long-chain molecules such as those found in natural fibers, rubber, and plastic products. This phase of their work resulted in the creation of a number of giant molecules called *macromolecules, polymolecules,* or *polymers.* The team also determined that linear polymers composed of relatively small molecules linked end to end, much like a chain of paper clips, could be man-made.

In 1930 the chemists discovered an unusual characteristic in one of the substances under investigation. They found that when a glass rod in contact with some viscous material in a beaker was pulled away slowly, the substance adhered to the rod and formed a fine filament that hardened as soon as it was exposed to cool air. Furthermore they observed that the cold filaments could be stretched several times their extruded length to produce a flexible, strong, and attractive fiber. After this discovery the scientists set out to produce such a fiber in a practical and economic manner.

The next few years were devoted to improving the polymer, finding efficient methods for manufacturing it, developing necessary mechanical equipment for its production, and, perhaps of most importance, finding possible uses for the new fiber. In 1938 DuPont set up a pilot plant, and one year later, a large-scale plant was placed "on stream" at Seaford, Delaware. It has been estimated that the first pound of nylon fiber produced at Seaford cost $27 million.

Nylon, in the form of knitted hosiery, was test-marketed in various parts of the United States in late 1939 and early 1940. Introduction of the fiber to the general public was well planned and coordinated; it was a classic example of successful mass marketing (Fig. 10.1). Throughout the nation, heralded by uniform advertising campaigns, nylon stockings were

Figure 10.1 Advertisement used to introduce nylon, October 30, 1938. (*E. I. DuPont de Nemours & Company*)

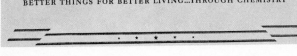

launched on May 15, 1940. They were a tremendous and immediate success. Despite the temporary absence from the consumer market during World War II, nylon hosiery has retained its early success and popularity.

The first nylon was and is referred to as type 6,6. The numbers derive from the fact that each of the two chemicals used in making this nylon has six carbon atoms. Nylon type 6,10—composed of one chemical with six carbon atoms and one with 10—was developed simultaneously, and DuPont used it in making bristles for brushes and similar products.

Since the 1940s, many other types of nylon or polyamide fibers have appeared, both in the United States and abroad. In addition, fibers that are modifications have replaced some of the early nylons.

DuPont has stated that the real importance of nylon lay in the fact that, for the first time, basic elements were specifically made into a molecule tailored to become a textile fiber. Human beings had stopped trying to imitate silkworms and had struck out on their own to create a fiber by using their intellect. To a large degree nylon bypassed the vagaries of animal and vegetable life and the capriciousness of nature.

The Textile Fiber Products Identification Act defines *nylon* as

> a manufactured fiber in which the fiber forming substance is a long-chain synthetic polyamide in which less than 85 percent of the amide (—C—NH—) linkages are attached directly to two aromatic rings.
> $\overset{\|}{\underset{O}{}}$

In many parts of the world nylon is actually identified by its scientific term *polyamide*.

Manufacturing

Nylon 6,6

Early advertising of nylon proclaimed that the fiber was made from coal, air, and water. This is, of course, an oversimplification, but it is true that

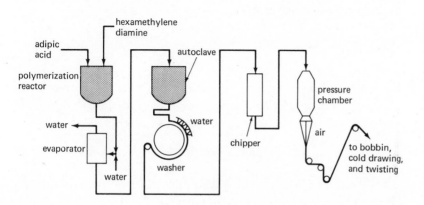

Figure 10.2 Flow chart showing steps in the manufacture of nylon 6,6.

the elements found in nylon are also found in coal, air, and water—that is, carbon, hydrogen, oxygen, and nitrogen.

Nylon 6,6 is a linear condensation polymer made from hexamethylene diamine and adipic acid. Specific amounts of the two chemicals are combined in solution to form *nylon salt*. This salt is purified, polymerized, extruded in ribbon form, and chipped into small flakes or pellets. Then the polymer is melted and extruded through a spinnerette into cool air, where the nylon filaments are formed. After cooling, the filaments are stretched, or cold-drawn, to orient the molecules in the fibers and develop fiber strength and fineness.

Well-known trademarks for nylon 6,6 include DuPont Nylon, "501," Antron, Astroturf, Blue "C" by Monsanto, Cadon, Cumuloft, and Action-wear. Several trademarks are controlled by certification standards and are authorized for use only when the fabrics satisfy the fiber producer's specifications. Among these are "501," Blue "C," and Cumuloft.

Nylon 6

Nylon 6 is manufactured by polymerization of caprolactam. Like nylon 6,6, the nylon 6 polymer is formed under pressure, extruded, chipped into pellet or flake form, and melt-spun through a spinnerette. The filaments are cold-drawn.

The most common trade names for nylon 6 are Ayrlyn, Caprolan, Crepeset, Enka, Nytelle, Touch, Celon, Grilon, and Perlon.

Fiber Properties of Nylon 6,6 and Nylon 6

Microscopic Properties

Nylon filaments are smooth and shiny. When viewed in cross section, nylon is usually perfectly round. Exceptions to this are trilobal nylons such as Antron, "501," Cadon, and Cumuloft. Longitudinal magnification shows relatively transparent fibers of uniform diameter with a slight speckled appearance (Fig. 10.4).

Physical Properties

Like other man-made fibers, nylon can be extruded in a variety of diameters and lengths, and its transparency and luster can be controlled.

One of the major advantages of nylon fibers is their strength and abrasion resistance. Nylon's tenacity ranks high among man-made fibers, and since it retains much of its strength when wet, it requires no special care. Its resistance to abrasion makes it appropriate to many different end-uses.

Nylon is a highly elastic fiber with excellent recovery from elongation. This quality assures outstanding shape retention of nylon fabrics. Nylon

Figure 10.3 Evening sheath of Antron nylon and Lycra spandex blend. (*E. I. DuPont de Nemours & Company*)

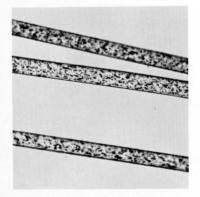

Figure 10.4 Photomicrograph of nylon 6,6 fiber, longitudinal view. (*E. I. DuPont de Nemours & Company*)

has good to very good resiliency and fabrics recover easily from crushing or wrinkling.

Compared with natural fibers, nylon has rather low moisture absorbency. In spite of this quality, nylons accept dyes well; because of it, fabrics dry quickly after laundering. However, the low moisture absorption, together with poor electrical conductivity, tends to cause an accumulation of static electric charges on nylon.

Thermal Properties

Nylon 6,6 melts at approximately 250°C (489°F) and nylon 6 at 210°C (400°F). All nylon can withstand temperatures to 149°C (300°F) for long periods of time without damage. But if temperatures approach 177° to 205°C (350°–400°F), the fiber softens, and discoloration and loss of strength occur.

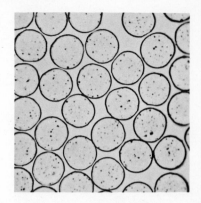

Figure 10.5 Photomicrograph of nylon 6,6 fiber, cross section. (*E. I. DuPont de Nemours & Company*)

Table 10.1 Physical Properties of Nylon 6,6 and Nylon 6

Property	Nylon 6,6	Nylon 6
shape	controlled by manufacture uniform in appearance length and diameter determined by manufacturer for end-use staple or filament translucent	
luster	controllable—bright to dull	
strength–gpd		
dry	4.6–8.8	4.9–8.5
wet	4.0–7.6	4.2–8.0
% elastic recovery	100% at 4% extension	
% elongation		
dry:		
regular filament	26–32	23–42
regular staple	37–40	23–50
high strength	19–24	16–19
wet:		
regular filament	30–37	27–34
regular staple	42–46	31–55
high strength	20–26	18–20
resiliency	good to very good	
density	1.14	1.14
moisture absorption		
20°C (70°F) 65% R.H.	4.2–4.5	3.5–5.0
saturation	8.0	8.5

Safe ironing temperatures for nylon 6,6 are considered to be between 149°C (300°F) and 177°C (350°F). Nylon 6 should not be ironed at temperatures above 149°C (300°F).

Nylon melts away from a flame and forms a gummy gray or tan ash that hardens as it cools. The fiber will burn if held in an open flame, but it does not support combustion.

Because nylon is heat sensitive or thermoplastic, it can be heat-set during processing so that it will retain its shape during use and maintenance. The fiber will stretch under stress but will return to its original size after release of the stress. Application of temperatures higher than those used for heat setting may cause fiber deformation and shrinkage. Therefore, in order to maintain dimensional stability, it is important to avoid high temperatures for most nylon products.

Chemical Properties

Nylon is not affected by alkalies, but acids—whether of the mineral variety such as hydrochloric, or the organic kind such as formic—will destroy the fiber.

Most organic solvents have little or no effect on nylon. Stain removal or dry cleaning substances do not damage it. Soaps, synthetic detergents, and bleaches can be used safely.

Sunlight is destructive to nylon and causes a marked loss of strength after extended exposure. For that reason nylon is not recommended as a window curtain or drapery fabric. Specially developed dyes, however, can inhibit sunlight damage in nylon to a certain extent. Age appears to have no effect on the fiber. If stored away from light, it will last for many years.

Biological Properties

Nylon is highly resistant to attack by most insects and microorganisms. However, some insects normally found outdoors, including ants, crickets, and roaches, will eat nylon if they are trapped in folds or creases. Mildew may attack finishes used on nylon, but it does not damage the fiber.

Other Nylons

Many other nylons, or polyamide fibers, are being manufactured in various countries or are in the developmental stages. A few of these nylons are cited here.

Nylon 11   Rilsan, or nylon 11, is produced in Europe, Asia, and South America. It is a polymer of aminoundecanoic acid. Its fiber properties resemble those of nylon 6 and 6,6, except that nylon 11 has a lower moisture regain and a lower melting point, and it does not discolor as quickly. It is frequently used in bulky yarns.

Nylon 4   Nylon 4, made by polymerizing 2-pyrrolidone, is said to combine the good properties of natural fibers with those of nylon. It is being developed by Radiation Research in the United States. The fiber has a high moisture absorbency and a higher melting point than nylon 6.

Nylon 7   Polyheptanoamide, or nylon 7, is manufactured in the Soviet Union under the trade name Enant. Although similar to nylon 6,6 and nylon 6, it has a higher melting point and a lower moisture regain than either of the common fibers.

Nylon 6T   Polyamide fibers made from hexamethylene diamine and terephthalic acid—nylon 6T—have a high melting point (370°C), a slightly higher density (1.21), and a lower elongation than nylon 6,6 or nylon 6.

Qiana   Qiana nylon was introduced by DuPont in high-cost apparel items during the late 1960s. Since then, the fiber has become available in medium- to upper-price merchandise. It resembles silk in hand and appearance, yet has excellent wash-and-wear properties. Qiana takes a variety of dyes in clear, brilliant colors—either solids or prints—and does not discolor. It is used most satisfactorily in weaves and knits.

Nylon 6,10   Nylon 6,10 is made from hexamethylenediamine and sebacic acid. It is widely used for bristles.

Nylon Modifications

In addition to developing new polymers, fiber scientists have been active in modifying existing forms of nylon. These modifications are frequently referred to as second- and third-generation fibers, and they can take several forms: changing cross-section shape; texturizing yarns by special processes; combining two or more types of nylon to form bicomponent fibers; and chemically modifying the polymers by cross linking, graft polymerization, or the addition of other chemicals.

Cross-Section Modifications   The original nylon fibers were round in cross section; modified cross sections include triangular, irregular, trilobal, and other multilobal shapes. These changes result from altering the shape, arrangement, and number of orifices in the spinning jet.

Modified cross sections can produce many desirable qualities, such as increased cover; a crisp, silklike, firm hand; reduced pilling; increased bulk; sparkle effects; and heightened resistance to soil. Trilobal nylon is available in various fiber diameters. It is widely used in apparel and home-furnishing fabrics.

Texture Modifications   Stretch yarns of nylon, manufactured by various texturizing processes, are popular alone or in blends to produce many of

Figure 10.6   Shirt and skirt of Qiana nylon. (*E. I. DuPont de Nemours & Company*)

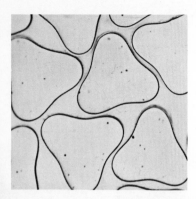

Figure 10.7 Photomicrograph of trilobal nylon, cross section of Antron® nylon. (*E. I. DuPont de Nemours & Company*)

the stretch fabrics on the current market. Other texturizing processes yield bulky yarns. These processes will be discussed more fully in Chapter 19.

Bicomponent Fibers Extruding two filaments of different composition results in bicomponent fibers. The spinnerette openings can be either side by side or one inside the other (Fig. 10.8). In order for the filaments to form a strong bond at the interface, they must be compatible. Filaments produced by this method usually differ in such characteristics as shrinkage and thermal behavior, which enables the processor to introduce fiber crimp by utilizing the shrinkage differential. Such fibers offer greater bulk, improved fit, retained sheerness, and attractive appearance in the ultimate fabric.

Cantrece is a bicomponent nylon and is considered a third-generation product. This fiber consists of two nylon components with different shrinkage potentials. Upon subjection to heat a latent crimp develops, and one component shrinks more than the other. The fiber has good resilience and fit retention; it serves primarily for women's hosiery. Crepeset nylon is designed to develop a special crimp during the fabric finishing processes. It is frequently used in knit structures for apparel.

Cross-Linking Nylon molecules can be cross-linked by adding a chemical characterized by reactive groups at both ends of the molecule. This chemical reacts with either the terminal amine group or the terminal carboxyl group on the nylon molecule to hook adjacent fiber molecules together. Such modifications increase the fibers' strength and reaction to stress and make them especially serviceable in vehicle tires.

Graft Polymerization Nylon fibers can be modified by grafting other chemicals onto the fiber molecules. One important property altered by graft polymerization is moisture absorbency, which increases, and, in turn, heightens the wet crease recovery and diminishes static buildup.

Chemical Addition Modified nylons can be produced also through the addition of small amounts of special chemicals to the nylon melt. Among these fibers are nylon 420 and nylon 22N.

Nylon 420, which was developed for use in blends with cotton, resembles cotton in its initial resistance to stretching. It adds strength and abrasion resistance to the nylon-cotton blends.

Nylon 22N, an antistatic nylon by Monsanto, is a modified fiber with built-in chemical and physical properties that reduce the static buildup to a point near that of cotton. The fiber has a silklike luster, good covering power, resistance to soiling, and superior whiteness retention.

Nylon in Use

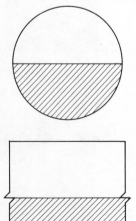

Figure 10.8 Diagram showing one type of bicomponent nylon. (*Allied Chemical*)

Nylon is popular in fabrics for apparel, home furnishings, and industry (Fig. 10.9). It has proved to be the leading fiber in the manufacture of

Figure 10.9 Carpeting of 100 percent DuPont nylon fibers. (*E. I. DuPont de Nemours & Company*)

hosiery and has considerable importance in the lingerie market. For outerwear, it is blended with other fibers to contribute dimensional stability, elastic recovery, shape retention, and abrasion resistance.

Much carpeting and upholstery are made of nylon, for the fiber wears well, is easy to clean, and does not require special protection against moths and carpet beetles. Trilobal nylons such as Cumuloft and "501" are popular in carpeting because they resist soiling (or do not show soil quickly) and crushing, as well as retaining their attractive appearance.

It is important to emphasize that nylon carpeting should be cleaned frequently. While nylon is easy to clean, the fiber has a tendency to scavenge color from soil during wear; this produces discolored or grayed products. Care reduces or eliminates this buildup of grayness and helps retain the original appearance.

Nylon is easy to launder. It can be washed safely at all laundry temperatures, drip dried, spun dry, or dryer dried. However, at low or medium low temperatures the fabric will be less likely to wrinkle. Drying in dryers at low temperatures, followed by prompt removal, frequently will produce smooth and neat products.

Bleaches can be used on nylon, and soaps and synthetic detergents will not damage the fiber.

Problems encountered in the laundering of nylon include the fact that nylon fibers tend to scavenge color and soil during the washing process. This produces gray, yellow, or discolored items that may be difficult to restore to their original appearance. White nylon fabrics are particularly vulnerable to discoloration by improper care techniques. There is some evidence that colored detergents may discolor white nylon if not thoroughly rinsed away.

Figure 10.10   Puckered nylon. The surface effect is obtained by special chemical processing of nylon.

Modern dyestuffs, if wisely selected and properly applied, produce fast colors on nylon fabrics. However, it is extremely important that proper techniques be used in applying the dyes to avoid streaky or uneven dyeing.

Pilling, the formation of tiny balls of fiber on the surface of the cloth, is a severe problem with fabrics made of spun nylon yarns and to a lesser degree with filament fiber fabrics. Since the nylon fibers are extremely resistant to abrasion, the pills are not rubbed off after they form as they would be on the surface of fabrics with low abrasion resistance.

Because of the low moisture absorbency of nylon, fabrics must have adequate spaces or interstices between yarns to permit water vapor passage and thus ensure the wearer's comfort. Various finishing techniques that improve surface absorbency have been developed. These finishes increase comfort by drawing moisture away from the body.

The capacity of nylon to be heat-set makes it possible to build surface designs, such as embossed effects, into the fabrics. Puckered or crinkled nylon can be made by shrinking certain areas of the fabric with a weak solution of phenol. Metallic substances such as copper and aluminum can be used to produce print designs on nylon. These treatments are durable if laundering and drying temperatures do not exceed those used in heat setting.

Aramid

Differing from nylons is a polyamide that has recently acquired a new generic name—*aramid.* It is defined by the Textile Fiber Products Identification Act as

> a manufactured fiber in which the fiber-forming substance is a long chain synthetic polyamide in which at least 85 percent of the amide linkages ($-\overset{\parallel}{\underset{O}{C}}-NH-$) are attached directly to two aromatic rings.

Aramid is spun as a multifilament fiber with outstanding characteristics. The fiber has no melting point, high strength, low flammability, good tenacity, and inertness to moisture.

At the present time the only trade name for an aramid fiber is Nomex, which is marketed by DuPont. Nomex does not ignite unless temperatures exceed 370°C (698°F), and it is self-extinguishing. It also resists nuclear radiation, chemicals, and abrasions. The fiber is finding considerable use in space suits, space vehicles, military applications and protective clothing for industrial plants. Nomex is not generally adaptable to consumer goods, because it tends to yellow in a short time and is difficult to dye.

Polyester Fibers 11

Historical Review

The first work on polyester fibers was done by the Carothers team of chemists during the early stages of their fundamental research for DuPont. However, when polyamides appeared to show more promise, this group was selected for development, and the polyesters were set aside. In fact, the early polyesters were poor in quality and threatened to be too expensive to produce.

While Carothers and his assistants directed their emphasis to the polyamides, chemists in Britain began experimenting with long-chain linear polyester polymers. In 1941 J. R. Whinfield and J. T. Dickson of Calico Printers' Association introduced a successful polyester fiber. Development of this fiber was delayed by World War II, and public announcement of the discovery was withheld until 1946. Imperial Chemical Industries, Ltd. (ICI) purchased the rights to manufacture the fiber for all countries except the United States, where DuPont obtained the manufacturing privilege.

DuPont's polyester fiber, known successively as Fiber V, Amilar, and finally Dacron, became available to the American consumer in small quantities in 1951. A large manufacturing plant was completed at Kinston, North Carolina, in 1953, and since that time polyester has been one of the most widely used and desirable of all synthesized fibers.

While Dacron polyester was becoming popular in the United States, the same fiber made by ICI and called Terylene was gaining status in England and several European countries. Recently, other companies have entered the polyester market. Fibers now available in the United States include Fortrel, Blue "C," Vycron, Kodel, Avlin, Encron, Quintess, and Trevira.

Polyester fibers found immediate consumer acceptance because of their ease of maintenance and excellent crease resistance. When the fiber was first previewed for the press, several products were exhibited, the most impressive being a man's business suit. To dramatize the superior wrinkle resistance and easy-care properties of the new fiber, the suit was worn for 67 days without ever being pressed. During that time it was submerged twice in a swimming pool and washed once in an automatic washing machine. When shown at the press preview, it was still presentable.

The Textile Fiber Products Identification Act defines a *polyester* fiber as

a manufactured fiber in which the fiber-forming substance is any long chain synthetic polymer composed of at least 85% by weight of an ester of a substituted aromatic carboxylic acid, including but not restricted to substituted terephthalate units

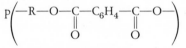

and parasubstituted hydroxybenzoate units.

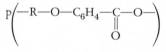

Production

Polyesters are the product of the reaction between a dihydric alcohol and dicarboxylic acid. The generic definition has recently been modified so that no specific acid is identified, as was the case before 1973.

As the substances are polymerized, they are extruded from the polymerizing vessel in the form of a ribbon, then cut into chips. The chips are diced and conveyed to a hopper, from which they are fed to the melt spinning tank. The hot solution is forced through the spinnerette and solidifies into fiber form upon contact with air. It is stretched while hot; the stretching contributes strength to the fiber and controls elongation. The greater the amount of stretch, the stronger the fiber will be, and the lower the elongation.

Figure 11.1 Mixing vessels for preparing polyester. (*Hoechst Fibers*)

Fiber Properties

Microscopic Properties

A longitudinal view of polyester fiber exhibits uniform diameter, smooth surface, and a rodlike appearance (Fig. 11.3). The cross section is usually round, but modifications can include trilobal and pentalobal filaments (Fig. 11.4).

Physical Properties

Polyester can be made in any length or diameter required for end-use. The fiber is partially transparent and white or slightly off-white in color. Pigment can be combined with the spinning solution, which permits control of the degree of luster. Optical brighteners are frequently added to produce clear, bright fibers.

The strength of polyesters varies widely. It, too, depends on end-use and is controlled by the manufacturer. Some fibers have the low tenacity of rayon, while others exceed the strongest nylon. There is no loss of strength when polyester fibers are wet.

Elongation is another controlled property in polyesters. But the fiber's elastic recovery overall is very good, and its resiliency is excellent. When properly heat-set, polyesters require little or no pressing to retain a smooth appearance.

The moisture regain of polyester fibers is very low—less than 0.5 percent. Because of the low regain, moisture has little effect on fiber strength, and static electric charges are accentuated. Furthermore, the low moisture absorption demands special techniques in dyeing and finishing. Like cotton and linen, polyesters have a high degree of wickability. This

Figure 11.2 Melt spinning. Polyester filaments emerging from spinnerettes. (*Hoechst Fibers*)

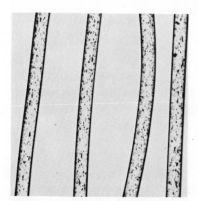

Figure 11.3 Photomicrograph of regular polyester fiber, longitudinal view. (*E. I. DuPont de Nemours & Company*)

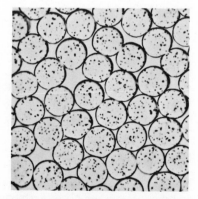

Figure 11.4 Photomicrograph of regular polyester fiber, cross section. (*E. I. DuPont de Nemours & Company*)

wicking property can produce end-use products that carry exterior moisture through to the inside, or body perspiration through to the outside.

If polyester is properly heat-set, it will not shrink or stretch during normal use.

Thermal Properties

Polyester fibers melt at temperatures from 238° to 290°C (460°–554°F) depending upon type and modification. As the fiber melts, it forms a gray or tawny-colored bead that is hard and noncrushable. Polyesters will burn and produce a dark smoke and an aromatic odor. In light fabric constructions the fibers melt and drip away from the source of ignition, preventing the propagation of flame.

Ironing temperatures for polyesters vary with fiber type. Generally, a temperature of 121°C (250°F) is considered safe.

Heat setting of polyester yarns and fabrics is essential if they are to have the easy-care, wrinkle-free properties associated with the fiber. Once heat set, polyester will hold creases, pleats, or any other shaping lines, as long as proper care procedures are followed.

Chemical Properties

Polyester has good resistance to weak alkalies but only moderate resistance to strong ones. Weak acids do not affect the fiber, nor do strong acids at room temperature. Strong acids at high temperatures, however, will destroy polyester.

In general, the fiber resists organic solvents. Chemicals used in stain removal and cleaning do not damage it. Bleaches can be used safely.

Direct sunlight weakens polyester, but it has good resistance to sunlight when behind glass. It is, therefore, satisfactory for window curtains and drapes.

Biological Properties

Insects will not destroy polyesters if there is other food available. However, if trapped, beetles and similar insects will cut their way through the fabric as a means of escape. While microorganisms will not harm the fiber, they may attack finishes that have been applied.

Modified Polyester Fibers

Polyester fibers are available in a variety of types, some of them second- and third-generation fibers. Each type has at least one special characteristic that alters its behavior in some way. These new fibers are created by altering the cross section shape from round to multilobal, by changing fiber formulas, or by varying the physical processing. The shape changes produce fibers with hand and appearance different from regular polyester,

Figure 11.5 Cross-dyed polyester fabric. Modification of polyester fibers can control dye acceptance to permit formation of checks and plaids after fabric is woven. (*E. I. DuPont de Nemours & Company*)

while chemical modifications result in fibers that are dye selective, have altered strength characteristics (and as a result altered pilling behavior), and are crush resistant.

Cross-sectional shape change usually occurs through alteration of the spinning jet. Chemical modification involves the addition of chemical compounds. For example, fiber dyeability changes with the inclusion of chemicals that add sulphonic groups and with the substitution of isophthalic acid for a portion of the terephthalic acid.

Trilobal and pentalobal cross sections contribute several desirable properties to polyester fibers. Yarns and fabrics constructed from such fibers are characterized by a silklike hand and appearance. In addition, the fabric appears to soil less quickly, because dirt lodged in the valleys between the lobes is inconspicuous. The fibers have improved covering power, and their luster and surface sheen are pleasing to the eye.

Other fiber changes can be obtained by modifying the spinning speed and degree of molecular orientation, which affects physical properties such as strength and pilling. Crimp can be set in the fiber during manufacture to increase bulkiness and resilience.

Research scientists are currently seeking ways to reduce the oleophilic property of polyester—that is, its propensity for absorbing oil.

Polyester in Use

The most important characteristics of polyester fibers are wrinkle-free appearance and ease of care. The fabrics require little or no ironing; they are easy to launder and quick to dry.

The care of 100-percent polyester products is minimal. Soaps, synthetic

Figure 11.6 Dress of 100 percent Trevira polyester. (*Hoechst Fibers*)

Figure 11.7 Upholstery on chair and sofa of 100 percent Dacron polyester. (*E. I. DuPont de Nemours & Company*)

Figure 11.8 Mainsails of Dacron polyester fiber. (*E. I. DuPont de Nemours & Company*)

detergents, and laundry aids do not damage them. It is advisable to pretreat heavily soiled areas with a lubricating detergent before laundering either by machine or by hand. Garments can be drip dried or dried in a dryer if removed before any wrinkles are set. Laundry equipment with durable press controls is preferred. Blends may require special care. For best results, all instructions on the label should be followed.

Frequent complaints about polyester fabrics arise from their tendency to absorb oily stains. One solution to this problem involves applying a liquid detergent or hair shampoo to the stain before laundering. This generally will ensure lift-off of oil and grease. Spray spot removers are often effective for tenacious stains.

Despite the easy-care characteristics cited, polyester may evidence a property that irks consumers—shrinkage. Unless the fabric has been well stabilized by heat setting, it may shrink during care. Knitted polyesters are particularly susceptible. To prevent shrinkage during care, avoid high drying temperatures. Knitted yardage should be preshrunk before use and care.

Fabrics of 100 percent filament polyester are used in apparel for men, women, and children (Fig. 11.6). There are limitless varieties available —ranging from sheer to heavy, smooth to crepe.

Blends of wool, cotton, rayon, or linen with polyester fibers are popular with both men and women. In blended fabrics polyester fibers contribute easy maintenance, strength, durability, abrasion resistance, relatively wrinkle-free appearance, shape and size retention; protein or cellulosic fibers enhance dyeability, comfort, and absorbency, while reducing static charges.

Various fiber manufacturers have established desirable minimum amounts of polyester for combination with different fibers. At least 65 percent and no less than 50 percent polyester is recommended with cellulosic fibers. With wools, acrylics, or modacrylics at least 50 percent polyester is advisable. Polyester fibers seem to be the most satisfactory choice for blended fabrics with durable-press finishes and for the easy-care, wrinkle-free, textured woven and knit fabrics so compatible with modern living.

In addition to apparel, polyester appears in home furnishings, industrial fabrics, tires, and protective clothing. The use of polyesters in rugs, especially shag rugs, has increased tremendously in the past few years. Polyester in tires seems to eliminate the flat spotting associated with nylon and increase the durability. Other industrial applications range from conveyor belts and fire hoses, through such products as laundry bags and press covers, to fishing nets, ropes, and sailcloth.

Acrylic and Modacrylic Fibers

Acrylic Fibers

Historical Review

The early success of nylon was so extraordinary that many manufacturers began experimenting with other chemicals in an attempt to find new fiber-forming polymers.

Early in World War II, DuPont, partly as a result of the fundamental research of Carothers, developed an acrylic fiber, Fiber A, that showed potential as a substitute for either wool or silk. In the staple form the fiber resembled wool; in filament form it resembled silk in texture and appearance. For the duration of the war the fiber was used in limited amounts for government purposes while DuPont continued its development. It was given the trademark *Orlon,* introduced in pilot-plant quantities to a test segment of the population, and then evaluated. Interest was found to be keen. The public liked the fiber, and DuPont decided to build a full-scale plant in Camden, South Carolina, where production of Orlon began in 1950.

While DuPont was developing Orlon, other companies were also working on acrylic fibers. In Germany, Farbenfabriken introduced two acrylic fibers, Pan and Dralon. The increased public acceptance of man-made fibers in the United States encouraged other companies to enter the industry. Chemstrand Corporation of Decatur, Alabama, was formed in 1949 as a joint operation of Monsanto Chemical and American Viscose Corporation. In 1950, Chemstrand began production of an acrylic fiber, *Acrilan,* in pilot-plant quantities. A broad advertising campaign introduced this new acrylic to the public in 1952, and the full-scale plant went "on stream" in 1953. However, the first quantities of the fiber were somewhat inferior, so the company made minor changes in formulations and manufacturing techniques. In 1954 an improved product appeared that has been extremely successful. Monsanto has since obtained sole ownership of the corporation that is now identified as Monsanto Textile Division.

American Cyanamid Corporation had begun working with acrylic and other polymers in the late 1930s, but the firm did not direct its efforts toward the production of textile fibers until the 1950s. American Cyanamid, too, saw the potential of acrylic fibers and in 1958 introduced commercial quantities of their acrylic fiber, Creslan. Also in 1958 the Dow Chemical Company released a new textile fiber called Zefran. While this is basically acrylic, the Dow chemists prefer to call it an acrylic-alloy fiber. During the last ten to fifteen years manufacturers of acrylics have directed most of their research toward modification of existing fibers.

At the present time the acrylic fibers produced in the United States include Acrilan, Bi-Loft, Creslan, Nandel, Orlon, and Zefran. Foreign acrylics found in consumer goods in the United States are marketed under the trade names Acribel, Crylor, Courtelle, Leacril, Toraylon, and Crysel. The Textile Fiber Products Identification Act defines an *acrylic* fiber as

a manufactured fiber in which the fiber-forming substance is any long chain synthetic polymer composed of at least 85% by weight of acrylonitrile units
$$(-CH_2-CH-)$$
$$|$$
$$CN$$

Production

Acrylic fibers are linear polymers formed by addition polymerization of at least 85 percent by weight of *acrylonitrile* (*vinyl cyanide*). Scientists had known for many years that acrylonitrile would polymerize to form high polymer compounds, but the resulting fiber was characterized by insolubility and degradation at melting temperatures. Finally, solvents were discovered that would dissolve the polymer to permit spinning. The dissolved polymer is extruded through spinnerettes into a heated spinning container, or into a coagulating bath where the filaments solidify. The filaments are stretched while hot to introduce molecular orientation and fineness.

Fiber Properties

Microscopic Properties

Acrylic fibers, viewed longitudinally, show uniform diameters, a rodlike appearance, and some irregularly spaced striations or parallel lines (Fig. 12.1). Cross-section views of the various acrylics exhibit considerable differences. Orlon possesses a dumbbell- or acorn-shaped cross section; Acrilan is round or bean-shaped. Creslan and Zefran are nearly round (Fig. 12.2).

Physical Properties

Like all man-made fibers, acrylics can be controlled in terms of length and diameter. In general, the fiber is marketed in staple or tow form and is used as a staple fiber. Acrylics are available in bright, semidull, or dull lusters.

Most acrylics are marketed in a pure white. However, Zefran can be obtained also in producer-dyed colors.

The strength of acrylics is slightly lower than that of cotton, but it is still adequate for a variety of end-uses. Although the fibers' tenacity is reduced when wet, this does not pose any problem in use and care.

The elongation of acrylic fibers varies from 20 to 55 percent. When fibers are wet, elongation increases. The elastic recovery of acrylics is good at extensions of 1 to 2 percent, but at higher degrees of extension the recovery drops sharply. Bicomponent acrylics, such as Sayelle and Wintuk, have good to very good elastic recovery; they can be tumbled dry after laundering and will recover their original size.

Acrylic fibers have good resiliency. Bulky fabrics are especially resilient and lofty; they retain their shape very well.

The moisture regain of acrylic fibers is relatively low, which results in speedy drying but contributes to difficulty in dyeing. Static electricity will build up in acrylics, a problem that increases when the humidity is low.

With proper heat setting and appropriate care, acrylic fibers show little dimensional change. However, the application of excess heat and steam will cause shrinkage and a loss of loft or bulk. This can be quite evident when knitted acrylic sweaters receive improper care.

Thermal Properties

Acrylic fibers have good resistance to heat. The fibers are thermoplastic and respond to heat-setting procedures. Upon exposure to fire, they burn with a yellow flame and form a gummy, hot residue that drips away from the burning fiber. This residue is hot enough to ignite combustible substances upon which it may fall.

Manufacturers recommend that these fibers not be subjected to boiling water, since excessive shrinkage can occur. Ironing temperatures should be below 161°C (325°F).

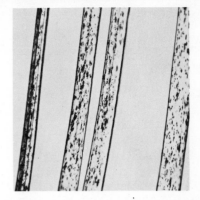

Figure 12.1 Photomicrograph of Orlon® acrylic fiber, longitudinal view. (*E. I. DuPont de Nemours & Company*)

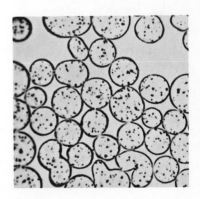

Figure 12.2 Photomicrograph of Creslan acrylic fiber, cross section. (*E. I. DuPont de Nemours & Company*)

Chemical Properties

Acrylic fibers have good resistance to weak alkalies, but strong ones cause rapid degradation. Weak acids have no destructive effect whatsoever; concentrated acids cause a loss of fiber strength.

The solvents used in cleaning and stain removal are not damaging to acrylic fibers. The same is true for soaps and detergents. Bleaches can be used if directions are followed. Acrylics have excellent resistance to sunlight.

Biological Properties

Mildew, other microorganisms, and common household pests will not attack or eat acrylic fibers.

Fiber Modifications

Trademarked acrylics are produced in several varieties that may differ in such characteristics as physical shape, appearance, and dyeability. These differences indicate minor modifications in chemical structure.

Among the most important modifications are bicomponent fibers. They are made of two different chemical formulations extruded simultaneously, so they form a fiber with an acorn- or mushroom-shaped cross section. Each component differs in properties. When dry, one component curls and gives a spiral crimp or coil to the fiber. The other may have a higher moisture regain and can accept a deeper shade of color because of easier dye penetration. It is essential that bicomponent fibers be dried without any tension, so that the spiral crimp develops properly and the yarn returns to its original size.

Recent acrylic modifications have had special chemicals added to reduce flammability. This feature assumes particular importance with the increasing use of acrylics in carpeting. Other chemical modifications alter the dyeing properties. Texturizing processes have developed special crimp.

Acrylic Fibers in Use

All types of acrylic fibers appear in knitted and woven fabrics. Blends of acrylic fibers with wool, cotton, other cellulosic fibers such as rayon, and fibers such as nylon (Fig. 12.3) are common. Acrylic fibers have low density, and they are soft. These properties contribute to producing fabrics that are bulky, soft, and light in weight compared to fabrics of similar construction made of natural fibers.

End-uses such as blankets, carpeting, and upholstery are excellent for acrylics because of the fiber's rapid recovery from deformation, its light weight, and the ease of maintenance (Fig. 12.4). Acrylic fibers are found in items of apparel where shape retention and easy care are important considerations. They are popular in sportswear. Their light, bulky, soft

Figure 12.3 Girl's bib skirt of Acrilan acrylic and Spectran polyester blend. (*Monsanto Textiles Company*)

Figure 12.4 Wall-to-wall carpeting of Acrilan acrylic fiber. (*Monsanto Textiles Company*)

properties make them prized in ski clothes, children's snow suits, and sport shirts. Deep-pile fabrics frequently have acrylic fibers in their construction to contribute resiliency.

Several yarns and fabrics are certified to conform to producer specifications. They are marketed under trademarks such as Wintuk, Sayelle, Nomelle, and Anywear.

Many acrylic fibers accept brilliant dyes in a wide variety of patterns. They have good wash-and-wear properties and will take permanent pleats and creases if heat-set properly.

Most acrylic fabrics can be washed safely in home laundry equipment and dried in home dryers with variable temperature controls. However, products bearing the trademarks Sayelle and Wintuk should be dried in an automatic dryer so the tumbling action can restore the fabric to its proper size. Fragile and delicate fabrics of acrylic fibers should be laundered by hand. The consumer should always heed labels attached to the product that give care information.

Modacrylic Fibers

Historical Review

Dynel, the first modacrylic fiber, was introduced to the public in 1950 by Union Carbide Corporation. In 1956 Tennessee Eastman brought out Verel. These modacrylics resulted from attempts to produce a fiber that could withstand higher temperatures than previous vinyl chloride fibers. Legislation calling for flame-resistant textile products for children fostered further development of modacrylics. Among the fibers currently made in the United States are Elura and Dynel. Several modacrylics are imported,

Figure 12.5 Boy's sweater of 100 percent Acrilan acrylic, a wear-dated garment. (*Monsanto Textiles Company*)

Figure 12.6 Knitting yarns of Orlon Sayelle and Wintuk.

including Kanekalon from Japan—a fiber widely used in the manufacture of wigs. Production of Eastman's Verel was discontinued but has been recently restored.

The Textile Fiber Products Identification Act defines *modacrylic* as

a manufactured fiber in which the fiber-forming substance is any long chain synthetic polymer composed of less than 85% but at least 35% by weight of acrylonitrile units ($-CH_2-CH-$) except fibers qualifying under
$$CN$$
category (2) of Paragraph j (rubber).

Production

Modacrylic is an addition polymer composed of vinyl chloride and acrylonitrile. The two substances are polymerized. The polymer is dissolved in acetone, filtered to remove any solids, and extruded into a water bath, where the filaments coagulate. The fibers are then dried and stretched.

Fiber Properties

Microscopic Properties

The longitudinal view of modacrylics shows clear, transparent striations. Cross sections are irregular. They may be **C**-shaped, peanut-shaped, or somewhat flat (Fig. 12.7).

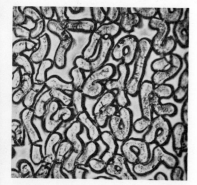

Figure 12.7 Photomicrograph of Dynel modacrylic fiber, cross section. (*E. I. DuPont de Nemours & Company*)

Physical Properties

Length and diameter of the fiber are controlled. Dynel is naturally a cream color, and it is crimped. Verel, a white fiber, was available in smooth or crimped contours. The strength of modacrylics is similar to that of cotton. The fibers have high elongation with excellent elastic recovery; the fibers' resiliency is very good. Moisture regain, on the other hand, is very low, and because of it dyeing requires special care.

Thermal Properties

Modacrylic fibers do not support combustion. They will burn when placed directly in a flame, but they self-extinguish as soon as the flame source is removed. The fibers do not drip while burning.

Dynel is more sensitive to heat than Elura. Ironing temperatures should not exceed 121°C (250°F). Higher temperatures will cause fiber shrinkage.

Chemical Properties

Modacrylic fibers have good resistance to most alkalies. Although concentrated solutions may cause discoloration, any reduction of strength is minimal. Hot concentrated acids affect Dynel, causing a loss of color and some loss of strength.

Most organic solvents used in cleaning and stain removal do not damage modacrylics. However, acetone will dissolve the fibers and some paint solvents may stiffen them.

Sunlight may cause Dynel to discolor and lose some strength. All types of soaps, detergents, and bleaches can be used safely.

Biological Properties

Modacrylic fibers are highly resistant to microorganisms and insects. Tests indicate that moth larvae will starve to death rather than eat their way through Dynel netting to reach desirable food.

Modacrylic Fibers in Use

The major end-uses for modacrylic fibers include "fake" furs, blankets, knitted goods, wigs and hairpieces, draperies, carpeting, industrial materials, and—a recent addition to the list—children's sleepwear. The fibers produce fabrics that are soft, resilient, stable in size, low in pilling, and resistant to fire damage. This last factor is of value in home furnishings as well as in apparel fabrics, where safety is of major importance. The fibers have proved extremely attractive for wigs, making them easy to

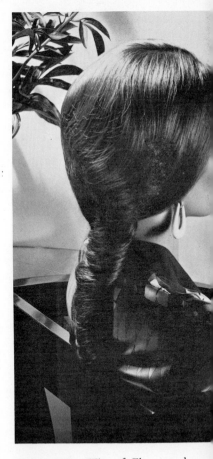

Figure 12.8 Wig of Elura modacrylic. (*Monsanto Textiles Company*)

style and easy to care for. For carpeting modacrylic fibers are sometimes blended with acrylics.

Modacrylics can be laundered with warm water in home equipment. Dryers with medium to low temperature controls can be used for Elura, but Dynel should not be dried in any dryer. Label information regarding care should always be carefully followed in order to avoid disappointment with modacrylic products.

Figure 12.9   Fake fur of modacrylic fiber. (*Collins & Aikman*)

Olefin Fibers

Historical Review

Olefin fibers were developed in the 1950s and early 1960s. Polyethylene in fiber form was the product of Imperial Chemical Industries, Ltd., in England. Polypropylene fibers were developed by Montecatini of Italy. By the mid-1970s there were approximately fifty American companies producing some type of olefin fiber, and foreign production had increased proportionately.

The Textile Fiber Products Identification Act defines *olefin* as

> a manufactured fiber in which the fiber-forming substance is any long chain synthetic polymer composed of at least 85% by weight of ethylene, propylene, or other olefin units, except amorphous (non-crystalline) polyolefins qualifying under category (1) of Paragraph j (rubber) of Rule 7.

Production

The olefin raw material is polymerized under pressure with a catalyst. To produce fiber filaments, the polymer is melt-spun into a current of cooling

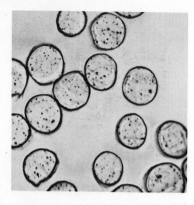

Figure 13.1 Photomicrograph of polypropylene olefin fiber, cross section. (*E. I. DuPont de Nemours & Company*)

gas. After the filaments have cooled, they are drawn or stretched to six times the spun length. This drawing process introduces molecular orientation and makes the fibers fine and pliable. In order to produce a fiber of quality, propylene must be polymerized in an *isotatic* form.

Fiber Properties

Microscopic Properties

Olefin fibers resemble glass rods in both longitudinal and cross-section views (Fig. 13.1). They are even, clear, and round. Polypropylene can be extruded from specially shaped spinnerettes, and it will then be irregular in cross section.

Physical Properties

Length and diameter of olefin fibers are controlled by the manufacturer. Polyethylene tends to be waxy, polypropylene considerably less so. Both types of olefin are smooth and white.

The strength of olefin fibers is good, but it varies with the degree of polymerization and molecular orientation from about 3.5 to 8.0 grams per denier. This is comparable to nylon.

Polyethylene has a wide range in elongation, and its elastic recovery is excellent. However, if it is stretched more than 10 percent, it can lose some of its shape. The elongation of polypropylene also varies widely, while the elastic recovery is outstanding. Properly heat-treated olefin fibers will retain their size and shape. They will stretch or shrink only if subjected to temperatures higher than the heat setting.

Both olefin fibers have good resistance to crushing. Because of this property polypropylene gives good service in carpeting.

The fibers have little or no moisture absorption, which creates a serious problem in dyeing.

Thermal Properties

Olefin fibers burn slowly and give off a sooty, waxy smoke. They shrink at low temperatures unless heat-set, and even then the fibers soften at temperatures above 65°–71°C (150°–160°F). Olefins should be ironed at the lowest setting possible with a press cloth.

Chemical Properties

Olefin fibers are highly resistant to alkaline substances. They also have good resistance to acids, except for oxidizing acids which weaken them.

Cleaning solvents containing chlorinated hydrocarbons should never be used, for they cause olefin fibers to swell and eventually to degrade. Laundry soaps, synthetic detergents, and bleaches are safe.

Figure 13.2 Olefin fibers used in floor coverings. Marvess olefin in locker room at Furman University. (*Phillips Fibers Corporation*)

Olefins will lose strength after prolonged exposure to sunlight. They are subject to staining by oil and grease, but normal laundering usually removes the stains.

Olefins do have static electric buildup, but it is considered to be less than on nylon, polyester, or wool.

Biological Properties

Olefin fibers are seldom attacked or damaged by either mildew or insects.

Olefin Fibers in Use

Olefins, particularly the polypropylene fibers, have a variety of industrial applications. They are also used in textiles for apparel and home furnishings. Several manufacturers have made fabrics for suits and dresses, and blends of polypropylene with wool, cotton, and rayon are being knitted for sportswear. Polypropylene has a woollike hand and feel. This property, coupled with the low density, has resulted in polypropylene coating and blanket fabrics.

One of the best-known uses for polypropylene fibers is in the production of carpeting and carpet tiles (Fig. 13.2). The fiber has been employed in needle-punched indoor-outdoor carpeting with great success. Indoor tufted carpeting of polypropylene is also popular. The fiber is easily cleaned and resists crushing, two factors that add to its desirability for floor coverings. The introduction of the polypropylene fibers in indoor-outdoor carpeting has led to a tremendous increase in the amount of carpet to be found in kitchens, work areas, patios, garages, and even in and around swimming pools.

Pigment can be added to the polypropylene solution to color the fiber. Furthermore, manufacturers have developed techniques for modifying the

Figure 13.3 Cable-knit sweater of Marvess olefin fiber. (*Phillips Fibers Corporation*)

Figure 13.4 Plush upholstery fabric and cut pile carpeting of Herculon olefin fibers. (*Hercules Incorporated*)

fiber so that a variety of dyestuffs can be employed to color end-use products. The success of these methods is evident in the wide choice of colors and patterns available in polypropylene yarns and fabrics.

Many olefin manufacturers do not trademark their fibers, partly because of the proportion of sales to other industries where trade names are not important. The general consumer most frequently encounters the following names: Herculon, Marvess, Polycrest, and Vectra.

Olefin fibers have one unusual application: specially shaped filaments locked into a durable but flexible base are used to form artificial ski slopes (Fig. 13.5). Sno-Mat is one of the better-known names for this product.

Olefin fibers and fabrics launder well, dry quickly, and require little or no ironing. Floor coverings are easily cleaned, and stains wipe off with a sponge or cloth and water. Detergents can be used on stubborn stains.

In general, olefin fibers should be machine washed in warm water. Fabric softeners will improve the hand and reduce static electricity. Olefin products should be dried either in machines if they have low-temperature settings, or they should be air dried. Stains should be removed before laundering. Fabrics must not be ironed unless they are blends that permit it. In any case, care instructions attached to the product should always be followed.

Figure 13.5 Sno-Mat artificial ski slope of olefin fibers. (*Dillon-Beck Manufacturing Company*)

The future of olefin fibers will depend to some degree on the energy shortage. Olefin fibers are made from petroleum. Oil and coal are sources of raw materials for several other fibers as well. The question of priority in the use of energy resources has not been answered. In any case, the cost of these fibers will increase as the cost of raw materials escalates. If petroleum and coal are needed for essentials such as heat and light, a scarcity of olefin fibers, in particular, as well as nylons, polyesters, and acrylics may occur in the very near future.

Elastomeric Fibers

14

Elastomers are elastic, rubberlike substances. They can be prepared in various forms, but discussion here is limited to fibrous forms used in textile products. All elastomers are characterized by extremely high elongation and outstanding elastic recovery.

Rubber

The Textile Fiber Products Identification Act defines *rubber* as

> a manufactured fiber in which the fiber-forming substance is comprised of natural or synthetic rubber, including the following categories:
> 1. a manufactured fiber in which the fiber-forming substance is a hydro-carbon such as natural rubber, polyisoprene, polybutadiene, copolymers of dienes and hydrocarbons, or amorphous (non-crystalline) polyolefins.
> 2. a manufactured fiber in which the fiber-forming substance is a copoly-mer of acrylonitrile and a diene (such as butadiene) composed of not

more than 50% but at least 10% by weight of acrylonitrile units

The term *lastrile* may be used as a generic description for fibers falling within this category.

3. a manufactured fiber in which the fiber-forming substance is a poly-chloroprene or a copolymer of chloroprene in which at least 35% by weight of the fiber-forming substance is composed of chloroprene units

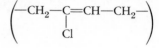

The thick gummy liquid obtained from trees of the Hevea species has been used for many hundreds of years. However, not until the 19th century did scientists become aware of the unusual characteristics of this substance. In 1839 Charles Goodyear discovered that the properties of rubber were greatly changed when it was heated with sulfur. Strength and elasticity increased, and cold temperatures no longer hardened the rubber or made it brittle. Goodyear's process—now known as *vulcanizing*—set the scene for the development of rubber in many forms. Consumption of rubber remained small until the beginning of the 20th century, when the growing automobile industry began to require large quantities for tires.

Rubber in fiber form originated in the 1920s as a result of research by the U.S. Rubber Company. Scientists discovered that liquid rubber (latex) could be extruded in round forms of minute fineness, which had high elongation and elastic recovery. These early fibers were not used alone but served as a central core for other fibers, such as cotton, which were wrapped around them. To some extent this is still true today.

Synthetic rubbers were first developed in the early 1930s, but it was not until the natural rubber supply was cut off by World War II that synthetic rubber gained consumer acceptance. Even then it was used chiefly by the Government until after 1946. Today, there is a good market for many products in both natural and synthetic rubber.

The properties that make rubber desirable in certain end-uses include

- a high degree of elasticity
- flexibility and pliability
- strength
- toughness
- impermeability to water and air
- resistance to cutting and tearing
- resistance to many chemicals

Rubber yarns contribute support and improved fit to end-use products. Fabrics with rubber are comparatively crease resistant and require a minimum of ironing.

Properties of rubber that can cause problems are

- deterioration by sunlight and smog
- loss of strength and elasticity through aging
- damage from body oils
- damage caused by solvents commonly encountered in cleaning
- sensitivity to temperatures over 93°C (200°F) that cause deterioration and loss of pliability

In general, synthetic rubber has fewer of these drawbacks than natural rubber.

Rubber products can be laundered in warm water. Strong soaps and synthetic detergents are recommended, because they remove oily dirt better than mild detergents. Drying in a dryer at medium temperatures is considered safe by some authorities, but others maintain that air drying is the only acceptable method. Probably the most important fact about cleaning rubber items is that they should be laundered after each wearing to reduce damage from body oils and perspiration. It is best to avoid dry cleaning.

Rubber yarns are used in foundation garments, swimwear, surgical fabrics (such as elastic bandages and support hosiery), underwear, elastic yarns for decorative stitching, shoe fabrics, tops of socks and hosiery, and elastic tape. Trade names frequently encountered for rubber fibers or yarns include Contro, Globe, Lastron, Lastex, and Laton.

During the 1960s one chemical company sought to establish a new generic term for an elastomeric fiber. As a result the Federal Trade Commission redefined rubber and specified the name *lastrile* as a substitute generic term for one group of rubber fibers. To date there has been no commercial development of lastrile fibers. Consequently, there is no published literature that describes properties, production, and characteristics of such a fiber.

Spandex

The first spandex was introduced by the DuPont Corporation as Fiber K in 1958. Volume production began in 1959, and the fiber acquired the trade name, Lycra. United States Rubber patented a spandex elastomer in 1956, but commercial quantities were not produced until about 1961. The amount of this fiber, trademarked Vyrene, is still limited.

During the 1960s several new spandex fibers were released in limited quantities. The products can be recognized by such trade names as Lycra, Numa, Glospan, and Unel.

The Textile Fiber Products Identification Act defines *spandex* as

a manufactured fiber in which the fiber-forming substance is a long chain synthetic polymer comprised of at least 85% of a segmented polyurethane.

Figure 14.1 Photomicrograph of Lycra spandex fiber, longitudinal view. (*E. I. DuPont de Nemours & Company*)

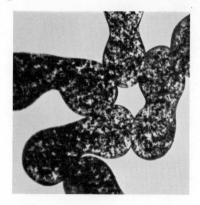

Figure 14.2 Photomicrograph of Lycra spandex fiber, cross section. (*E. I. DuPont de Nemours & Company*)

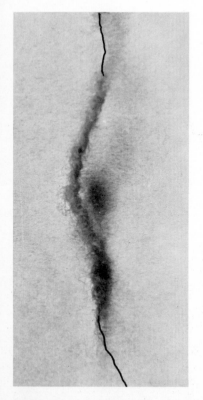

Figure 14.3 Core-spun yarn, showing the staple covering fibers pulled away at each end to reveal the core.

Although textile authorities predicted during the mid-1960s that spandex fibers would ultimately be included in a large percentage of all fabrics manufactured to give them stretch properties, this has not occurred to date. The current interest in knit fabrics has, at least temporarily, overshadowed stretch fibers.

Spandex fibers are relatively weak, but because of their tremendous elongation (500–800 percent), they have good durability. Their elastic recovery is excellent. They accept dyestuffs easily and evenly.

Spandex fibers will burn and form a gummy residue. They can be ironed safely at temperatures below 149°C (300°F).

The resistance of spandex to chemicals is good. Concentrated alkalies at high temperatures cause eventual degradation. Acids have little effect. Soaps and synthetic detergents do not damage the fiber; however, chlorine bleaches may cause yellowing and some loss of strength. Dry cleaning agents with chlorine compounds may alter colors, so laundering is recommended.

Spandex has several advantages over rubber, including resistance to degradation by sunlight and smog and to damage from body oils and perspiration; superior flex life; ability to be dyed and to be laundered easily and dryer-dried safely. Spandex is lighter in weight than rubber and has a higher initial modulus of elasticity, which results in garments that are lighter and sheerer but still provide the same degree of figure control.

Spandex is utilized in the bare filament or uncovered form; in yarn constructions where the fibers are wrapped spirally with other fibers to produce covered yarns; and in core-spun yarns where staple fibers are fed around the core filament to make a single yarn (Fig. 14.3). The amount of stretch can be predetermined and controlled by yarn spinning machine adjustments.

Spandex can be found in articles such as foundation garments, bras, lingerie straps, sock tops, hosiery, and medical products requiring elasticity. In addition, stretch fabrics using spandex fibers appear in many items of wearing apparel, some home-furnishing fabrics such as slipcover materials, and some domestic fabrics, particularly fitted sheets.

Spandex fibers can be laundered by hand or machine and dried in the air or in a dryer at medium or low temperatures. Any type of detergent can be used. Some manufacturers maintain that chlorine bleach is safe for spandex, but DuPont recommends perborate bleaches. All spandex producers state that normal concentrations of chlorine in swimming pools will not damage the fiber, but a color loss may occur. White spandex may yellow as a result of smog, body oils, and perspiration; however, this does not affect the fiber properties of stretch, strength, or holding power. Frequent laundering will reduce the discoloration.

Anidex

The Federal Trade Commission added the generic term *anidex* to the Textile Fiber Products Identification Act in 1969. It is defined as

> a manufactured fiber in which the fiber-forming substance is any long chain synthetic polymer composed of at least 50% by weight of one or more esters of a monohydric alcohol and acrylic acid ($CH_2{=}CH{-}COOH$).

Rohm and Haas, the company that developed the fiber, introduced it in 1970 under the trade name ANIM/8. According to the company, it has the following properties:

1. Its recovery from stretching is superior to any previous elastomeric fiber.
2. It can be bleached successfully with chlorine.
3. It blends well with all natural and man-made fibers.
4. It is equally adaptable to weaving and knitting.
5. It can be used core-spun, covered, plied, or bare.
6. It can be dyed, printed, and finished by traditional processes.
7. It takes permanent-press and soil-release finishes.
8. It retains its elasticity after washing and dry cleaning.
9. It has excellent affinity for disperse dyes.
10. It is described as an acrylate.

To date, this fiber has not been produced in any significant volume.

Figure 14.4 Swimsuit of Antron nylon and Lycra spandex. Skirt of nylon jersey. (*E. I. DuPont de Nemours & Company*)

15 Other Organic Noncellulosic Fibers

The fibers discussed in this chapter are not well known or widely used by the general public. Occasionally, however, they are encountered in fabrics for home furnishings and apparel, so it is important for the consumer to know something about them.

Saran

Saran fibers were introduced to the retail market by the Dow Chemical Corporation in 1940. Subsequently, other saran fibers, under license, were manufactured by Firestone and National Plastic Products—now Enjay Fibers. Only small amounts of the fiber are being produced at the present time. The Textile Fiber Products Identification Act defines *saran* as

> a manufactured fiber in which the fiber-forming substance is any long chain synthetic polymer composed of at least 80% by weight of vinylidene chloride units

$$(-CH_2-CCl_2-)$$

Saran is made from vinylidene chloride and vinyl chloride or vinyl cyanide. The filaments are melt-spun and cold-drawn.

Saran fibers are transparent, even, smooth, and almost perfectly round in cross section. They are highly lustrous and silky in appearance. Staple fibers are less lustrous and have a built-in crimp.

Saran is not strong, but it has good elongation, very good resiliency, and excellent elastic recovery. These properties contribute to make the fiber a good choice for carpeting.

The moisture absorbency of saran is very low, which makes coloring difficult. If it is properly processed and if high temperatures are avoided, the fiber does not stretch or shrink.

Saran is practically nonflammable. It will melt and burn slowly if held in a flame, but it does not support combustion, and as soon as the source of flame is removed it self-extinguishes. However, the fibers do have a relatively low melting point; therefore, if ironing is needed, it should be done with a low-temperature setting.

Acids have no effect on saran, and the only alkalies that damage it are sodium hydroxide and ammonium compounds. Most cleaning solvents and stain-removal agents are entirely safe, but acetone, carbon tetrachloride, and alcohol cause a loss in fiber strength if used at temperatures over 65°C (150°F).

Sunlight causes saran to tan or discolor, but there is little or no loss in strength. Soaps and synthetic detergents have no damaging effect. The fiber does develop static electric charges. Saran is immune to attack by household pests and microorganisms.

The best use of saran fiber is in furnishing fabrics such as upholstery, draperies, and carpeting. It is frequently utilized for automobile upholstery and outdoor furniture, because it is easily cleaned with soap and synthetic detergents. Application of the fiber has not proceeded as expected due to increased production of olefin fibers, which have many of the same properties and are less expensive.

Figure 15.1 Fabric containing saran fibers. (*Isabel Scott*)

Vinyon

The first vinyon fibers were made experimentally in 1933 by the Carbide and Carbon Corporation, but commercial quantities were not available until 1939. At that time the American Viscose Corporation began to convert the polymer into filament fibers. This fiber, a true synthetic, was introduced the same year as nylon.

Vinyon is defined by the Textile Fiber Products Identification Act as

a manufactured fiber in which the fiber-forming substance is any long chain synthetic polymer composed of at least 85% by weight of vinyl chloride units ($-CH_2-CHCl-$).

Trade names for vinyon include: Avisco Vinyon HH, Clevyl, Fibravyl, PVC, Rhovyl, and Voplex.

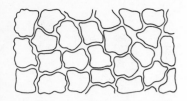

Figure 15.2 Sketch of the microscopic cross section of vinyon fibers.

The fiber has round, dog-bone, or dumbbell-shape cross sections and smooth, even, relatively clear longitudinal views. It can be made in any length or diameter.

The tenacity of vinyon is similar to that of dry rayon, but there is no difference in dry and wet strength. There is a tremendous spectrum of elongation; resilience is good; elastic recovery is fair.

Vinyon fibers have extreme heat sensitivity, which makes them soften at temperatures greater than 65°C (150°F) and limits their use to applications where no ironing is required.

The fibers offer excellent chemical resistance. Acids and alkalies have no effect, and solvents used in cleaning do no damage except for ketones and aromatic hydrocarbons. Soaps and synthetic detergents are quite safe.

Vinyon fibers are widely used in industry. Because of their low softening and melting temperatures, they seldom occur in fabrics for apparel or furnishings. They are generally found in products such as women's handbags, hats, and floor matting. In nonwoven fabrics vinyon is occasionally used as the bonding agent.

Vinal

Vinal is manufactured principally in Japan. Its trade name in the United States is Kuralon. The Textile Fiber Products Identification Act defines *vinal* as

> a manufactured fiber in which the fiber-forming substance is any long chain synthetic polymer composed of at least 50% by weight of vinyl alcohol units ($-CH_2-CHOH-$), and in which the total of the vinyl alcohol units and any one or more of the various acetal units is at least 85% by weight of the fiber.

As extruded, the fibers are water soluble and must be treated with formaldehyde to make them insoluble.

Under magnification vinal fibers are smooth, somewhat grainy, and characterized by faint striations. They are white in their natural form. The cross section may be bean-shaped, U-shaped, or nearly round.

The fiber has good strength and moderate elongation, but it is weaker wet than dry. Its moisture absorbency is slightly higher than that of nylon, which permits relatively easy dyeing.

Vinal does not support combustion; it softens at 200°C (390°F) and melts at 220°C (425°F). Its resistance to chemicals is good. Chlorine bleaches as well as soaps and detergents can be used safely. The fiber has a high tolerance to sea water and excellent resistance to microorganisms and insects.

Except for limited industrial applications, vinal has not been used in the United States in any sizable quantity. In Japan and some other countries it is employed in protective apparel—raincoats, jackets, hats, umbrellas, suiting fabrics, lining fabrics, socks, and gloves. Combinations

Figure 15.3 Infant's garment of vinyon/vinal. (*Macy's*)

with cotton or rayon in blends are said to be very attractive and silky. Industrial uses include fishing nets, filter fabrics, tire cord, tarpaulins, and bristles.

Although vinal is usually produced so that it is insoluble in water, limited amounts of the water-soluble product are manufactured for special fabrics, in which the soluble vinal is dissolved, leaving unusual designs. The soluble fiber also has some surgical applications.

Nytril

The Textile Fiber Products Identification Act defines *nytril* as

> a manufactured fiber containing at least 85% of a long chain polymer of vinylidene dinitrile ($—CH_2—C(CN)_2—$) where the vinylidene dinitrile content is no less than every other unit in the polymer chain.

The B. F. Goodrich Company developed nytril fibers and introduced the first commercial product in 1955. The original fiber name, Darlan, was soon changed to Darvan. In 1960 Celanese Fibers Company purchased the rights to manufacture Darvan, and in 1961 Celanese joined with Farbe-werke Hoechst of Germany in an agreement to manufacture the fiber in Europe. There it was called Travis. For unexplained reasons, the fiber is currently not produced anywhere in the world.

Darvan had many desirable properties and may eventually return to the market. It was an easy-care fiber, extremely soft, nonpilling, and resilient. Care procedures were similar to those used for acrylic fibers.

Novoloid

The generic term *novoloid* was approved by the Federal Trade Commission in 1973. It is defined as

> a manufactured fiber containing at least 85% by weight of a cross-linked novolac.

The fiber is currently manufactured by the Carborundum Company as Kynol. It is characterized by resistance to flames and chemicals, minimal shrinkage, and easy care.

Novoloid fibers appear mainly in situations where flame-resistant products are required—for example, in garments for firefighters, welders, and the military. Since Kynol fabrics are not only fireproof but also comfortable, they are ideal in suits for racing car drivers, and as such they have received international recognition. The fiber is useful also in airplane fabrics, draperies, and protective apparel for laboratory workers.

Figure 15.4 Protective apparel of Kynol novoloid fiber. (*American Kynol Incorporated*)

16 Mineral and Miscellaneous Fibers

Natural Mineral Fiber

Asbestos

Figure 16.1 Asbestos rock, showing both rock and fiber form. (*Johns-Manville Incorporated*)

Asbestos is the only mineral matter used as a textile fiber in the form in which it is obtained from natural sources. The substance is a fibrous vein in serpentine or amphibole rock (Fig. 16.1). It has been known since the days of early Greece and Rome. In fact, the word *asbestos* is of Greek derivation.

The use of asbestos was recorded by Pliny the Elder in the first century A.D. Legends concerning this amazing fiber have been told for centuries. It is said that Emperor Charlemagne delighted in mystifying guests by throwing a tablecloth of asbestos into a roaring fire and then removing it, unharmed and clean, from the flames. A few centuries later, Marco Polo told his friends in Italy about a substance he observed in Siberia that could be woven into attractive textiles that would not burn, even in direct flame. These stories all point out the salient property of asbestos: It is completely resistant to fire.

Early uses for asbestos included such unexpected items as handkerchiefs and cremation fabrics, as well as wicks for oil lamps and the aforementioned table coverings.

Chrysotile is the asbestos most often found in textiles because of several properties making it especially adaptable to fabrics. The fibers have good strength, flexibility, toughness, low conductivity, and adequate length for spinning into yarns. They also have a silky texture.

Asbestos fibers may be blended with 5 to 20 percent cotton or rayon for yarns and fabrics. The same techniques of yarn processing are employed as with other fibers.

Yarns of asbestos may be plain; they may have a core of wire, glass, or nylon filament; they may be singles, plies, or cords.

Asbestos cords have many industrial applications. Yarns can be used in fabrics of various structures. Treated to produce exceptionally smooth and uniform surfaces, they can be made into materials for asbestos curtains; protective clothing for firefighters; fire-smothering blankets; protective mitts for cooking; protective pads for tables and stoves.

Asbestos is as resistant to chemicals as it is to fire. Fabrics can be washed carefully or simply wiped clean with a sponge. In extreme cases they may be subjected to open flames to burn out the dirt. Of course, for this technique the fabric must be 100 percent asbestos or there will be damage to other fibers.

It is important to comment on the manufacturing of asbestos yarns and fabrics. Special care and safety precautions are required to prevent workers from developing lung ailments. The fine bits of asbestos settle in workers' lungs unless they wear protective masks.

Man-Made Mineral Fibers

Glass Fiber

The origin of glass and glass fibers is uncertain. One legend credits Phoenician fishermen with the discovery of glass fiber. It is said that these men noticed pools of a molten substance under fires they had built on a sandy beach of the Aegean Sea. Natural curiosity caused them to poke at the molten material, and as they withdrew the sticks, glass pulled out in a long, stringlike form. This was, perhaps, the first glass fiber. During the Middle Ages Venetian artisans developed spun glass, which they used as decoration on blown glass forms, such as goblets and vases. This, too, was a form of glass fiber.

Serious efforts to create glass fibers for textiles began in the late 19th century. Edward Drummond Libbey succeeded in attenuating glass into fiber and made sufficient yarn to manufacture fabric for a dress, which was exhibited at the Columbian Exposition of 1893. The garment was attractive and not transparent as the public had anticipated. However, the fibers were coarse and low in strength and flexibility. A concentrated development plan for glass fiber got underway in 1931, and by 1938 usable

Figure 16.2 Fire-resistant coverall, hood, and gloves of aluminized asbestos and cotton fabric. (*American Crafts Council's Museum of Contemporary Crafts, New York*)

glass textile fibers were available in commercial quantities. The Owens-Corning Fiberglas Corporation was formed as a joint venture of Owens-Illinois Glass Company and Corning Glass Company, both of whom had been working on glass fibers. Owens-Corning was the first producer of glass fiber, marketed as *Fiberglas*.

Today, glass fibers are manufactured by several corporations and sold under such trade names as Unifab, Unistrand, Modiglass, Fiberglas, Beta, Pittsburgh PPG, and Uniglass.

The Textile Fiber Products Identification Act defines *glass* as

a manufactured fiber in which the fiber-forming substance is glass.

Production

The raw materials for glass are primarily silica sand and limestone, with small amounts of modifiers such as aluminum hydroxide, sodium carbonate, and borax. These materials are melted at high temperatures and formed into clear marbles (called *cullet*) about $\frac{5}{8}$ inch in diameter. Only perfect marbles are selected for the fiber-making process.

The marbles are then fed into a small furnace, where they are remelted, and the molten glass falls by gravity through a platinum spinnerette. As the melted glass leaves the spinnerette, it solidifies. For filament yarns the fibers are pulled together, lubricated for ease in handling, and wound on tubes in strand form for fabric manufacture.

To form staple fibers a different procedure is followed. As the fibers leave the spinnerette and begin to solidify, they are hit by a jet of steam under high pressure. This breaks the filaments into short lengths and blows them onto a drum. The fibers are pulled into a sliver and processed as for cotton or wool (see p. 134).

During the last few years several manufacturers have installed direct processing equipment. In this method the molten glass is fed directly to the spinnerette, thus avoiding the intermediate cullet step.

Fiber Properties

Glass fiber is strong. Its elongation is low—only 3 percent—but elastic recovery is 100 percent. It has excellent dimensional stability. The fibers do not absorb moisture and have excellent resistance to wrinkling. They are smooth, even, and transparent. The cross section is circular.

Fibers of glass will not burn. They will soften at about 815°C (1500°F), and strength begins to decline at temperatures greater than 315°C (600°F). However, as soon as the heat is reduced, fiber strength returns.

Hydrofluoric and hot phosphoric are the only acids that attack glass fibers, but most alkalies do. The fibers are damaged by strong alkalies at any temperature and by weak ones at high temperatures. Organic solvents and mild laundry agents have no effect.

Although glass fibers are pliable and flexible, they lack abrasion resistance. When folded, as for hems in draperies, the edge will tend to crack if it is subjected to rubbing against another surface, such as the floor or window sill. Through the development of special techniques glass fibers can be dyed or printed in a variety of colors and patterns.

In the early 1960s, Owens-Corning introduced a new superfine glass filament, trademarked *Beta*. This fiber has been very successful and is used in draperies, bedspreads, and table coverings. Beta has been tried in upholstery fabric and apparel but has not been widely adopted in such applications. Beta glass is one of the finest and softest fibers manufactured. It blends successfully with other fibers, particularly the modacrylics and olefins.

Figure 16.3 Window curtain of glass fibers. (*Owens/Corning Fiberglas*)

Glass fibers are considered nonallergenic by most authorities. However, there is growing evidence that the fibers do produce serious allergic reactions in some people. Whether this reaction is due to the fiber ends causing irritation, to finishing compounds, or to the actual fiber composition has not been established. Because the fiber can cause allergic reactions for some, it is suggested that consumers handle the fiber on an experimental basis before selecting for use.

Glass Fibers in Use

The use of glass fiber has tripled since 1955, but much of this growth has been in products for industry. Various plastic materials reinforced through impregnation with glass fibers are often called fiberglass products. This group includes such items as sports car bodies, bodies for sand-dune buggies, poles for pole vaulting, boats, and furniture.

Major home uses of the fiber are in window curtains and tablecloths, ironing-board covers, lampshades, screens, and recently in some facets of actual building construction. Glass is not utilized for apparel as yet because the sharp fiber ends that are found at cut edges frequently cause skin irritations.

Glass fabrics should not be dry cleaned but laundered—separately. They should not be washed in a machine because the residue from the fibers may be left behind and transferred to articles washed in the

Figure 16.4 Fiberglas Beta fabric was used as the roof of the United States Pavilion at Expo '70 in Osaka, Japan. The translucent Beta fabric glowed from the interior light at night and allowed sunlight to pass through the dome during the day. (*fabric: Owens/Corning Fiberglas; architects: Davis, Brody & Associates*)

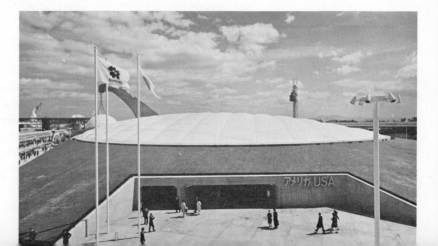

Figure 16.5 Boat hull reinforced with fiberglass fibers. (*Owens/Corning Fiberglas*)

following loads. Glass fiber residue also can cause skin irritation. Mild soaps, detergents, and bleaches can be used. Fabrics should be rinsed thoroughly, then rolled or wiped with a towel. Window coverings can be rehung immediately while other fabrics should be laid smooth to dry or hung over padded lines. In sum, the major points to remember are the following: never wring or spin dry glass fibers; do not rub; do not use strong alkaline detergents; rinse laundry equipment after use to prevent transfer of fiber residue to other items.

Metallic Fibers or Threads

Metallic threads are truly the oldest form of man-made fiber, dating back to ancient Persia and Assyria. Actually, the first metallic fibers were not real fibers but were the result of slitting very thin sheets of metal into narrow, ribbonlike forms. Even today most metallic yarns are manufactured by variations of this old process.

The Textile Fiber Products Identification Act defines *metallic* fiber as

a manufactured fiber composed of metal, plastic-coated metal, metal-coated plastic, or a core completely covered by metal.

Gold, silver, and aluminum are the metals most often used in textile products. Gold and silver yarns are extremely costly. Occasionally they are pure metal, but since these metals are soft, it is more common for thin strips of the product to be wrapped around a central core of a strong, flexible product, generally silk or very fine copper wire. Silver tarnishes quickly in the air, and gold may discolor, so aluminum has replaced these fibers in Western countries. Some fabrics from the Orient are still made with pure gold or silver threads.

Modern aluminum yarns are made by one of two basic procedures. First, aluminum may be encased in a plastic coating of either a polyester, such as Mylar, or cellulose acetate-butyrate. The second product is cheaper, but the polyester is more desirable. Color is applied either to the plastic coating or directly to the aluminum by an adhesive. The second technique for manufacturing involves mixing finely ground aluminum, color, and polyester together, and then laminating this product to clear Mylar polyester.

Both types of metallic yarns can be obtained in a variety of colors —most frequently with gold and silver effects. The yarns are bright and colorful and do not tarnish. The plastic coating prevents damage from salt water, chlorine, and alkaline detergents.

Metallic yarns are not especially strong, but they are quite adequate for normal decorative purposes. Polyester-coated yarns are stronger than those coated with acetate-butyrate and are often used in fabrics for evening wear. The yarns are colorfast to light and laundering.

The care of metallic yarns is determined to a considerable degree by the type of plastic coating, the core substance in wrapped yarns, and other fibers in the final product. Careful observance of all labels is recommended. Warm, never hot, temperatures should be used in the care process.

The popularity of metallic yarns is affected tremendously by the dictates of current fashion. A wide variety of home-furnishing fabrics —including drapery and curtain materials, upholstery, bedspreads, towels, and tablecloths—contain metallic yarns. Metallics will enhance apparel, from evening gowns and cocktail dresses to sportswear, such as slacks, shorts, and bathing suits. The luxury of gold and silver, once available only to kings and queens, may be enjoyed today by almost everyone.

A recent addition to metallic fibers is stainless steel, which may be made into yarn as a monofilament fiber or in combination with other fibers. Stainless steel in fabrics contributes strength, tear and abrasion resistance, and thermal conductivity. It also reduces static buildup in floor coverings. Steel fibers may be utilized in resistance wiring for draperies, floor coverings, and upholstery. These wires can radiate heat when properly connected to a power source. One of the better known trade names for steel fibers is Brunsmet.

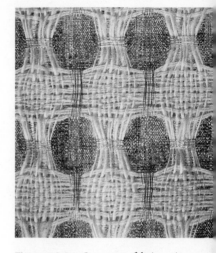

Figure 16.6 Casement fabric using metallic yarn of silver for accent. (*Jack Lenor Larsen, Inc.*)

Miscellaneous Fibers

The textile industry is ever changing. New fibers are constantly introduced and either accepted or rejected. Many fibers serve only in industry for highly technical purposes. The following are important examples of new fibers for both industrial and commercial applications.

Graphite   Continous-filament yarns of graphite are made by converting filament fibers such as rayon or acrylic into pure carbon. The graphite fibers are extremely strong and resist high temperatures. They are widely used in aerospace products. A recent application is plastic matrixes, which add strength to the form.

Boron   Fibers from boron and from boron nitride are employed in industries where heat resistance, strength, and flexibility are important. Boron nitride is a flexible white fiber. It has been used in space fabrics and protective apparel.

Chromel   Alloys of nickel and chromium (chromel) are important to the aerospace industry for space suits and other products. These fibers can be knitted, woven, and braided on standard equipment, and they blend satisfactorily with other fibers. Chromel resists extremely high temperatures; it is nonflammable and static free.

PBI Fiber   Polybenzimidazole, or PBI, resists temperatures greater than 177°C (350°F) for very long periods of time and temperatures above 538°C (1000°F) for a short time. The fiber has been used in apparel for

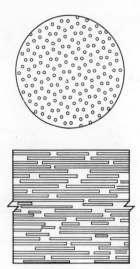

Figure 16.7 Diagram of a biconstituent fiber. (*Allied Chemical*)

space and for drogue chutes. It is nonflammable, comfortable, and flexible. One special product is the soft, flexible undersuit worn by astronauts.

Source   Allied Chemical introduced a biconstituent fiber in the late 1960s. This fiber, called *Source,* is composed of a nylon 6 matrix, with polyester fibrils—running parallel to each other and to the longer dimension of the nylon matrix—embedded in each filament (Fig. 16.7).

A-Tell   At the same time that Qiana was introduced in the United States, a fiber described as having similar properties to Qiana and to silk was released in Japan. This fiber, named *A-Tell,* is a benzoate produced from a benzoic acid and ethylene oxide. The fiber was listed as having the following characteristics: no waxiness, resistance to abrasion, resistance to sunlight, no damage by acids or alkalies, dimensional stability, and close resemblance to silk in texture and hand. Knitted fabrics of A-Tell, which are on the market in the United States, are very soft and drapable, and have easy-care properties.

Monvelle   A biconstituent fiber composed of nylon and spandex was introduced recently by the Monsanto Corporation. The fiber's excellent holding power makes it ideal for hosiery; stockings appear smooth during wear. The fiber is easy to care for, has durability, and can be dyed in many shades.

Polycarbonate Fibers   The fiber *Lexan,* made by General Electric Corporation, is listed as a polycarbonate. Data concerning its properties are not available.

Polyurea Fibers   Polyureas are strong; they have a low moisture regain, good resistance to chemicals, and average resistance to heat. In hand polyurea fibers resemble silk, while in mechanical properties they are similar to nylon. As yet the fibers have been used only in industrial applications.

Yarn Structure III

To weave or knit a fabric it is necessary to have yarns. Thus, the making of yarns is nearly as old as the manufacture of fabric and definitely predates recorded history. In prehistoric time fibers were twisted together in simple ways to form yarns. It is reasonable to suppose that the first technique for yarnmaking involved rolling fibers together between the palms of the hands, between fingers, or between a hand and another part of the body, such as the thigh. This latter process is still used by some peoples in isolated parts of the world.

The next development was the invention of spindles. Various types of spindles have emerged from archaeological digs, but the most common device seems to have employed a distaff, a spindle, and a whorl. Loose fibers were tied to a distaff. The spindle was a short stick notched at one end and pointed at the other. The spinning whorl was secured near the pointed end. The spinner held the distaff under the arm to free both hands for the actual spinning. Fibers were attached to the spindle notch, and the whorl pulled the fibers and spindle downward in a twirling motion. As the spindle dropped, the spinner drew out the fibers and formed them into a thread with the fingers while the whirling spindle twisted them into a

left: Figure III.1 Design on an early Greek vase (c. 560 B.C.), clearly showing a spindle, whorl, and distaff used in spinning yarn. (*Metropolitan Museum of Art, New York: Fletcher Fund, 1931*)

right: Figure III.2 Spinning wheel with foot pedal for power. (*Don Cyr*)

tight strand. When the spindle neared the ground, the spinner took it up, wound the finished thread around it, and caught the new yarn in the notch. The process was then repeated.

Yarns were spun by these hand methods until late in the 14th century, at which time a crude spinning wheel was developed. The Saxony spinning wheel (Fig. III.2), seen in many antique shops and museums today, was introduced in the 16th century. It is still used in some parts of the world and is currently enjoying a revival among handcraftsmen. This spinning wheel formed the yarn mechanically, but the power was human. Either a hand-propelled wheel or a foot treadle operated the wheel.

During the 18th century multiple spinning frames were developed, and shortly thereafter waterpower was incorporated. The basic machine-spinning techniques still used today follow the principles of the early multiple frames. A number of men played major roles in the perfection of spinning processes and equipment. Lewis Paul and John Wyatt developed the roller method of spinning in 1737; James Hargreaves invented the spinning jenny in 1764; Richard Arkwright introduced the waterpower spinning frame about 1770; and Samuel Crompton created the spinning mule in 1779. Theirs are the basic inventions upon which all modern spinning is dependent.

Today yarns are manufactured by several processes. The type of yarn used may produce variations in fabric appearance, durability, maintenance, and comfort. The following three chapters are concerned with the processes by which yarns are manufactured and the yarn variations available.

Yarn Construction 17

Basic Principles

Yarns are composed of textile fibers. The different methods by which these fibers are joined create the variety of yarn structures available to fabric manufacturers. The term *yarn* has been defined in several ways, but the definition given by the American Society for Testing Materials (ASTM) is representative:[1]

> a generic term for a continuous strand of textile fibers, filaments, or material in a form suitable for knitting, weaving, or otherwise intertwining to form a textile fabric. Yarn occurs in the following forms:
>
> *a.* a number of fibers twisted together
> *b.* a number of filaments laid together without twist
> *c.* a number of filaments laid together with more or less twist
> *d.* a single filament . . . monofilament
> *e.* one or more strips made by the lengthwise division of a sheet of material such as a natural or synthetic polymer, a paper, or a metal foil.

[1] American Society for Testing Materials, *Yearbook,* Part 32 (1974), p. 46.

Figure 17.1 Staple and filament fibers.

The varieties available include single yarn, plied yarns, cabled yarn, cord, thread, and fancy yarn. Insertion of the phase "or strands" following "continuous strand" in the foregoing definition will serve to broaden and clarify the use of the word *yarn,* as it is interpreted in this text.

Yarns can be made from short, staple-length fibers or from long filament fibers (Fig. 17.1). If filaments are used, the yarns may be either *multifilament* (composed of several filaments) or *monofilament* (composed of a single filament). The staple fibers may derive from those natural fibers that are available only in short lengths, or they may be composed of man-made fibers (or silk) that have been cut short. In any case, yarns made of short fibers require considerable processing.

Yarn Processing

Yarns composed of staple fibers are frequently called *spun yarns,* and this term will be used interchangeably with the term *staple fiber yarns.* In general, spun yarns are manufactured by either the cotton or the wool system.

The Cotton System

Sorting and Blending   Cotton or other staple fibers of similar length arrive at the processing unit in a large bale. To make cotton yarns, yarns of other fibers of similar length, or yarns that are an intimate blend of several fibers with uniform quality, the fibers from several bales and sources will be combined. Once the bales are opened, thin layers of fibers from several bales are fed into the blending machines. The machines will loosen and separate the closely packed fibers, remove any dirt and other heavy impurities either by gravity or by centrifugal force, and blend the fibers into a uniform mixture.

left: Figure 17.2 Close-up of metal "fingers" that pull small tufts of fibers from the bale, loosen them, and free them for processing. (*Springs Mills*)

right: Figure 17.3 The picker lap is delivered to the card frame, where it supplies fibers to form the card sliver. (*Springs Mills*)

Picking   From the opening and blending equipment, the fibers are conveyed to the *pickers.* These machines clean them further and form them into a *lap* about 45 inches wide of randomly oriented fibers. The laps resemble absorbent cotton in form and shape. Quality of the yarn is

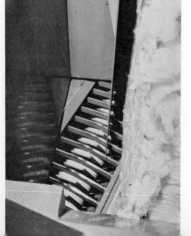

above: **Figure 17.4** A card frame. At the back, or right, is the picker lap; at the front, or left, is the card sliver as it is taken from the carding unit. (*Springs Mills*)

above right: **Figure 17.5** Fibers leave the carding frame in a filmy, sheer layer. This web is pulled into the sliver for the next step in manufacture. (*Springs Mills*)

right: **Figure 17.6** A card frame, showing automatic fiber feed at rear and doffing of card sliver at front. (*Springs Mills*)

dependent to a considerable degree upon the thoroughness of the picking operation and the uniformity of the picker lap.

Carding   The picker lap is next fed into the carding machine. This step continues the cleaning process, removing fibers too short for yarns, and separating and partially straightening them so that their longitudinal axes are somewhat parallel. The fibers are then spread into a thin, uniform web. The web moves into a funnel-shaped device, where it is gathered into a soft mass and formed into the *card sliver,* a ropelike strand of fibers about $\frac{3}{4}$ inch to 1 inch in diameter. The card sliver is not completely uniform in diameter, and the fibers are considerably more random in arrangement than a combed sliver. Carded yarns go directly to the drawing machine; combed yarns receive additional processing before drawing.

Combing   For high-quality yarns of outstanding evenness, smoothness, fineness, and strength, the fibers are combed as well as carded. In the combing operation several card slivers are combined and then drawn onto the comb machine where they again are spread into a web form and subjected to further cleaning and straightening. Short fibers are removed. After combing, the fibers are pulled from the combing wires and formed into a *combed sliver.* This sliver will produce yarns of high quality.

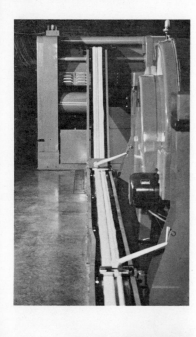

far left: Figure 17.7 Slivers—in this case, five—are fed together into the drawing frame, where they are combined and drawn into a new sliver ready for combing, blending, and roving. (*Springs Mills*)

left: Figure 17.8 Drawn slivers of yarn are combined in a sheet and wrapped onto rolls. These lap rolls provide the fiber supply for combing units, where short fibers are combed out and a new sliver is formed. (*Springs Mills*)

Drawing Depending on the quality of yarn desired, drawing follows either carding or combing. Several slivers are combined and conveyed to the drawing machine, where they are pulled together and drawn out into a new sliver no larger than one of the original single slivers.

If the yarn is to be an intimate blend of two or more fibers, the slivers will be of different fibers. For example, one sliver of cotton fibers for each sliver of polyester fibers will produce a blend of approximately 50 percent polyester and 50 percent cotton. As yet, no twist will have been introduced into the yarn.

Roving The sliver from the drawing machine is taken to the roving machine, where it is attenuated until it measures from $\frac{1}{4}$ to $\frac{1}{8}$ of its original diameter. As the roving strand is ready to leave the roving frame, a slight twist is imparted to the strand, and it is then ready for the spinning frame. The fineness and intimacy of blending of the yarn depends to some degree on the number of times the slivers are doubled and redrawn during the roving operation.

Spinning The final process in the manufacture of yarn is the spinning operation. In the spinning frame the yarn is stretched to its ultimate diameter, and the desired amount of twist is inserted. Several methods are used for imparting twist during the spinning operation. For cotton yarns as well as for other fibers processed on the cotton system the most common technique is *ring spinning*.

In ring spinning, the drawn-out roving is guided in a downward direction through the *traveler,* a small inverted U-shaped device. The traveler moves around the ring at the rate of 4000 to 12,000 revolutions

Figure 17.9 Slivers from the combers are combined and fed into a drawing unit where the slivers are pulled and drawn to form a single sliver. (*Springs Mills*)

Figure 17.10 Roving frame. Slivers from the comb or card drawing frames are pulled and drawn out to form the roving. A slight amount of twist is imparted to hold fibers together. (*Springs Mills*)

per minute. As the spindle revolves to wind the yarn, the latter has to pass through the traveler, which carries it around on the ring. This process imparts the desired twist. The yarn as it comes from the spinning machine is a single yarn.

Other methods of spinning include the flyer and cap systems. The flyer process was the original method of continous spinning, but it is seldom used today because it is slow and production is low. However, yarns made by the flyer process are smooth and have a high luster.

Figure 17.11 Spinning frame, which converts roving to the final simple single yarn. An average frame has 360 spindles of roving hung from the top, each supplying a spinning area. The roving is guided down into the spinning area, where it is pulled and attenuated to form the spun yarn. The yarn is wound onto bobbins at the lower level of the frame. (*Springs Mills*)

Figure 17.12 The traveler, the metal ring through which the yarn is guided, moves around the ring and imparts twist as the yarn is wound onto the bobbin. (*Springs Mills*)

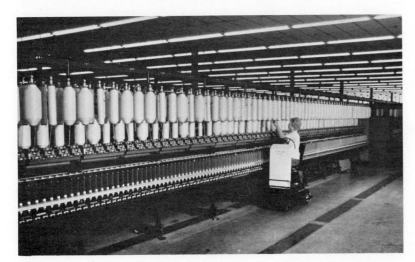

The Wool Systems

Wool and man-made fibers can be spun into yarns by the woolen or the worsted system. The woolen system is comparable to that used in spinning carded cotton, where the yarns are carded, drawn, and spun. Yarns made by the worsted system are similar to combed cotton yarns in that the fibers are combed after carding to produce smoother and finer-quality yarns.

Sorting   Each fleece is carefully opened, and an expert grader pulls the fleece apart and sorts the fibers according to fineness or width and length of fiber, and sometimes according to strength. The grade of fiber determines the type of product for which it will be used. Fine fibers that are relatively long are reserved for sheer wool fabrics and for worsteds; medium fibers of shorter length are suitable for woolens; coarse fibers, both long and short, go into rough fabrics and carpets. The best-quality fibers come from the sides and shoulders of the sheep. Lamb's wool, sheared from animals about eight months old, is used in making very fine-quality, soft-textured sweaters or similar products.

Scouring   After sorting, the wool is scoured. This involves washing in warm soapy water several times, followed by thorough rinsing and drying. Scouring is essential, for it removes the natural grease in the fiber, the suint or body excretions, dirt, and dust. Natural grease is recovered and purified and becomes lanolin, used in the cosmetic industry. Scouring is, of course, not required for man-made fibers.

Carding and Combing   Wool fibers are carded by passing them between cylinders faced with fine wire teeth. This procedure removes considerable vegetable matter—such as twigs and burrs that remain in the fiber after scouring—and begins to disentangle the fibers and straighten them. It can be compared with the carding of cotton fibers.

Before combing, it must be decided whether the fibers are to be used for woolen or worsted yarns and fabrics. Woolen yarns are carded only, and the fibers are quite random in arrangement. Considerable foreign matter remains in woolen yarns, and if this is to be removed, it is eventually taken out by carbonization. The latter involves passing the fabric through a sulfuric acid bath and applying heat, which combines with the acid to burn out vegetable matter. A final rinse removes acid and carbonized matter.

Fibers for worsted yarns are combed by passing them through the combing machine, where they are arranged parallel to each other. Short fibers are removed, and the remaining fibers are pulled into an untwisted strand called *top*. Wool tops can be dyed in this form, or the worsted yarns can be constructed and dyed later.

Spinning   The spinning of wool yarns usually is done by either the *ring* method or the *mule* method. Large amounts of wool are spun by the ring

method today, because it is faster, it produces good-quality yarn, and the equipment occupies less space than the mule frame.

Mule spinning is classified as an intermittent system. It is still used for the best-quality soft yarns, so a brief description of the process is included. Unlike the systems previously mentioned, which are continuous-spinning techniques, the mule spinning frame accomplishes the drawing and twisting in one operation and the winding in a second operation. The carriage moves away from the spools of roving a distance of approximately 60 inches, and during this outward move the yarn is drawn and twisted. As the carriage moves back to its original position, the yarn is wound onto the yarn package. Although this machine occupies a considerably greater amount of space than other spinning frames, it does produce a soft yarn that is excellent for filling and for both warp and filling in blankets and other soft fabrics.

Staple Man-Made Fibers

Staple man-made fibers can be processed by any of the spinning systems discussed, depending on the cut length of the fibers. Conversely, the yarn manufacturer orders the staple length needed for the type of equipment available. If man-made fibers are to be used in blends with a natural fiber, the blending may be part of the preliminary blending process; however, it usually occurs at the drawing stage. Spun yarns of a single type of man-made fiber do not require blending, for they are relatively uniform as they come from the producer.

Yarns of staple fibers can be made with various diameters, from relatively fine to comparatively heavy and thick. All yarns composed of staple fibers must possess sufficient twist to hold the fibers in place, the amount depending upon the intended use. Yarns for warp, filling, or knitting have varying degrees of twist because of different requirements in fabric manufacturing. Additional twist is imparted to produce crepe yarns.

left: **Figure 17.13** Woolen carding. Fibers are opened or loosened, mixed, made into a uniform web, and condensed into roving. (*Wool Bureau*)

right: **Figure 17.14** Worsted carding. Carding teases out the fibers and removes impurities. On the lower right, wool in a filmy web is gathered together into a sliver. (*Wool Bureau*)

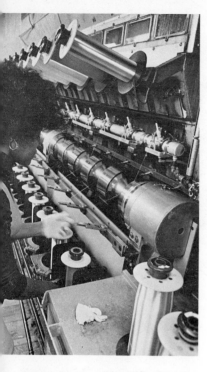

Figure 17.15 Filament fibers are combined with minimal twist to produce filament yarns. All the filament fibers required to make a specific size filament yarn are extruded simultaneously through the spinnerette. (*Celanese Corporation*)

Filament Yarns

The manufacture of yarns from filament fibers—whether natural or man-made—is a much more simple and direct process than that required for staple fibers. Silk is the only natural filament fiber, and the size of the silk yarn depends upon the number of cocoons reeled off at one time (see Chap. 8).

Filament yarns of man-made fibers are produced by either the continuous or the discontinuous process. In the continuous process the filaments are collected in groups (the number of filaments in each group is determined by the desired number in the finished yarn) as they are extruded from the spinnerette. Then, a specified amount of twist is added, and the yarn is ready for processing into fabric. In the discontinous method the filaments are extruded, placed on cones or cakes, and shipped to yarn manufacturers, who combine the filaments into the desired arrangement, impart twist, and prepare the yarn for fabric construction.

Filament yarns are smooth and even unless they have been deliberately made irregular for novelty effects. They can be thick and heavy, gossamer sheer and light, or of any intermediate weight and diameter.

Simple yarns of filament fibers are lustrous and somewhat silklike in appearance. The luster can be reduced considerably by the addition of delusterants, but even delustered filaments tend to have more sheen than staple yarns. Filament yarns have no protruding fiber ends, so they do not pill (unless the filaments are broken), and lint is not formed. Textured filament yarns may pill, however. Round filaments tend to shed soil, while multilobal filaments camouflage dirt.

The strength of filament yarns is determined by a combination of factors: fiber strength, number of filaments, denier of the actual yarn, and denier of each individual filament. Because the fibers are long, they receive equal pull, and fiber strength is maximized in the yarns.

The amount of twist in filament yarns is usually relatively low, but it is possible to make high-twist crepe yarns successfully.

New Methods of Yarn Preparation

During the past few years yarn manufacturers have developed new techniques in order to deal with rising operating costs and to develop some degree of automation in the textile industry. These new methods include continuous automatic spinning devices that

1. move the fiber directly from bale to sliver
2. move the sliver or tow directly to completed yarn
3. move the fiber directly to the yarn stage—open-end spinning —without intermediate stops.

Fiber to Sliver   Automatic feeding of fibers from the bale to the sliver is accomplished by several types of equipment. The fiber is plucked automatically from the bale, fed to the blender, then moved to the carding equipment and, if desired, to combers. The resulting yarns are more uniform than regular yarns, and strength tends to be superior. Production speed is increased, and labor costs are reduced.

Sliver to Tow to Yarn   The sliver-to-yarn method utilizes a direct spinning frame. It eliminates separate drawing, roving, and twisting machines and provides for continuous movement from the sliver stage to the final yarn. Yarns tend to be coarser than those produced by older methods, but the new technique is less costly, more efficient, and faster. For end-uses where fineness is not important, particularly in woolen yarns, it is quite acceptable.

Tow-to-yarn processing is becoming very popular. Formerly, man-made fibers used in staple yarns had to be extruded as filaments, cut into short lengths, and then processed into yarns by either the cotton or the wool system. The tow-to-yarn procedure bypasses many of these steps. The tow is fed into a machine in which rollers, operating at different speeds, cause fiber breakage. The breakage occurs at various points, so no groups of fibers are broken at the same spot. Throughout this step parallel arrangement of fibers is maintained. The fibers are then fed to regular drawing and spinning equipment and converted into yarns.

Yarns made by this process are even, soft, uniform, and comparatively strong; they may have high bulk if desired. Considerable economy,

Figure 17.16 Karousel picker. Modern yarn manufacturing is highly automated. In this Karousel the yarns are picked from the bales, loosened and fluffed, and fed automatically to carding and drawing equipment. In open-end spinning, fibers may move automatically from opening to final spinning. (*American Textile Manufacturers Institute*)

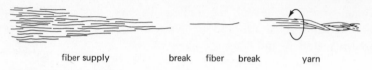

fiber supply   break   fiber   break   yarn

Figure 17.17 The basic principle of break spinning.

reduced waste, and flexibility in the production of special effects are the virtues of this technique.

Fiber to Yarn   Fiber-to-yarn processing is frequently called *open-end spinning*. (It is also referred to as *break spinning* and *element spinning*.) This procedure converts fibers directly into yarns without separate carding, combing, drawing, and spinning operations. The major advantages include fewer knots in yarns, rapid yarn production, greater economy, and the ability to prepare yarn packages of any size.

Three basic fiber-to-yarn methods are in use: mechanical spinning, fluid spinning, and electrostatic spinning.

Mechanical spinning involves the contact of fibers with devices such as funnels, cones, baskets, sieves, or needled surfaces. The fibers are carried by gas or liquid current to the mechanical device, where they are collected. They are then taken off the collecting unit mechanically and delivered to the yarn-forming unit. Finally, twist is inserted. Fluid systems are very similar, except that in the final stage the fibers are delivered to spinning and twisting operations by fluid feeds instead of mechanically. Electrostatic systems utilize an electrostatic field to produce a parallel arrangement of fibers, transport and collect the fibers, and deliver them to mechanical twisting equipment.

Split Film Yarns

Split or slit film yarns are produced from film or tape that is cut into narrow ribbons. These ribbons are fed by conveyor through a heat-stretching or orientation zone to a stabilizing zone. They are then broken down into fibrils. The process can be used on all thermoplastic fibers but is most commonly applied to polyethylene and polypropylene (olefins). Not only is it rapid and economical, but it can produce yarns of varying texture, denier, and appearance.

Yarn Properties

Thread and Yarn

Thread and yarn are basically similar. *Yarn* is the term usually applied when the assemblage of fibers is employed in the manufacture of a fabric, while *thread* indicates a product used to join pieces of fabric together to create textile products. Thread is frequently of plied construction. It is

Figure 17.18   An assortment of threads. (*Educational Bureau, Coats & Clark, Inc.*)

fine, even, and strong. One authority explains that thread is made from yarn but that yarn is never made from thread.[2]

Thread must be so constructed that it can be adapted to either hand or machine sewing as well as to embroidery or lacemaking. A satisfactory thread must have high strength and adequate elasticity, a smooth surface, dimensional stability, resistance to snarling, resistance to damage by friction, and attractive appearance. Several types of thread are available: simple-ply threads, cord threads, elastic threads, monofilament threads, cord threads, elastic threads, monofilament threads of man-made fibers, and multifilament threads.

Yarn Twist

As fibers, staple or filament, are formed into yarns, twist is added to hold the fibers together. The amount of twist is sometimes suggested broadly by such terms as low, medium, and high, but it is more accurately indicated by the number of turns per inch. The turns per inch (TPI) needed to form the best possible yarn varies with the yarn diameter. As the yarn becomes finer, it requires more twist.

The strength of yarns is due, in part, to the amount of twist that has been imparted. Strong yarns require considerable twist. However, beyond an optimum point, additional twist will cause yarns to kink and finally to lose strength and become almost brittle.

Balanced yarns are those in which the twist is such that the yarn will hang in a loop without kinking, doubling, or twisting upon itself. *Unbalanced yarns* have sufficient twist to set up a "torque" effect, and the yarn will untwist and retwist in the opposite direction. Smooth fabrics require balanced yarns, but for crepe and textured effects, unbalanced yarns are frequently used. Crepe yarns are also produced by balanced yarns with enough twist to produce kinking.

[2] G. E. Linton, *The Modern Textile Dictionary,* 2d ed. (New York: Duell, Sloan & Pearce, Meredith Press, 1963), p. 946.

Figure 17.19   Balanced yarn (left) and unbalanced yarn (right).

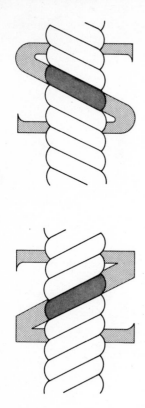

Figure 17.20 Diagram of S and Z twists in yarn.

The direction of twist is also important. Yarns can be twisted with either a right-hand twist (Z twist) or a left-hand twist (S twist). The direction of the twist conforms to the center bar of the letter.

Various effects can be obtained by combining yarns of different twist direction, and durability may be increased by efficient plying of S and Z twist single yarns.

Yarn Number

Yarn number is a measure of linear density. *Direct yarn number* is the mass-per-unit length of yarn; *indirect yarn number* is the length-per-unit mass of yarn. Yarn number is frequently called *yarn count* in the indirect system. To some extent the yarn number is an indication of diameter when yarns of the same fiber content are compared.

Over the years various methods of determining yarn number have been developed. Cotton yarns are numbered by measuring the weight in pounds of one 840-yard hank; the count is then reported as the number of 840-yard hanks required to weigh 1 pound. For example, if 840 yards of cotton weigh 1 pound, the yarn number is 1s; if it requires 30 hanks to weigh 1 pound, the yarn is a 30s. A heavy yarn would be the 1s, a medium yarn a 30s, and a very fine yarn a 160s.

Woolen yarn is measured by the number of 300-yard hanks per pound, while worsted yarn is measured by the number of 560-yard hanks per pound.

Silk and man-made fiber yarns are usually measured using the denier system. The denier is equal to the weight in grams of 9000 meters of yarn. This is an old system and dates back to early Roman times, when a coin, the *denier,* was the medium for buying and selling silk.

Some time ago the textile industry, or a segment thereof, proposed a universal system for yarn numbering or yarn count. This method, called *Tex,* would determine the yarn number by measuring the weight in grams of one kilometer of yarn. The result would be the tex yarn number. While the Tex system is favored by research groups, it has not met with commercial acceptance. This may happen automatically, however, when the United States adopts the metric system.

Simple and Complex Yarns

Simple Yarns

Yarns that are even in size, have an equal number of turns per inch throughout, and are relatively smooth are called *simple yarns*. A simple, single yarn is the most basic assemblage of fibers suitable for operations such as weaving and knitting. These yarns can be made from any of the fibers and by any of the basic systems.

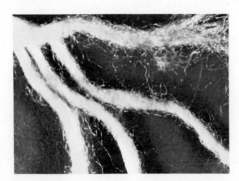

Figure 18.1 Simple yarn. A four-ply yarn with the singles separated and with fibers slightly separated in one of the singles.

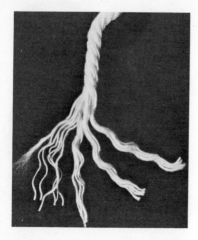

Figure 18.2 Cord yarn composed of four plies, each with seven single yarns.

A simple-ply yarn is composed of two or more simple single yarns plied and twisted together. In naming a ply yarn the number of singles included usually precedes the word *ply*. For example, if two singles are used, the yarn is called a 2 ply; if four are used, a 4 ply.

Simple cord or cable yarns consist of two or more ply yarns twisted together. In identifying a cord, it is necessary to indicate the number of plies in the cord. Thus, a "3,5-ply cord" indicates that each ply has five singles and that three of these 5-ply yarns are combined in making the cord.

Crepe yarns are a variation of simple yarns. However, a crepe yarn possesses a high degree of twist, so the yarn tends to kink. This kinkiness results in the rough texture characteristic of crepe fabrics. Nevertheless, the yarns are evenly twisted and even in size, so they are truly simple yarns rather than complex or novelty yarns.

Except for the textured effect achieved by crepe yarns, simple yarns, in themselves, do not create variation in fabric appearance. However, a combination of simple yarns of different sizes, different amounts of twist, and/or different fiber content can produce many interesting effects. The arrangement of yarns in groups (as in dimity) can also yield visual variety. Other changes in appearance depend on the number of warp and filling yarns per inch and the type and amount of twist. A large number of the simple yarns are used in fabrics where design applied through color or finish is the important thing.

In general, simple yarns tend to produce smooth fabrics. But as previously indicated, the arrangement of the yarns and combinations of various sizes in the fabric structure will influence the end product.

Simple yarns are usually considered to be durable, although the durability is affected by such factors as yarn number, amount of twist (turns per inch), and structure (single, ply, cord). The uniformity of simple yarns helps prevent snagging and tearing. Except for the highly twisted crepe yarns, which tend to shrink during care, simple yarns are most often easy to maintain. The arrangement of the yarns, the yarn structure itself, and the degree of yarn balance will determine maintenance procedures to some degree. Even yarns, balanced yarns, and uniform arrangements of yarns produce fabrics that are comparatively easy to care for.

The preceding statements concerning simple yarns are mere generalizations, however. Differences in fibers, fabric structure, coloring methods, and finishing processes will all have a drastic effect. It is, therefore, essential that students of textiles be aware of the influence of fabric "dimensions" on durability, maintenance, appearance, and comfort before evaluating specific statements about any fabric.

Complex Yarns

Complex or novelty yarns are made primarily for their appearance value. They differ from simple yarns in that their structure is characterized by

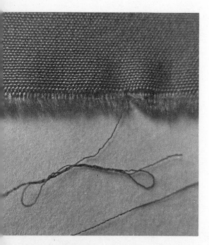

Figure 18.3 Crepe yarn. Note the knotted or crinkled effect resulting from the high twist that gives the fabric its characteristic surface.

irregularities in size, twist, and effect. Most complex yarns are either single or ply; occasionally a cord or modified cord construction is used in complicated novelty yarns.

Complex ply yarns are usually composed of the following: a base, an effect, and a tie or binder yarn. The base yarn controls the length and stability of the end product. The effect yarn forms the design or effect. The tie or binder yarn holds the effect yarn so it will remain in position.

Complex Single Yarns

Slub Yarns   A *slub yarn* may be either a single yarn or a 2 ply. In the single slub the yarn is left untwisted or slackly twisted at irregular intervals in order to produce soft, bulky sections. In a 2-ply slub the soft and fluffy portion is held in place by a second yarn that has more twist. The lack of twist in the bulky areas of slub yarns causes the yarn to be fluffier and softer at those points. Slub yarns are found in such fabrics as shantung, butcher rayon, and some linen.

Thick-and-thin yarns are similar in appearance to slub yarns. However, the manufacturing process differs, as does the length of fiber used. Slub yarns are made from staple fibers, thick-and-thin yarns of filament fibers. As the filaments are extruded, the pressure forcing the spinning solution through the spinnerette is varied, so the filaments are thicker in some sections than in others. The resulting group of filaments forms a yarn of irregular size with thick-and-thin characteristics.

Flock Yarns   Flock yarns, frequently called *flake yarns,* are usually single yarns in which small tufts of fiber are inserted at irregular intervals and held in place by the twist of the base yarn. These tufts may be round or elongated. Flock yarn is used for fancy effects in suiting and dress fabrics. Tweeds, for example, usually contain flock yarns. One drawback to these yarns is that the flock tufts are easily pulled loose. However, since this occurs over a long period of time, it is not considered serious. Some authors classify flock or flake yarns as one variety of slub yarns.

Complex Ply Yarns

Several systems exist to classify complex ply yarns, and definitions of the various yarns differ. The history of textile yarns and fabrics dates back thousands of years, so it is understandable that various descriptions for irregular and decorative yarns have evolved.

Bouclé Yarns   Bouclé yarns are characterized by tight loops projecting from the body of the yarn at fairly regular intervals. These yarns are of 3-ply construction. The effect yarn that forms the loops is wrapped around a base yarn, and then a binder or tie yarn holds the loops in position. Bouclé fabrics can be constructed by either knitting or weaving. The yarn is also available for hand knitting.

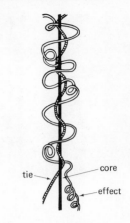

Figure 18.4   Diagram of the basic units in a three-ply complex yarn: the core or base yarn, the decorative or effect yarn, and the binder or tie yarn.

Figure 18.5   A complex slub yarn, slightly magnified.

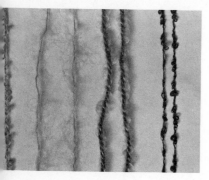

Figure 18.6 Complex-ply yarns, loop types.

Loop and Curl Yarn   The loop yarn is of at least 3-ply construction. The base yarn is rather coarse and heavy. The effect yarn, which forms loops or curls, is made of either a single or a ply of two or more singles. The loops are held in place by an additional single yarn (or two singles) that serve as ties. These binder yarns are fine and securely twisted. In the 1960s loop yarns became quite popular. They were frequently used in suit and coating fabrics of mohair and in fabrics of other fibers that were (incorrectly) called mohair. The popularity of loop yarns appears to be on the wane.

Ratiné and Gimp Yarns   Ratiné and gimp yarns are very similar to each other and, in addition, are rather like bouclé and loop yarns. The major difference between the yarns is that the loops are close together in ratiné or gimp, while in bouclé they are more widely spaced and in loop yarns they are larger and more open. The structure of ratiné and gimp is similar to that of other complex ply yarns, with the loop or effect yarn wrapped around the base and held in place by a binder or tie. Ratiné yarns have a rough-surface appearance. The manufacture requires two distinct twisting operations: after the yarn is first made, it is twisted in the opposite direction to establish the desired effect. The term *gimp* is used frequently as a synonym for ratiné. When a distinction is made, a yarn that has the loops formed by a very soft and slackly twisted yarn is referred to as a *gimp yarn,* while the loops on the ratiné yarn are of a soft but securely twisted yarn.

Nub or Spot, and Knot or Knop Yarns   The terms *nub, spot, knot,* and *knop* are often used interchangeably; however, there are minor differences. A *nub* or *spot yarn* is made on a special machine that permits the base yarn to be held almost stationary while the effect yarn is wrapped around it several times to build up an enlarged segment. Sometimes the effect yarn is held in position by a tie, but in many cases the nub (or spot) is so secure that no binder is required. The *knot* or *knop yarn* is produced in much the same way, except that brightly colored fibers are frequently added to the enlarged knot.

Seed or Splash Yarns   While seed and splash yarns resemble nub or knot yarns, there is a difference in the shape of the enlarged knot segment—that of the splash yarn is elongated, that of the seed yarn tiny.

Spiral or Corkscrew Yarns   Spiral or corkscrew yarns are complex yarns in which the desired effect is obtained either by twisting together yarns of different diameters or different fiber content, or by varying the rate of speed or the direction of twist. A *spiral yarn* consists of two or more single yarns of different size: one fine with a hard twist, the others bulky with a slack twist. The heavy yarn is wound spirally around the fine yarn. A *corkscrew yarn* can be made by twisting together two yarns at an uneven rate, by twisting together two yarns of different size, or by twisting a fine yarn loosely around a heavy yarn so it gives the appearance of a corkscrew.

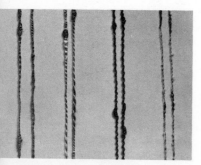

Figure 18.7   Complex-ply yarns: bouclé, nub or knot, and flock or flake.

Chenille Yarn   Chenille yarns create special effects in fabrics and in chenille rugs. The yarn resembles a hairy caterpillar—chenille is French for caterpillar. A special doup-weave fabric (a leno-weave structure, see p. 194) is constructed and then slit into narrow warp-wise strips that serve as yarn. This yarn is then used as filling in chenille fabrics. As the special fabric is slit, the loose ends of the crosswise yarns, which are soft and loosely twisted, form a pilelike surface. The yarn can be folded so the pile is all on one side of the final fabric, or it may be arranged so the loose ends form a raised surface on both sides.

Figure 18.8 Fabric of complex yarns, chenille type.

Core and Metallic Yarns

Core and metallic yarns are included here because they are novelty yarns and have surface design, although they may not necessarily conform to the strict definition of complex yarns.

Core Yarn   A core yarn is one in which a base or foundation yarn is completely encircled or wrapped by a second yarn. For example, the core may be rubber wrapped with cotton to give a comfortable, relatively durable, but highly elastic yarn. Or the core may be silk that is wrapped with gold or silver yarn.

Metallic Yarns   Metallic yarns are not new, but modern developments have produced varieties that are more durable and require less care. American-made metallic yarns are usually produced either by a sandwich-type construction or by a lamination process. In the sandwich construction, aluminum foil and pigment are "sandwiched" between layers of plastic. In the lamination method a metallized polyester is laminated or bonded to clear polyester. Color can be added to the adhesive in the lamination process or to the polyester.

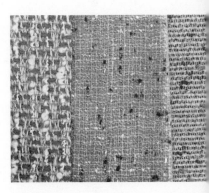

Figure 18.9 Fabrics of complex yarns, flock or flake type.

Metallic yarns are primarily decorative. Thanks to the plastic coatings, they resist tarnishing, but care must be taken in pressing because the plastic is easily softened or melted by high temperatures.

Complex Yarns in Use

Complex or novelty yarns are valued mostly for their appearance. They add texture and design to a fabric. However, there may be problems in comfort, maintenance, and durability. Some complex yarns are rough and harsh, so they may actually be uncomfortable. On the other hand, many loop yarns are soft and pleasant to touch, and they also increase warmth.

The rough surface of many novelty yarns and the irregular twist and loops that characterize many complex yarns may cause them to snag easily, and the flat abrasion resistance is reduced. These properties can contribute to inferior service, particularly when they are used in upholstery fabrics. Although complex yarns usually require careful handling, they are often selected for their appearance regardless of problems they might present.

Figure 18.10 Drapery fabric of complex yarns. (*Robert Tait Fabrics*)

19

Textured Yarns

For many years the term *textured yarns* was just one of several expressions employed in describing complex yarns. More recently, however, the term has been applied to a specific group of yarns.

Today's textured yarns are composed of filament or spun fibers. Most are processed directly from manufactured filament fibers. They may be regular or irregular in construction, so they often bear superficial resemblance to either simple or complex yarns. However, textured yarns do possess individual properties of their own, and for this reason they require special attention.

Textured yarns are characterized by a greater apparent volume than conventional yarn of similar fiber (filament) count. There are many variations in appearance. They may be bulky or relatively smooth and fine; or they may combine bulk or sheerness with stretch. The major concepts of stretch are discussed in a separate chapter (see Chap. 28). This chapter deals with stretch whenever it is an important aspect of textured yarns.

Most textured yarns are manufactured from thermoplastic fibers. The ability to be *heat-set*—to be influenced in character by the application of controlled heat—is a necessary property for the production of many, but not all, textured yarns. In recent years several manufacturers have developed finishing and treatment techniques that impart stretch in completed yarns. However, in this chapter discussion is confined to those textured yarns formed as a result of fiber manipulation.

There are several processes used in the manufacture of textured yarns. These include stuffer-box crimping, gear crimping, tunnel crimping, knit-deknit, false twisting, air-set, and edge crimping. Filament fibers are preferred for texturizing, because they produce yarns with little or no pilling, yet they have softness and bulk.

Texturizing Processes

False-Twist Methods

To create textured yarns by false-twist methods, twist is inserted into simple filament yarns and set in place by the application of controlled heat. The yarn is then cooled and untwisted. As the twist is removed, the fibers kink or crimp sinusoidally because of the distortion resulting from the presence of the heat-set twist. (A *sinusoidal curve* is defined as a wavy line that has identical amplitude on each side of a central axis.) When stretchy yarns are desired, the yarns are heated during the twisting process only, and for stabilized false twist yarns they are passed through a second heating zone after the untwisting operation. The entire process, including variations, is accomplished in a matter of seconds.

Simple yarns made by this method are characterized by either a left- or a right-hand torque, so they tend to be unbalanced and subject to distortion, especially if not stabilized by the second heating. To prevent the distortion, a right-hand and a left-hand twisted single are combined to form a balanced ply yarn. The best-known yarn made by this process is probably Helanca, manufactured by the Heberlein Corporation. Yarns produced on Whitin ARTC equipment are also in this category. Helanca yarns were originally made of nylon fibers, but any thermoplastic fiber is suitable, and currently there is a noticeable increase in the use of polyester fibers as well as the various polyamides.

The degree of stretch produced in yarns by the twist method can be controlled by the amount of turns per inch heat-set into the filaments. Yarns are available in a wide range of stretch, from those that can be elongated up to 400 percent and still return to the original size to those with a small amount of stretch but with high bulk. It is possible to stabilize these yarns so the bulk remains but no noticeable stretch occurs.

Some false-twist machines are designed to process two yarns side by side imparting **S** twist to one and **Z** twist to the other. These yarns are then plied together to produce balanced yarns, which possess many of the same properties as spun yarns manufactured on conventional yarn-spinning equipment.

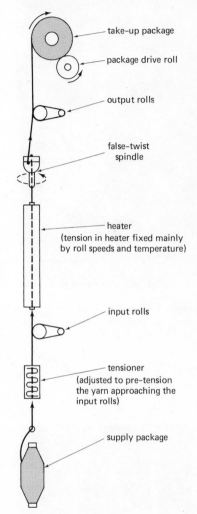

Figure 19.1 Schematic drawing showing the yarn path through a typical false-twist machine. (© *1970 National Knitted Outerwear Associates*)

- take–up package
- package drive roll
- output rolls
- false–twist spindle
- heater (tension in heater fixed mainly by roll speeds and temperature)
- input rolls
- tensioner (adjusted to pre-tension the yarn approaching the input rolls)
- supply package

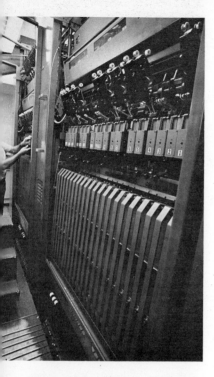

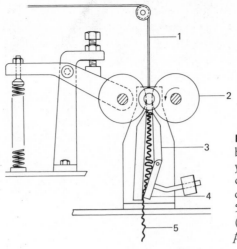

Figure 19.3 Diagram of stuffer-box texturizing: 1) filament yarn feeding into unit; 2) crimping rolls; 3) stuffer box; 4) control to release textured yarn; 5) textured yarn leaving unit. (*E. I. DuPont de Nemours & Company, Patent 3,237,270*)

Figure 19.2 Heat-set equipment used in producing false-twist textured yarns. (*Celanese Corporation*)

Yarns made by the false-twist systems are often softer and more uniform than those made on other texturizing equipment. They have excellent stretch and/or high bulk properties.

The Knife-Edge Method

Textured yarns made by the knife-edge method possess a spirallike curl or coil. The yarns are passed over a heated knife edge or heated and then passed over a knife edge while still hot. It is easy to visualize this process if one takes a paper ribbon—the kind frequently used for gift wrapping —and draws it quickly over a sharp knife or scissor blade. The best known yarn of this kind is Agilon, a nontorque yarn manufactured by Deering-Milliken Research Corporation, which is used extensively in hosiery.

The technique consists of drawing a thermoplastic yarn (usually nylon) over a hot, sharp knife blade. The edge of yarn in contact with the heat and knife is changed in molecular structure, so that the resulting yarn has a bicomponent quality somewhat similar to wool. Agilon yarns show a high degree of elasticity but retain their sheerness so they are desirable for stretch hosiery. Recent research has found the yarns to be satisfactory in knitted fabrics for sweaters and in certain types of upholstery and carpeting.

The amount of stretch in yarns produced by the knife-edge process can be controlled. Because they are nontorque in nature, yarns can be used as either singles or plies. They produce comfortable items of apparel and can be combined with other types of yarns for novelty effects.

The Stuffer-Box Method

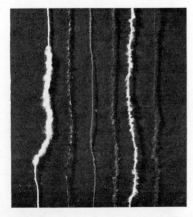

Figure 19.4 Taslan textured yarns that have been processed to simulate complex yarn structures. (*E. I. DuPont de Nemours & Company*)

In the stuffer-box method filament fibers are forced into a narrow box or tube that causes them to develop a saw-toothed crimp. The crimp is heat-set, so when the filaments are removed from the tube, the crimp remains. The greatest amount of bulk and a controlled amount of stretch can be created by this method. Yarns are torque free and, therefore, produce satisfactory textured singles as well as plies. The best-known stuffer-box yarn is Ban-Lon. The Ban-Lon process, which is owned and controlled by the J. Bancroft & Sons Company of Wilmington, Delaware, can be applied to any thermoplastic fiber. Nylon is most frequently used, with the polyesters ranking second. While the Ban-Lon process is adaptable to both short staple fibers and filament fibers, it is most satisfactory with the second variety because pilling is drastically reduced.

Ban-Lon fabrics are soft, strong, and easy to care for. They have a lively hand, excellent moisture absorption, controlled stretch, minimum pilling, dimensional stability, and adequate air circulation for comfort.

Another product that utilizes the stuffer-box method is Spunize. To make Spunize the technique is modified so that multiple ends of yarn can be handled at the same time. While Ban-Lon is generally used in wearing apparel, Spunize yarns are more common in carpets and upholstery fabrics and in industrial applications.

Air-Jet Method (*Loop Yarns*)

Taslan, manufactured and licensed by DuPont, is the best example of a yarn textured by the introduction of loops into the filaments. The process is a highly refined rewinding operation that provides for a brief exposure of multifilament yarn to a turbulent stream of compressed air. The air, in concentrated jets, blows the filaments apart and forms loops in the individual fibers. The resulting yarn is bulky, but it does not exhibit stretch. Since no heat is involved, filament yarns of any manufactured fiber can be bulked by the air-jet method. It has proved highly successful on glass fiber yarns for upholstery and drapery fabrics. Skyloft yarns, manufactured by the American Enka Corporation, depend upon a similar air-jet principle.

Yarns that are bulked by the introduction of loops exhibit the following properties:

- a permanent change in the physical structure of the yarn
- a unique appearance, hand, and texture
- increased covering power
- subdued luster
- lower yarn strength and elongation

Gear Crimping

In gear crimping, yarns under controlled tension and temperature are carried between rotating, intermeshing gears that give a saw-tooth configuration to the filaments. Novelty textured yarns can be formed by an intermittent crimping.

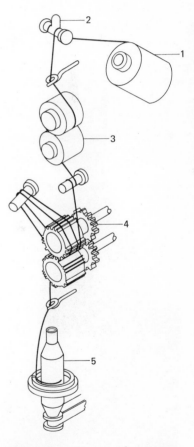

Figure 19.5 Diagram of gear-crimping process for texturizing: 1) yarn supply; 2) tension controls to maintain uniform yarn feed; 3) thread advancing rolls, which pull yarn from supply and feed it to the actual texturizing area; 4) gears used to produce crimp; 5) take-up spindle. (*Monsanto Company*)

Figure 19.6 Knitted tubing that has been heat-set and deknitted to produce textured yarn. (*Celanese Corporation*)

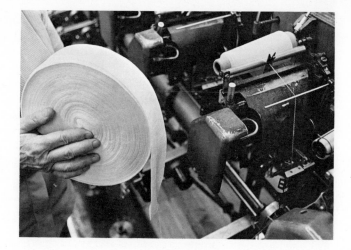

Tunnel Crimping

Tunnel-crimped yarn is fed into a tunnel in such a way that it arranges itself in a winding or sinuous form of desired amplitude. The filaments are then set by heat. Controlled vibrations facilitate proper shaping.

Knit-Deknit

The knit-deknit process involves knitting filament yarns into fabric, heat-setting the fabric, then deknitting or unraveling the yarn. The unraveled yarns exhibit crimp and are ready for fabric manufacture.

Other Texturizing Processes

Bicomponent Texturizing   Two different formulas or modifications of a polymer fiber can be extruded simultaneously from spinnerettes positioned side-by-side or one inside the other to produce a bicomponent fiber. If desired, the fiber can have built-in texturing potential. A crimp can be developed as the filament is formed or during later processing (latent crimp). Examples include Cantrece, Sayelle, Bi-loft, and Wintuk.

Figure 19.7 Apparel of Ban-Lon texturized nylon. (*Indian Head*)

Spinnerette Modification   A spiral or helical crimp (texture) can be introduced into filaments by modifying the shape of the spinnerette openings, by changing the air flow speed at the spinnerette, or by vibrating the spinnerette.

Chemical Texturizing (Crimping)   Chemical texturizing can be applied to any man-made fiber. Immediate or latent crimp is possible, and several processes are in use or development.

Textured Yarns in Use

Textured yarns are found in a wide variety of fabrics. They can be uniform in appearance or plied in special ways to resemble complex yarns. The major factors in the development and acceptance of textured yarns include comfort, appearance, and versatility.

Man-made filament fibers often prove to be uncomfortable apparel fabrics, because the filaments pack tightly together and prevent the movement of moisture or air through the fabric. However, texturizing creates bulk and space between the filaments, so the yarn itself will absorb moisture and provide a greater degree of comfort. In addition, fabrics of textured yarns may be considerably warmer than those of smooth, closely packed yarns, because the bulk acts as insulation.

The stretch property that is often a part of textured yarns has several advantages. For the manufacturers it means they can produce apparel items in a smaller range of sizes, since one size will fit a variety of figures. For consumers it can mean a firmer and more comfortable fit with adequate freedom of movement. On the other hand, stretch can create problems. Some consumers find that stretch fabrics tend to bind or they may blame them for doing so because they are wearing stretch apparel that is too tight. In addition to being uncomfortable, fabrics that are too tight are also unattractive in appearance.

Maintenance of fabrics made from textured yarns is similar to the care given the same fiber in other forms. The added moisture retention increases the drying time for these fabrics, but washing procedures remain unchanged. Care must be taken to avoid snagging, for the texturing technique creates raised or rough surfaces that are easily damaged. Durability is similar to that of other fabrics made from the same fiber. However, the problem of snagging may lead to broken filaments or pilling and, perhaps, broken yarns that would shorten the life of the product.

Fabric Construction

Fibers, yarns, and single fabrics are combined in many different ways to produce the multitude of fabrics available to the modern consumer. Part IV outlines the techniques used in the manufacture of fabrics and the appearance, durability, maintenance, and comfort of finished textiles.

Chapter 20 discusses the production of fabrics directly from fibers. Chapter 21 pertains to the construction of fabrics by knitting or interlooping of yarns and by stitch-knit methods. Woven fabrics are discussed in Chapter 22, while other methods of constructing fabrics—such as knotting, braiding, and multicomponent structures—are described in Chapter 23. Finally, Chapter 24 examines engineered yarns and fabrics, such as blends and combinations.

Figures IV.1 and IV.2 illustrate a number of time-honored methods of fabric construction. Fabrics can be knitted, knotted, and coiled from one thread, while plaiting, tapestry, and weaving employ two or more sets of threads. Many of these techniques are still in use today, but the repertoire of the fabric manufacturer has been enormously expanded by modern technology.

fabrics from one thread

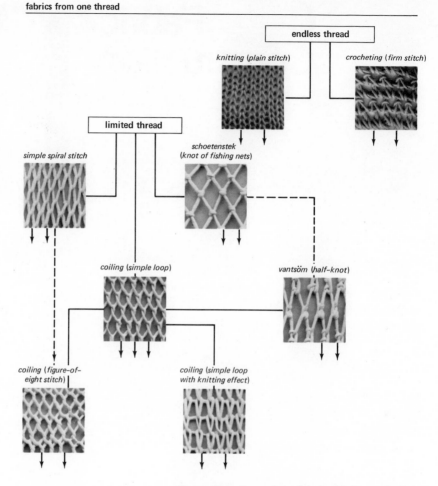

Figure IV.1 Examples of early fabrics made from one continuous thread, such as knitted and knotted fabrics. (*Ciba Review*)

fabrics from several sets of threads

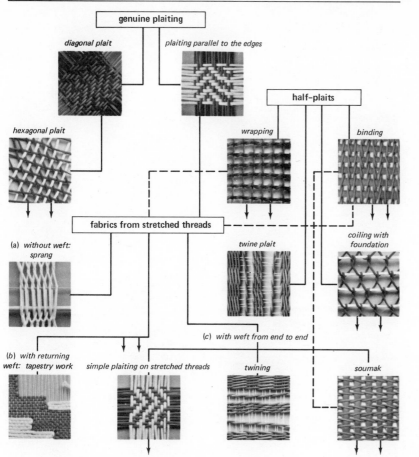

Figure IV.2 Examples of early fabrics made from several threads, including plaited and braided fabrics. (*Ciba Review*)

Felts and Nonwoven Fabrics 20

Felts

The construction of fabric directly from fibers is both the oldest and the newest method of making cloth. The ingenuity of human beings in forming flexible covering materials first expressed itself in felts. Felt manufacture depends upon special characteristics of wool, hair, or fur fibers. The most practical fiber for felt making is wool, but fur fibers are used in hat bodies and are sometimes blended with wool when certain properties are desired.

Felt made wholly or partly of wool is defined by the American Society for Testing Materials as

a structure built up by the interlocking of fibers by a suitable combination of mechanical work, chemical action, moisture and heat without spinning, weaving, or knitting. It may consist of one or more classes of fibers: wool, reprocessed wool or reused wool, with or without admixture with animal, vegetable, and synthetic fibers.[1]

[1] American Society for Testing Materials, *Standards on Textile Materials.* Part 32 (1974), p. 25.

A second definition of *felt* cited by the American Society for Testing Materials is

> a textile (fabric) characterized by the densely matted condition of most or all of the fibers of which it is composed.[2]

The ability of wool fiber to coil upon itself, interlock, and shrink when subjected to heat, moisture, and pressure (including friction and agitation) is responsible for the felting action. In ancient times, long before recorded history, it was somehow discovered that when heat and water were applied to wool fibers and the resultant mass was pounded with rocks, it would create a cloth that would hold together and conform to the general outlines of the body or add warmth to floors.

Today the manufacture of felt is highly mechanized. Wool fibers are cleaned, blended, and carded. After carding, two or more layers of fibers are arranged at right angles to one another. The number of layers depends on the planned ultimate thickness of the felt, but every layer alternates in fiber direction to the one immediately beneath it. The final thickness can vary from $\frac{1}{32}$ inch to 3 inches or more. Apparel felts are usually between $\frac{1}{16}$ inch and $\frac{1}{18}$ inch thick.

The layers or batts of carded fibers are passed through machines where they are trimmed and rolled. Moisture and heat are applied, and the batts are placed between heavy plates. The top plate vibrates, producing friction, agitation, and pressure, which cause the fibers to become entangled and pressed tightly together. The machinery is controlled automatically, so it stops when the desired thickness and hardness is attained. Fulling is the next step. This consists of shrinking the felt into a compact mass by the application of soap or sulfuric acid and then pounding with wooden hammers. Finally, felt is neutralized, scoured, rinsed, dried, and then stretched to the desired width.

Wool from the sheep is the animal fiber most frequently used in making felt, since it possesses the best felting properties. Until the mid-20th century, felts were composed only of animal fibers; however, the increased popularity of felts has encouraged the blending of nonfelting fibers with wool to produce lower-cost products. For example, rayon fibers are frequently blended with wool to make felts. Acceptable felt fabrics can be produced with up to 50 percent nonfelting fibers.

Felts have many industrial and domestic applications. Felt fabrics

- show good to excellent resilience
- are good shock absorbers
- are easy to shape
- will not ravel, so edges need no finish
- are sound absorbent
- have good insulating properties, with resultant warmth

[2] *Ibid.,* p. 24.

- will not tear, though fibers may pull apart
- can be finished to be mothproof, water repellent, fireproof, and fungi-resistant

The breaking load of felts is low when compared with many woven or knitted fabrics. However, with intelligent selection of type and thickness, the consumer can obtain a felt that will be satisfactory for almost any end-use. The shopper seeking felts for apparel must remember that, because of low breaking elongation, felt garments should be loose to be durable. Other properties that may cause dissatisfaction include the fact that holes cannot be mended invisibly and there is little or no elastic recovery. Felt will not return to shape after deformation caused by stretching or other forces.

Felt fabrics are used for wearing apparel, home-furnishing items, crafts and decorative accents, and industrial purposes. The method of construction permits considerable variation in the thickness of the completed fabric and, therefore, enables the manufacturer to produce both flexible fabrics and comparatively stiff products. Flexible felts are desirable for apparel, such as skirts and jackets, as well as for tablecloths, pillow covers, and similar items. The thick fabrics are more appropriate to such products as rug pads and insulating materials.

Proper care procedures for felts are similar to those required of any wool fabric. However, because of the absence of yarn formation, the softer, thinner felts have comparatively low tensile strength; therefore, they should be handled carefully and never subjected to strenuous pulling or twisting. Dry cleaning is recommended for most felt products.

Needle Felts

Needle felts or needle-punched fabrics resemble felt in appearance, but they are made wholly or primarily from fibers other than wool. These fabrics are characterized by an intimate, three-dimensional fiber entanglement produced by the mechanical action of barbed needles, rather than by the application of heat, moisture, and pressure.

The fibers are first blended by the same techniques used for any other manufacturing process. The blended fibers are then arranged into a web or batt by mechanical or air-lay systems. This arrangement may be completely random, which gives the fabrics equal strength in all directions; or it may be parallel, so the resultant fabrics have increased strength in one direction. A layer of scrim or filament fibers may be added to the web for greater durability. Next, the web (and scrim if used) is fed to the needle-punching equipment. In some cases the assemblage is tacked, using between thirty and sixty punches per square inch. The layer is then ready for actual needling.

While there are several types of needle-punching machines, the operation of all is similar. The needles, which have barbs protruding from the shaft, move through the layer of fibers, and the barbs push the fibers

Figure 20.1 Needle plate used in punching fiber mats to form needle felts. (*Monsanto Company*)

into distorted and tangled arrangements. The web is contained by metal plates above and below, so the fibers cannot be pulled or pushed beyond the web layer. As the web moves slowly through the machine, the needles punch as many times as desired for the end product. The number of punches per square inch varies from less than eight hundred to more than 2500. The higher figure is common for blanket fabrics, while low-cost carpet padding may use eight hundred or less.

The properties of needle-punched fabrics depend on

1.   the length and characteristics of the fibers used
2.   the thickness, evenness, and weight of the fiber web
3.   the arrangement of fibers in the web—parallel, criss-cross, or random
4.   the density and pattern arrangement of needles in the needle board
5.   the number of punches per second and the number per square inch
6.   the speed of movement of the web
7.   the size of the needles and the number and arrangement of the barbs

Products commonly made by needle punching include indoor-outdoor carpeting, fiber-woven blankets, padding materials, insulation, and industrial fabrics.

Bonded Fiber Fabrics

Bonded fiber or nonwoven fabric employs one of the newest techniques of fabric construction. The term *bonded fabric* was formerly applied to consumer products, while *nonwoven* designated industrial materials. Currently there is much disagreement about these terms. While "nonwoven" is considered by many authorities to be preferred, this text will use "bonded fiber" and "nonwoven fabric" interchangeably, in order to distinguish between these structures and multicomponent fabrics that may be called *bonded* or *laminated*.

A definition frequently cited for *nonwoven fabrics* states that they are materials made primarily of textile fibers held together by an applied bonding or adhesive agent or by the fusing of self-contained thermoplastic fibers.

Nonwoven fabric dates back to the early 1930s. At that time a few textile companies began experimenting with bonded materials as one way of utilizing cotton waste. After World War II more firms became interested in nonwovens, and by 1960 approximately thirty-five firms were manufacturing products technically classified as nonwoven fabrics.

The sequence of steps in manufacturing these fabrics is fairly standard:

1.   The fibers are cleaned and separated into fluff.
2.   They are formed into a web considerably thicker than the final fabric.
3.   The web is flattened and bonded.
4.   It is dried and cured.

Most nonwovens or bonded fiber fabrics are sold in an unfinished state. If dyeing and finishing are involved, these processes become the fifth step.

Modern bonded fiber fabrics are no longer produced from waste fibers only. Although a small percentage of waste is still used, manufacturers have turned increasingly to good-quality fibers. Furthermore, while early bonded products were made of cotton, today's nonwoven fabrics utilize almost any type of fiber or combination of fibers. The length of fibers varies from $\frac{1}{2}$ inch to 2 inches, and some structures are actually fused filament fibers. Since there is no yarn spinning involved, fibers of different lengths and different chemical compositions can be successfully combined in a single bonded structure. The choice of the fibers used depends upon the desired cost and performance of the end product. When the fibers have been selected, they are cleaned, bleached if necessary, and thoroughly blended.

The three techniques of web formation involve oriented, crosslaid, or random fiber arrangements. Oriented webs are those in which the fibers are parallel to the longitudinal axis. They can be formed on cotton or wool cards. Cotton cards result in uniform webs and fabrics with a texture similar to that of woven cloth. However, the production rate is low. Wool cards and garnetts produce webs at a rapid speed, but the web is less uniform. All webs of the oriented group are comparatively weak in the direction perpendicular to the lay of the fibers.

Cross-lay webs are made by combining two or more layers of fibers at right angles to each other. They are expensive to produce and are no more satisfactory than random webs. Consequently, this technique is seldom used.

Random web formation is steadily gaining popularity with manufacturers, largely because special machines have been developed. These

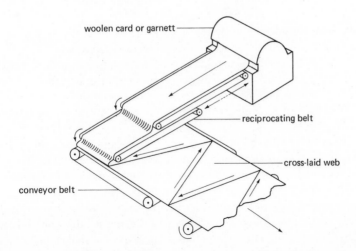

Figure 20.2 Diagram showing formation of a cross-laid web for making a nonwoven fabric. (*Monsanto Company*)

machines employ an air-doffer principle. They are often described as *air-lay systems*.

The air-doffer principle involves the spreading and laying of fibers by controlled air currents. Air suction pulls the fibers from the supply or feeder rolls or belts and deposits them in a random arrangement on a condenser roll. The fiber mat is then fed into a compressor, which forms the fabric. Advantages of this method include uniformity in thickness, equal strength in all directions, and reasonable cost of manufacture.

Some manufacturers have tried producing nonwoven bonded fiber fabrics with papermaking equipment. Fabrics made by this process have been used for disposable products such as cleaning and polishing cloths, "paper" garments, and interfacings. Consumers have welcomed the interfacings and polishing cloths, but acceptance of the apparel has not been very successful, because the garments tend to be stiff and drape poorly. In addition, except for interfacings, the fabrics are usually considered disposable and, therefore, lack any durability. This method of manufacture is comparatively inexpensive, however.

Two basic techniques are employed in bonding fiber webs together:

1. An adhesive or bonding agent, either a dry powder or a liquid, is applied directly to the web in a separate step. The powder is usually a thermoplastic substance that is fused into the web by the application of dry heat. If a web solution is used, it is spread uniformly over the web and then set by chemical action or by heat.
2. Thermoplastic fibers are uniformly blended in the fiber mix and are evenly distributed within the web. Heat is applied, and the thermoplastic fibers soften and fuse over and around the other fibers. As the web cools, the fibers are all held firmly together.

The adhesive technique is most commonly used. But the methods behave differently on different fibers or fiber blends, so the manufacturer must have considerable technical knowledge to make the right choice of bonding agent for the specific end-use of each fabric type.

The final stage in the manufacture of nonwovens is drying and curing. This step is extremely important when liquid binders are utilized. Drying devices include hot air ovens, heated cans, infrared lights, and high-frequency electrical equipment. The choice is dependent on the particular binding agent.

Nonwovens can be dyed or printed with standard techniques. However, at the present time, only a small percentage of these fabrics receive finishes or color, since most nonwoven yardage is sold in the same form in which it leaves the drying and curing ranges.

Nonwoven fabrics appear in a number of products. One writer lists nearly two hundred items in a range that begins at birth and ends with death. Nonwoven fabrics are found in diapers, handkerchiefs, skirts, dresses, apparel interfacings, bandages, and shrouds. Other products include curtains, decontamination clothing, garment bags, industrial

Figure 20.3 Nonwoven fabrics used for medical purposes. (*International Nonwovens & Disposables Association*)

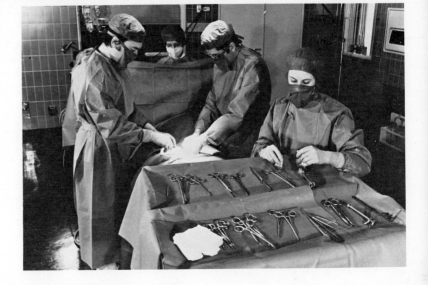

apparel, lampshades, map backing, napkins, place mats, ribbon, upholstery backing, and window shades.

Many nonwovens are manufactured for one-time use only, so care of the fabric is inconsequential. However, nonwoven fabrics can be laundered or dry cleaned if handled with care. The temperature of the laundry water should be that recommended for the specific fibers in the fabric, and agitation should be kept to a minimum. Twisting, wringing, or pulling must be avoided. Nonwovens in interfacings or underlining usually respond satisfactorily to the care demanded of the outer fabric. Nonwoven fabrics available by the yard include Pellon and Keyback, used for interfacings.

In considering the future of the nonwoven fabric industry, a steady increase in industrial fabrics and in disposable items can be expected for some time. However, if bonded fiber fabrics are to be accepted for consumer goods, particularly apparel items, the industry must develop fabrics with good draping qualities and adequate strength. Furthermore, present-day finishing techniques and dye procedures will have to be adapted to these fabrics in order to create products for specific end-uses. Finally, nonwoven fabrics will require good styling and merchandising to be successful in a competitive fabric market.

21 Knitted Fabrics

At the present time, knitted fabrics enjoy unprecedented consumer demand. Not only are traditional knitted products gaining in popularity, but knits are making sizable inroads in areas heretofore dominated by woven fabrics. In 1971 a market report stated that the ratio of knitted fabrics in apparel increased from 24 percent in 1963 to nearly 36 percent in 1969 and that by 1975 more than 52 percent of all apparel fabrics would be of knit structures. In 1973 knits made up 62 percent of men's sports coats; 60 percent of men's suits; 60 percent of men's trousers; 85 percent of women's suits; 48 percent of medium-priced and 58 percent of high-priced women's dresses; 40 percent of women's blouses; 48 percent of women's skirts; and approximately 70 percent of all underclothes, excluding hosiery.

There are several reasons for this burgeoning acceptance of knitted fabrics. Knits can be made rapidly, so yarn-to-fabric expenses are much lower, and quality fabrics can be produced at comparatively low cost. The increase in travel, especially by air, has resulted in the need for lightweight, comfortable clothes that require little care and keep their neat appearance after sitting or packing. Knitted fabrics fit these qualifications. The tendency for knits to resist wrinkling is a factor in their acceptance in

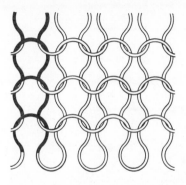

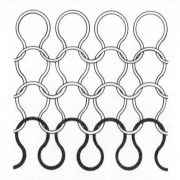

Figure 21.1 Diagram of a filling knit. The darkened vertical row indicates the wale.

Figure 21.2 Diagram of a filling knit. The darkened horizontal row indicates the course.

many end-uses. Fashion always plays a role in the selection of fabrics, and for several seasons leading fashion designers have included a wide range of knit fabrics in their creations.

In the construction and analysis of knits, two terms are used frequently: *wale* and *course*. Wale refers to a column of loops that are parallel to the loop axis. The wales also run parallel to the long measurement of a knit fabric. A *course* is a series of successive loops lying crosswise of a knit fabric, that is, at right angles to a line passing through the open throat to the closed end of the loops (Figs. 21.1 and 21.2).

Machine knitting consists of forming loops of yarn with the aid of thin, pointed needles or shafts. As new loops are formed, they are drawn through those previously shaped. This interlooping and the continued formation of new loops produces knit fabrics. Two general methods are used: *filling* or *weft knitting* and *warp knitting*.

Filling Knitting

Filling or weft knitting, in simplified terms, involves the use of a single thread. The term *weft* is taken from handweaving techniques, where it is

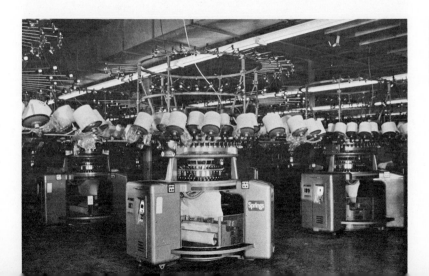

Figure 21.3 Circular knitting machine. This unit includes a Jacquard mechanism that produces decorative knits as well as plain knitted fabric. (*Springs Mills*)

Figure 21.4 Knitted fabric is rolled onto a take-up roll at the base of the machine. When the roll is full, it is removed for finishing. (*Springs Mills*)

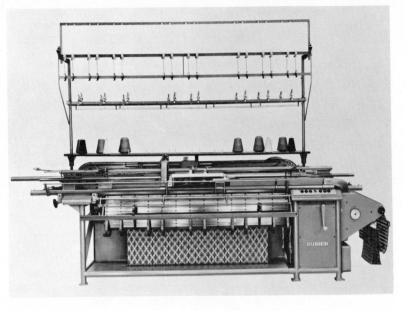

Figure 21.5 A flat-bed knitting machine. (*Dubied Machinery Company*)

used synonymously with *filling* to refer to the horizontal or crosswise direction of a fabric. Fabrics can be manufactured by machine or by hand. Some knitting machines employ needles arranged in a circle to produce tubular fabrics, which can be used in circular form or cut, shaped, and stitched. In others the needles operate from a flat bed or a V-bed to create

Figure 21.6 Close-up of a section of a flat-bed knitting machine.

flat fabrics. The latter are fashioned or shaped during knitting, then stitched into such items as sweaters and hosiery. In both types the basic procedures are similar. A series of horizontal loops is formed on the needles, then for each succeeding row new loops are added as the needles hook into the thread, catch a new loop, and pull it through the preceding loop. The old loop is forced off the needle, and the fabric is built. The resulting filling or weft knit fabric has slightly raised horizontal ridges (courses) and comparatively flat vertical rows of loops (wales).

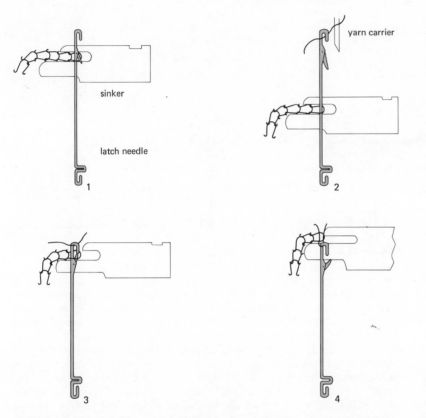

Figure 21.7 Stitch formation, single knit. The major knitting components for a single-knit latch needle machine are the latch needle, a holding down sinker, and the yarn carrier. 1) In this step the needle and sinker are in the rest position. 2) The needle is pushed by the cam to the uppermost position, where the yarn carrier feeds yarn to the hook. The needle rises until the latch is completely clear of the previously formed loop. The sinker remains in the forward position, holding down the formed loops. 3) After the yarn has been fed into the hook the needle begins to lower. The holding sinker retracts to permit the needle to drop low enough to pull the new loop through the previous loop. The old loop closes the latch on the needle in order to hold the new loop. 4) When the needle drops to its lowest position it has formed the new loop. The sinker begins to move forward to hold the newly formed loop down for the repeat of the operation. (*Springs Mills*)

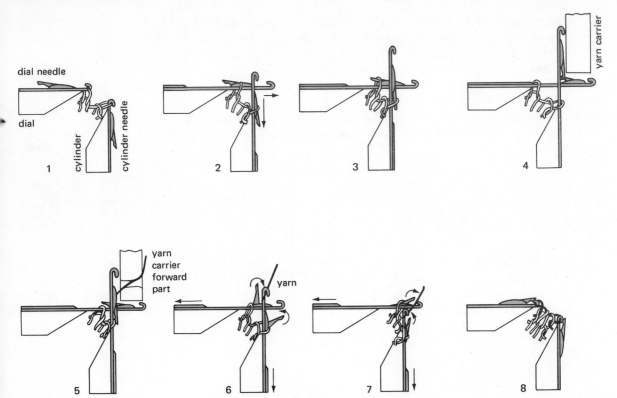

Figure 21.8 Stitch formation, double knit. 1) Needles are in the nonknit position with the old loops in the hooks of both cylinder and dial needles. 2) As the dial needle moves forward, the cylinder needle holds back the stitches on the dial needle. 3) The cylinder needle moves up and the dial needle holds back the stitches on the cylinder needle. 4) Both needles are in position to receive yarn, and the back of the yarn carrier moves into position to prevent the closing of the latches. The previously formed loops are below the latches. 5) The yarn carrier is about to lay new yarn in the hooks. The old loops are just moving under the tip (spoon) of the open latches. 6) The cylinder needle begins to move down and the dial needle to retract into the dial slot. The old loops move under the latches and begin to force the latches to close. 7) The cylinder and dial needles have the yarn in the hooks, the latches are closed, and the old loops are nearly ready to move over the end of the needles. 8) The needles are back in position, the new loops are in the hooks, and the old loops are in the "knock over" or cast off position. (*Springs Mills*)

Figure 21.9 A plain single-knit fabric, magnified slightly.

There are four basic stitches used in manufacturing weft knits:

1. the flat or jersey stitch
2. the purl stitch
3. the rib stitch
4. the interlock stitch

Flat or jersey knit fabrics have distinct but flat vertical lines on the face and dominant horizontal ribs on the reverse side. Hand knitters recognize this effect as the *stockinette stitch* (Fig. 21.9). Flat or jersey stitches are used more frequently than others because the process is rapid and inexpensive. Furthermore, flat knitting can be varied to provide run-resist and fancy patterned fabrics. Jersey stitch knits are used in making hosiery, sweaters, sportswear, and similar items.

A major disadvantage of regular flat knits is the ease with which they drop stitches if the yarn is broken. This results in vertical "runs" or "ladders," which destroy the appearance of the fabric. Some flat knits, such as wool jersey, resist running because of the tendency for the wool fibers to cling together. A variation of the filling knit stitch (Fig. 21.11) will resist running.

The purl stitch (Fig. 21.12) produces fabrics that are similar to the reverse of the jersey stitch on both sides. This method is often used in the manufacture of bulky sweaters and in some children's wear. Many attractive designs and patterns can be created. Since the standard purl stitch forms a fabric identical in appearance on face and back, it presents no problems in construction and is considered reversible. The major disadvantages of this technique are that production is slow and machine maintenance is higher than for other types of knitting equipment. The purl stitch is satisfactory in fabrics for such products as stoles and furniture throws, where stretch in both directions of the fabric is not required.

The rib stitch (Fig. 21.13) is usually made on a V-bed machine with two sets of needles that face each other. The stitches intermesh in opposite directions on a wale-wise basis, and the frequency of intermeshing determines the type of rib. If intermeshing occurs at every other wale, it is a 1 × 1 rib; if it occurs every two wales, the result is a 2 × 2 rib. Uneven ribs can be produced by interlacing in one direction for a certain number of wales and a different number in the other direction. Rib fabrics can be knitted also on circular machines equipped with two rows of needles.

The rib stitch is used whenever stretch is desired, and the resulting fabric has an excellent degree of elasticity. Rib knits are also warm. Their only disadvantage is high cost resulting from the added fabric weight and the relatively low output of the machines. Ribbing is usually found at the lower edge of sweaters, on sleeves, and at necklines. In current fashions, however, rib knits are used in apparel items designed to hug the body, such as shirts, blouses and body stockings.

The interlock stitch (Fig. 21.14) is a variation of the rib stitch. In construction it resembles two separate 1 × 1 rib fabrics that are inter-knitted. Interlock stitch fabrics are thicker and heavier than regular rib stitch fabrics of the same gage. They are identical on both sides and are characterized by a soft hand, good moisture absorbency, and high dimensional stability. These fabrics cut easily, do not ravel, and will not curl at the edges. Even with fine yarns, the result is a firm, closely knit fabric.

Figure 21.10 A single knit with a design. (*Springs Mills*)

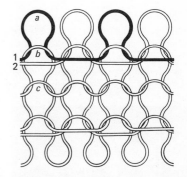

Figure 21.11 Diagram of a run-resist filling knit stitch used in some hosiery and similar fabrics. Numbers indicate the horizontal rows, letters the vertical loop rows.

Figure 21.12 The purl stitch.

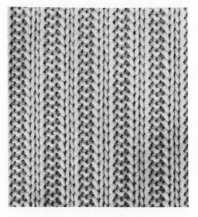

Figure 21.13 The rib stitch.

Figure 21.14 The double-knit inter-lock stitch.

Figure 21.15 Face and back of a double-knit fabric.

Figure 21.16 One type of electronic controls on a knitting machine. The tape with pattern holes, like a set of Jacquard cards, can be seen between the actual knitting areas. (*Springs Mills*)

Double Knits

Double knits are produced by the interlock stitch and by variations of that process (Fig. 21.15). Both surfaces of the fabric are somewhat riblike in appearance. Decorative effects can be achieved on double knits by the use of a Jacquard attachment for individual needle control on the knitting machine. This gives the designer much greater scope in developing interesting patterns.

In the past few years the production of patterned knit fabrics has become highly sophisticated. The use of electronic controls and computer-assisted design formation is common in modern plants. These devices can prepare knitting machines to make reproductions of detailed art work or other complicated designs in a matter of minutes.

Double knits have good dimensional stability and resistance to runs. They are generally easy to cut and sew. Because they do not ravel, they require little or no seam-finishing. Compared to single knits, they are relatively firm, heavier, less stretchable, and more resilient. Double knits are commonly made from polyester, triacetate, or wool fibers. Polyesters, the most popular, offer easy-care fabrics that pack and travel well and retain their attractive appearance during wear.

Knitted Pile Fabrics

Knitted pile fabrics are usually made by filling knit procedures and are based on double knit techniques (Fig. 21.17). To produce the pile, an extra set of yarns or a yarn sliver is drawn out in long loops and then cut or left uncut depending on the desired effect. The base fabric is generally a plain filling knit. Many pile coat fabrics are of knit pile construction. Fabrics in which soft yarn sliver is used in place of twisted yarn are fluffy with a full, rich, and luxurious pile. Many of the "fake furs" available today are sliver knit fabrics.

Figure 21.17 A pile fabric with a filling knit base.

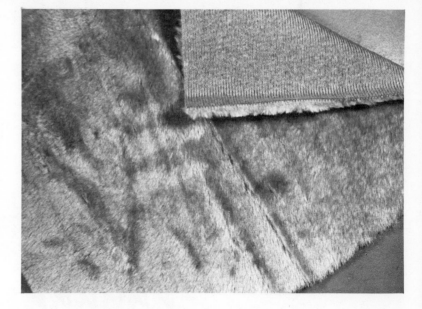

Warp Knitting

The term *warp knit* is also adopted from weaving techniques. In warp knitting the loops are formed in a vertical or warp-wise direction (Fig. 21.18). All the yarns required for the width of the fabric under construction are placed parallel to each other on a beam that resembles a warp beam for weaving (see p. 185). The beam is set into the warp knitting machine, and all yarns feed into the knitting area simultaneously. Each yarn and its needle are manipulated by guide bars, and all the yarns form loops at the same time. Jacquard and dobby attachments can be added to warp knitting equipment to provide for the individual control necessary to create elaborate designs. The machine knits yarns into fabrics by interlooping parallel threads in adjacent wales. Because of the interlooping action, warp knitting machines are frequently referred to as *knitting looms*.

Essentially, warp knit fabrics are flat with relatively straight side edges. They can be manufactured rapidly. Warp knits are classified according to the type of equipment employed. The most common types are tricot, milanese, and raschel.

Tricot Knits

Tricot knits originated in England during the latter part of the 18th century. The first tricot machine was used in knitting silk hosiery cloth. Nearly a century later a large-scale mill was established in the United States. Current tricot knits are much like the products of that early mill.

Either plain or decorative tricot fabrics can be made on the same machine. This results in a saving to the consumer, because patterned tricot knits can be produced at approximately the same price as plain ones. The

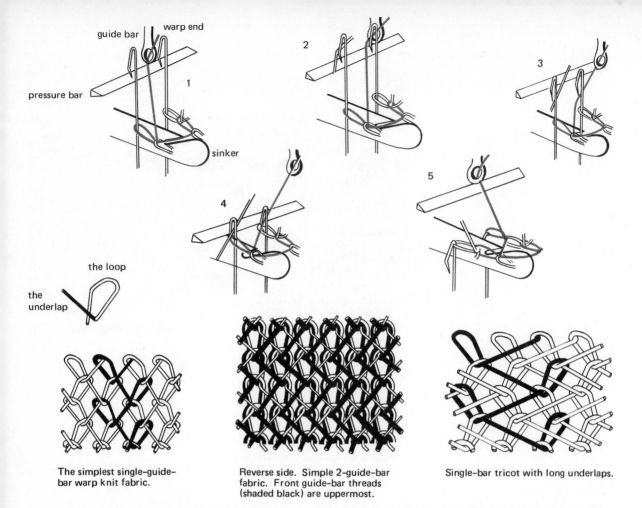

The simplest single-guide-bar warp knit fabric.

Reverse side. Simple 2-guide-bar fabric. Front guide-bar threads (shaded black) are uppermost.

Single-bar tricot with long underlaps.

Figure 21.18 Diagrams of five steps in tricot knitting with beard needles; a simple warp knit stitch; a single-guide-bar fabric; a two-bar fabric; a single-bar tricot with long underlaps.

Steps 1 through 5 show the formation of a single-bar tricot fabric using beard needles. Two needles and two yarns are shown in order to illustrate the movement of yarns during the knitting process. 1) The important parts of the knitting process for tricot knitting with beard needles are identified: the warp end, the guide bar, the pressure (presser) bar, and the sinker. At this point the needles are in their highest position; the sinkers are forward holding down the underlap of the previous loop; the loops formed previously are on the needle stems. 2) The guide bar carrying the yarn that has formed the loop on the needle to the left now swings over to place the thread around the needle on the right. A yarn from the far left is moving in to be placed on the left needle. 3) The yarn is on the needle stem. The needles start down to entrap the yarn in the hook. As the needles move down the pressure bar moves toward the needles. 4) With the yarn in the hook the pressure bar moves in to force the beard tip of the needle tight to the needle stem and the needle starts to pull the yarn through the previous loop to form a new loop. 5) The needles continue to descend, pulling the new loop through and "knocking off" the previous loop. For the next stitch, the yarn guide that laid the yarn in the right needle moves to the left to place yarn on the left needle.

The parts of the warp knit stitch include the loop, the underlap, and the closed end of the stitch.

The single-guide-bar fabric illustrates the vertical interlooping of parallel yarns. Follow the dark yarn: it moves from one vertical row of loops (wale) to the one beside it. The operation is repeated for the length of the fabric.

The two-guide-bar tricot (two-bar tricot) requires two yarn ends for each needle. However, the guide bars move independently. This type of tricot is more stable and less apt to run than a single-bar tricot.

The second example of a single-bar tricot shows that the guide bars carry the yarn for two or more needles instead of moving from one needle to its adjacent needle. This is one technique for forming designs. (*Springs Mills*)

needles looping the adjacent yarns can be controlled in tricot knitting to create delicate, sheer, and attractive patterned fabrics. Even lacelike fabrics are made easily.

The general characteristics of tricot knits are good air and water permeability, softness, crease resistance, good drapability, nonfray properties, run resistance, and elasticity. In addition, finishes are available for controlling the dimensional stability of the fabric and for providing good to excellent strength. It is important to note that fiber content also affects these properties.

The thickness of tricot is influenced by the size of the yarns, the tightness or compactness of the stitches, the length of the guide bar movement, and finishing processes.

Strength of knit fabrics is increased by strong yarns, balanced construction, and fine gage. A combination of yarns of different fibers may increase or decrease the strength of the final fabric, depending upon the strength of the fibers used.

Tricot knits generally are higher-priced than weft knits, and they may be even more expensive than woven fabrics of comparable weight and fiber content. Most often, however, warp knit fabrics are less expensive than woven fabrics, and they enjoy widespread acceptance because of many desirable characteristics. Tricot knits are frequently employed for lingerie fabrics.

Figure 21.19 A tricot knit fabric, with a printed design on a white base. (*Springs Mills*)

Milanese Knits

Milanese is a method of warp knitting similar to tricot. The resultant fabric is similar, but the machinery is quite different. Milanese equipment is not capable of producing as wide a variety of patterns. Despite the fact that milanese knits are smoother, more regular in structure and elasticity, and higher in tear strength than tricot, they are disappearing from the market because the production rate is low and the pattern possibilities are severely limited.

Raschel Knits

Raschel knitting is a warp knit technique that deserves special attention. It is one of the most versatile methods for constructing patterned knit fabrics. Among the many products of raschel knitting are crochet-effect dress materials (Fig. 21.21); close-knit fabrics with designs produced by planned, "laid-in" yarns; laces of all types and in all widths; powernets and similar elastic fabrics for foundation garments; swimwear; curtain and drapery materials.

The machinery for raschel knitting is quite versatile. It works with any type or weight of yarn and can be adjusted to almost any gage. It is especially suitable to heavy, complex, or textured yarns, and to coarse-gage designs.

Figure 21.20 A luxurious peignoir in tricot knit fabric. (*J. P. Stevens & Co., Inc.*)

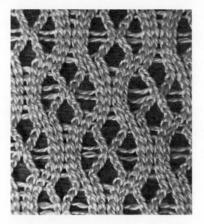

Figure 21.21 A raschel knit fabric with "crochet" design.

Figure 21.22 Raschel knit.

Knitted net structures can be made on either raschel or tricot equipment, but the current emphasis is on raschel machines. Nets result when, at planned intervals, there is no connection between two adjacent wales. The fabric spreads at those areas, leaving openings characteristic of nets.

Figure 21.23 A raschel knitting machine. (*Springs Mills*)

Knitted Fabrics in Use

Knitted fabrics possess many desirable properties. Probably most important to the average consumer are excellent elongation and elastic recovery, plus good wrinkle and crush resistance. Knits are preferred for traveling because they require little space in a suitcase, and wrinkles hang out quickly when the clothes are unpacked.

If knits are not properly constructed and finished, or if the fiber choice is not appropriate, the fabrics may stretch, sag, or shrink. This was a serious fault for many years. But recent improvements in manufacturing and finishing techniques, along with the introduction of heat-treated synthesized fibers, have resulted in products that are stable and durable.

Knitted structures are porous and permit the free circulation of air, so they are comfortable. Most knitted fabrics used in apparel are characterized by good stretch and elastic recovery. They allow freedom of movement without permanent fabric deformation. These fabrics are soft, usually light in weight, and require little or no ironing. It can be expected that knit fabrics will proliferate in both numbers and variety in the years to come.

Stitch-Knit Structures

It is difficult to isolate stitch-knit fabrics into a specific chapter or category. Although the word "knit" is included in the classification name, they are not truly knits. However, the equipment for stitch-knit resembles warp knitting machines, and the stitch is similar to a chain stitch used in basic knitting. Therefore, the textile industry tends to group stitch knits with regular knits.

This group of fabrics has three basic subcategories: (1) comparatively flat fabrics composed of yarns; (2) pile fabrics; (3) fabrics utilizing fiber mats and yarns. The two major products are called *mali fabrics* and *arachne fabrics,* after the machines employed in their manufacture.

Figure 21.24 Suit of knitted wool and blouse of knitted polyester. (*Kimberly Knitwear, Inc.*)

Fabrics Made of Yarns

Yarns are arranged in a planned pattern to produce the first type of stitch-knit fabric. They are then fed into a machine, where they are stitched in parallel rows across the width of the fabric to hold the yarns in position. The process utilizes chain stitch techniques and is very similar to the formation of knit loops. Single bar tricot techniques may be used.

The characteristics of the fabric depend on the relative weights of the base and stitching yarns. If the stitching yarns are considerably finer than the base yarns, the fabric resembles a woven structure on the face and a knitted structure on the back; if the stitching yarns dominate, the product has a distinct knitted appearance.

Fabrics in this category sometimes employ two sets of base yarns and one set for the stitch-knit operation. In that case the yarns are not

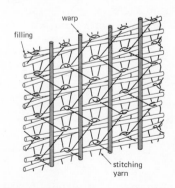

Figure 21.25 Diagram of the malimo stitch-knit technique utilizing three yarns. (*Crompton & Knowles Corporation, Textile Machinery Group*)

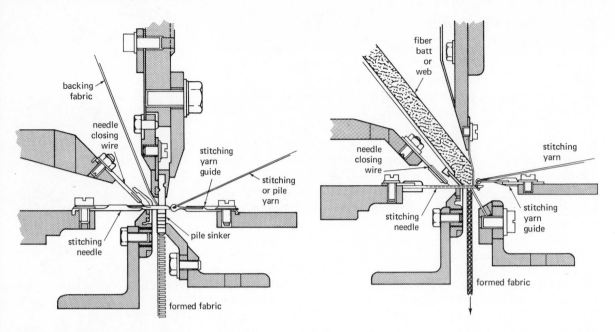

left: Figure 21.26 Diagram of the Malipol pile stitch-knit process. (*Crompton & Knowles Corporation, Textile Machinery Group*)

right: Figure 21.27 Diagram of the Maliwatt web stitch-knit process. (*Crompton & Knowles Corporation, Textile Machinery Group*)

Figure 21.28 Face and back of a Malimo type stitch-knit fabric.

arranged at a 90-degree angle as in woven fabrics but in a crisscross manner, with the stitching yarns perpendicular to one set of the base yarns.

Stitch-knit fabrics from yarn have pleasing drape and hand. They can be finished like woven or knit structures. The fabric properties are the result of the yarn arrangement, stitch-knit pattern, size and compactness of yarns, and fibers selected.

Pile Fabrics

Pile structures can be made with a yarn base or a fiber mat base, but the latter is more common. The base is fed into the stitching equipment, and, as the stitching occurs, the yarn is held in a loop to one side. When completed the loops can be cut or left uncut. For cut loops the procedure

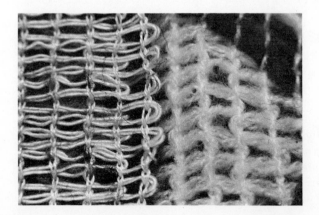

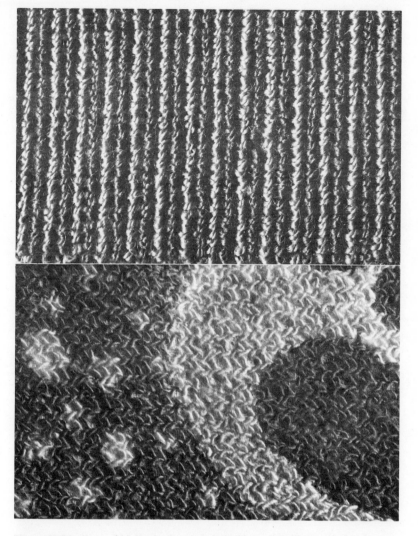

Figure 21.29 Face of Malipol pile stitch-knit fabrics. (*Bahlo Textile Corporation*)

usually allows for the inclusion of special stitching yarns that hold the base and pile yarns in position.

A recent innovation in pile stitch-knit employs a base composed of a preformed fabric, as well as yarns or fiber mat. This results in a product similar to tufted fabrics.

Fabrics Utilizing Fiber Mats

Fabrics for special end-uses can be made by forming a fiber web and stitching it together for stability. The web can be very thin (less than $\frac{1}{8}$ inch), or it may be $\frac{1}{2}$ inch or more in thickness. These fabrics resemble needle-punched materials to some degree.

Figure 21.30   Maliwatt type stitch-knit fabric. (*Bahlo Textile Corporation*)

Stitch-knit fabrics are economical to construct, for the process eliminates many steps involved in other techniques, and capital investment in space, materials, wages, and equipment is reduced. The design potential is great: fabrics that resemble woven structures, knit structures, and needle-punched structures can be made without all the different types of machinery. However, despite the many advantages, there has been little progress in the manufacture of stitch-knit fabrics in the United States. The reasons for this are not clear, but it must always be borne in mind that, despite a fabric's impressive list of qualities, the buying public may simply not like it. Perhaps this is the case with stitch-knits.

Because of their limited production, there is little information available about the care of stitch-knit fabrics. The consumer is advised to follow the maintenance instructions on any accompanying labels.

Woven Fabrics 22

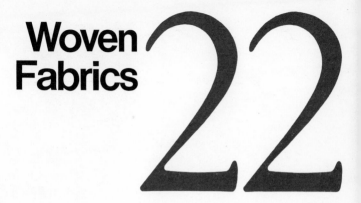

Weaving is one of the oldest arts known. While no actual looms from early civilizations survive, fabrics of fine quality have been found in the tombs of ancient Egypt, and designs on very old pottery provide indisputable evidence of early skill in weaving. Painted pottery also gives us some idea of the type of loom that was in use in the ancient world. Fig. 22.1 shows a Greek vase from the 5th century B.C. depicting the legend of Penelope, wife of Odysseus. Throughout the long voyage of Odysseus the constant Penelope refused to marry anyone else until she had completed a winding sheet for her father-in-law. By day she would sit at her loom and weave, and at night she would unravel everything she had done. At last, betrayed by her servant, she was compelled to finish the shroud and choose a suitor. But Odysseus returned just before the fateful decision was made, and the couple were happily reunited.

Woven fabrics consist of sets of yarns interlaced at right angles in established sequences. The yarns that run parallel to the selvage or to the longer dimension of a bolt (or length) of fabric are called *warp* yarns or *ends;* those that run crosswise of the fabric are called *filling* yarns, *weft* yarns, *woof* yarns, or *picks*. Warp and filling are the terms in common use today.

Figure 22.1 Vertical warp-weighted loom. Penelope at her loom. Greek, 5th century B.C. (*Chiusi Museum, Italy*)

Early looms were very crude compared with modern mechanical weaving contrivances. Nonetheless, all looms, old and new alike, have a few basic principles in common: There is some system to hold the warp yarns under tension; there is a way to spread yarns apart so the crosswise thread can move through the opening or *shed;* and there is a device to pack the crosswise threads tightly together.

Until the early 19th century weaving was primarily a hand or manual process. In the late 1700s and early 1800s scientists and inventors such as Joseph-Marie Jacquard and Edmund Cartwright developed weaving looms that were partially machine powered. Later manufacturers produced looms that were entirely mechanical and power driven. Weavers were hostile to these first mechanical looms, for they feared the machines would take away their jobs. Consequently, the Industrial Revolution was well under way before its effects were felt in the weaving mills. During the late 18th and early 19th century, developments in weaving involved the addition of automatic features to existing looms to increase the speed of operation and reduce the frequency and amount of damage due to faulty functioning.

The parts of the basic handloom are shown in Fig. 22.2. The *warp beam* holds the lengthwise yarns. It is located at the back of the loom and is controlled so it releases yarn to the loom as it is needed. The *heddles* are wire or metal strips with an eye located in the center through which the warp ends are threaded. The *harness* is the frame that holds the heddles in position. Each loom has at least two harnesses and may have twenty or more. Harnesses can be raised or lowered in order to produce the *shed* through which the filling thread is passed and thus control the pattern of the weave. The *shuttle* moves back and forth in the shed, passing the filling threads between the warp threads. The *reed* is a comblike device, and the openings between wires in the reed are called *dents*. Warp threads

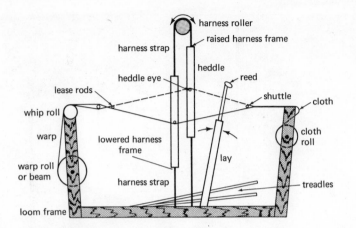

Figure 22.2 Diagram showing a simple loom.

pass through the heddles and then through the dents. The reed keeps the warp ends from tangling and beats and packs the filling threads into their proper position. The reed is parallel to the harness. The *cloth beam* is located at the front of the loom and holds the completed fabric.

The basic weaving operation consists of four steps:

1. *Shedding* is the raising and lowering of the warp ends by means of the heddles and harnesses to form the shed of the loom, so the filling yarn can be passed from one side of the loom to the other. Filling yarns can be carried by a *shuttle,* a jet of water, a metal arm called a *rapier,* or a metal gripper.
2. *Picking* is the actual procedure of placing the filling yarn into the shed. The shuttle or other device moves across the shed, laying the pick or filling as it goes.
3. *Battening,* sometimes called *beating, beating in,* or *beating up,* consists of evenly packing the filling threads into position in the fabric.

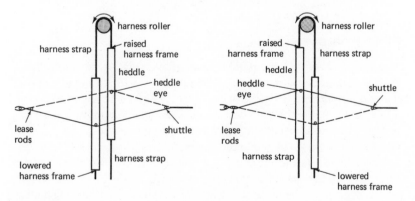

Figure 22.3 Movement of harnesses and warp thread to form a shed.

Figure 22.4   A modern loom for general weaving. (*Springs Mills*)

4. *Taking up and letting off* involves taking up the newly manufactured fabric onto the cloth beam and letting off or releasing thread from the warp beam. The operation maintains uniform distance and tension from harnesses to cloth.

Most fabrics are woven on a simple loom (Fig. 22.4). For elaborate fabrics, modification of the basic loom, addition of special attachments to the loom, or specially designed looms are used. Basic looms once had only two harnesses, but today most looms have several harnesses so that one loom can weave a variety of fabrics. Three or more harnesses are required for twill weaves; five or more for satin weaves. Weaving dobby patterns involves as many as 32 harnesses. The Jacquard attachment fits onto special looms and maintains individual control of every warp thread. It is used to manufacture elaborate weaves—often called *Jacquard weaves*—such as those found in brocades, damasks, brocatelles, and matelasses.

Plain Weaves

The plain weave is the simplest form of weaving. It consists of the alternate interlacing of warp and filling yarns, one warp up and one down, the entire width of the fabric (Fig. 22.5). This is referred to as a 1/1 weave. In the figure the black squares indicate that the warp yarn is on the surface. The squares paralleling the vertical direction of the diagram can be visualized as warp yarns, while the horizontal rows represent filling yarns.

Many woven fabrics are constructed by plain-weave interlacing. Unless colors or finishes are added on one side only, plain-weave fabrics are usually reversible. The yarns can be packed loosely or compactly. The warp

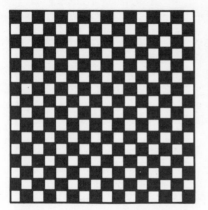

Figure 22.5 Diagram of a plain weave.

Figure 22.6 A plain-weave fabric.

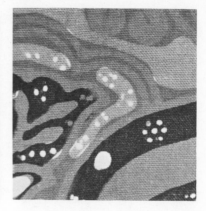

Figure 22.7 A plain-weave fabric with a printed design.

threads may equal the filling threads in number, but unequal arrangements can be produced by variations in yarn size and by unequal spacing of warp or filling yarns. When the number of warp yarns per inch is approximately the same as the number of filling yarns per inch, the thread count is considered balanced. Conversely, when the number of yarns per inch differs considerably between warp and filling, the fabric is unbalanced. The plain weave is comparatively inexpensive. Moreover, some of the most durable fabrics are manufactured by this technique.

Examples of plain weave include muslin, percale, print cloth, cheese-cloth, chambray, gingham, batiste, nainsook, lawn, organdy, taffeta, linen toweling, handkerchief linen, dress linen, seersucker, chiffon, challis, shantung, china silk, some wool tweeds, and homespun.

Rib Variation of the Plain Weave

Interesting and attractive fabrics can be obtained from the plain weave by utilizing the rib variation. A diagram of this weave is identical to the regular plain weave. The rib appearance is produced by using heavy yarns in the warp or filling direction, by grouping yarns in specific areas of the warp or filling, or by having more warp yarns than filling.

Many rib-weave fabrics have heavy yarns inserted as picks. Examples of this construction include poplin, faille, bengaline, and ottoman. Dimity derives from alternation of fine and heavy yarns at planned intervals in the warp. Such alternation in both warp and filling is used for cross-bar dimity and some tissue ginghams. Broadcloth results from a highly unbalanced yarn count in which there are many more warp yarns per inch than filling.

Comparative size of the ribs in some of the more commonly en-countered rib weaves serves as a basis of fabric identification. Some rib-weave fabrics listed in order from fine to heavy are broadcloth, poplin, faille, grosgrain, bengaline, and ottoman.

Figure 22.8 Rib-weave variations of the plain weave.

Basket Variation of the Plain Weave

The basket weave is generally defined as having two or more warp ends interlaced as a unit with one or more filling yarns. This construction is not so firm as regular plain weaves and frequently has lower strength, but basket weaves are attractive and have interesting surface effects. A basket variation in which two warps pass over and under one filling would be called 2/1 weave. Other fabrics of the basket-weave type can be found in 2/2, 2/4, 3/2 constructions.

Oxford cloth is an example of a 2/1 basket weave. The two warp yarns equal in size the single filling yarn. The cloth is frequently used for shirts because it is soft and comfortable. Some authorities consider oxford cloth a separate weave variation of the plain construction.

Monk's cloth is one of the best-known examples of basket weave. It is available in 2/2, 3/3, 4/4, 8/8, and in uneven arrangements such as 4/3 and 2/3. Rather coarse yarns are used in monk's cloth. Yarn slippage may occur because of the loose weave. Basket weaves are found also in coat and suit fabrics, hopsacking, and flat duck.

Other Plain-Weave Variations

In addition to the variations produced in plain-weave fabrics by modifications of the weaving pattern, other design effects can be introduced without structural change. The use of complex yarns, at either regular or irregular intervals, may create surface texture. The amount of twist in the yarns is the basis for diverse results: high-twist yarns are used in making crepe fabrics or voiles; low-twist yarns are required for napped fabrics.

Yarns of different fiber content or of different colors can be combined to develop distinctive patterns. Spacing of the yarns produces a wide variety of plain-weave fabrics, from loose, sheer cheesecloth to compactly woven taffetas.

Figure 22.9 Diagram of a 2/2 basket weave.

Figure 22.10 A basket-weave fabric.

Twill Weave

The second basic weave pattern used in the manufacture of fabrics is the twill weave. This technique is characterized by a diagonal line on the face, and often on the back, of the fabric. The face diagonal can vary from a low 14-degree angle (*reclining twill*) to a 75-degree angle (*steep twill*). At 45 degrees the angle is considered a medium diagonal (*regular twill*); it is the most common. The angle of the diagonal is determined either by the closeness of the warp ends or by the number of yarns and the actual pattern of each repeat.

Twill-weave fabrics have a distinctive and attractive appearance. In general, they are strong and durable. Twills differ from plain weave in the number of filling picks and warp ends required to complete a pattern. Whereas a plain weave uses two picks and two ends, the simplest twill needs three.

The warp yarn goes over (*floats* over) two filling yarns and under one in the 2/1 twill (Fig. 22.11). In a regular twill each succeeding float begins one pick higher or lower than the adjacent float. In more complicated twills the progression may vary, but the diagonal effect will remain visible. The number of pick yarns required to complete the twill pattern determines the number of harnesses needed on the loom. There must be at least three, and some twill patterns require as many as fifteen.

Twill fabrics have either a right-hand or a left-hand diagonal. If the diagonal moves from the upper right to the lower left of the fabric, it is referred to as a *right-hand twill;* if it moves from the upper left to lower right, it is a *left-hand twill.* In even twill fabrics the filling threads pass over and under the same number of warps, while in uneven twills the pick goes over either more or fewer warps than it goes under. Uneven twill fabrics have a right and wrong side and are not considered reversible materials. Even twills, unless they are altered by finishing or coloring processes, can be reversible.

above: **Figure 22.11**   Diagram of a 2/1 right-hand twill.

below: **Figure 22.12**   A right-hand twill fabric.

Figure 22.13   Diagram of a 2/2 right-hand twill.

Figure 22.14   A 2/2 twill-weave fabric.

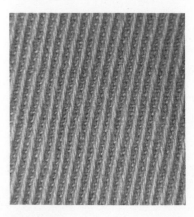

Figure 22.15   Face of a twill-weave fabric.

left: Figure 22.16 Diagram of a twill-weave variation, the herringbone.

right: Figure 22.17 A herringbone twill-weave fabric.

The twill weave permits packing yarns closer together because of fewer interlacings. This close packing can produce strong, durable fabrics, but if the yarns are packed too closely, the fabric will have reduced breaking and tear strength, abrasion resistance, and wrinkle recovery.

In addition to good properties and appearance, twill fabrics tend to show soil less quickly than plain weaves, but they are also more expensive than the latter because of more complicated weaving techniques and the added labor costs.

A common variation of the twill weave is the herringbone. In this design the twill is reversed at frequent intervals to form a series of inverted Vs (Fig. 22.16).

Examples of fabrics made by the twill weave include denim, drill, jean, covert, gabardine, foulard, serge, surah, wool broadcloth, wool sharkskin, cavalry twill, flannel, and some tweeds.

Satin Weave

Satin fabrics are characterized by long floats on the face. These floats are caught under cross threads at intersections (interlacings) as far apart as possible for the particular construction. Adjacent parallel yarns do not interlace in a position of contact. This reduces the possibility of a diagonal effect occurring on the face of the fabric. In a satin fabric it is the warp ends that float on the surface. A variation of the satin weave, in which the filling yarns float, is referred to as *sateen*. Filament fiber yarns are generally used for satins, while staple fiber yarns, frequently of cotton, are more common in sateens. There are, however, exceptions; cotton satins do exist and so do filament sateens.

The long floats of the satin weave create a shiny surface and tend to reflect light. This is accentuated if bright filament fiber yarns with a low twist of $\frac{1}{2}$ to 1 turn per inch comprise the floating yarns. The floats become snagged easily, and thus satin-weave fabrics are not as durable as plain or

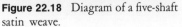

Figure 22.18 Diagram of a five-shaft satin weave.

Figure 22.19 A five-shaft satin fabric.

twill weaves. Two factors govern the length of the floats: the number of harnesses, which determines the number of filling yarns over which the warp yarns float, and the number of yarns per inch. A fabric with a high yarn count has shorter floats than one with a low yarn count when the same number of harnesses and the same repeat pattern are used.

Satin weave fabrics are lustrous. People select them for their appearance and smoothness. Satins are frequently used as lining fabrics, because they are easy to slip on and off over other materials. Satin and sateen fabrics have a definite face and back. Variations in satin can be produced by using highly twisted yarns in the filling to create a crepe effect on the back. With these so-called *crepe-back satins,* either side can be the face.

Examples of satin weave include antique satin, slipper satin, crepe-back satin, satin-back crepe, faille satin, bridal satin, sateen, moleskin, and Venetian satin.

Decorative Weaves

Decorative weaves, called *fancy, figure,* and *design weaves,* are formed by predetermined changes in interlacing of the warp and filling yarns. This can be done by various attachments on the loom that increase its flexibility. Weaving processes in this category include dobby, Jacquard, leno, pile, and double cloth weaves, as well as the use of extra warp or filling yarns.

Dobby Weaves

Dobby designs have small figures—such as dots, geometric designs, and floral patterns—woven into the fabric (Fig. 22.20). These designs are produced by the combination of two or more basic weaves, and the loom (Fig. 22.21) may have up to 32 harnesses. The design is produced by a dobby pattern chain, which consists of a series of wood crossbars with metal pegs or special pattern rolls of paper or plastic. Each crossbar

Figure 22.20 Dobby weave fabrics. (*Springs Mills*)

Figure 22.21 A loom with dobby attachment. (*Springs Mills*)

controls a row of the pattern and mechanically determines which warp yarns will be raised and which lowered to produce the desired shed. Recent developments in pattern weaving include the double-cylinder dobby. This improvement vastly increases the number of potential designs.

Examples of fabrics produced by dobby weaving are Bedford cord, piqué, waffle cloth, shirting madras, and huck toweling. The Bedford cord and piqué frequently employ heavy yarns, called *stuffer yarns,* to accentuate the cord effect.

Jacquard Designs

Fabrics with extremely complicated and decorative woven designs are manufactured using Jacquard attachments on looms. The Jacquard attachment was developed by Joseph-Marie Jacquard and first exhibited at an industrial exposition in France in 1801, where the Emperor Napoleon saw it and, apparently, visualized its potential. The French government bought the idea in 1806. When the loom was first introduced, many weavers believed it would replace them and cause widespread unemployment. As a result, there were a number of riots and other protests. However, the transition to the factory system gained momentum and the importance of Jacquard's invention became evident. Ultimately, it was considered a tremendous contribution to the textile industry.

The major advantage of the Jacquard machine is its ability to control each individual warp thread instead of a series of threads as in regular harness looms. This separate yarn control provides great freedom for the fabric designer, and large, intricate motifs can be transferred to fabric. Within the last few years extremely elaborate patterns, including paintings, narrative scenes, and photographs, have been reproduced in fabric by the Jacquard attachment.

The pattern for the Jacquard loom is transferred to a series of perforated cards, one for each filling pick in the pattern. The card is

Figure 22.22 Diagram of Jacquard mechanism. The Jacquard cards with holes corresponding to the pattern are placed in position by a turn of the cylinder, which also moves forward and back. The warp thread passes through the eye in the cord (harness), which is suspended on the hook. The hook passes through an eyelet in the needles and hangs on the griffe, which moves up and down. The cylinder moves forward with each motion of the loom; when a warp thread is to be lifted, the needle is presented with a hole in the pattern card, the griffe consequently lifts the hook harness and thread. When the thread is not to be lifted, the needle encounters a solid area in the pattern card. (*Springs Mills*)

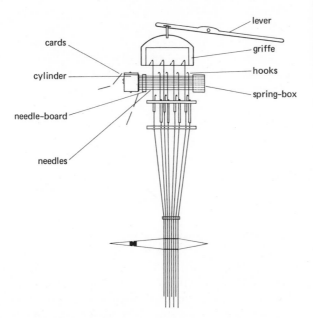

above: Figure 22.23 Jacquard pattern cards that control the warp yarns to produce the pattern in the woven fabric. (*Springs Mills*)

below: Figure 22.24 Jacquard loom. (*Springs Mills*)

Figure 22.25 Bobbins in a battery provide flexibility in color for filling as well as continuous loom operation. (*Springs Mills*)

punched to permit the lifting of certain knives on the machine to pass through the card while the others remain down. The shed is formed and the pick passes through. The punched cards, similar to a player-piano roll or a computer card, are laced together and pass over a cylinder at the top of the machine. Each card stops on the cylinder for its particular pick, moves on, and a new card takes its place. This continues until all cards are used. When one repeat of the pattern or design is completed, the cards start over.

The Jacquard loom is tall and requires a room with a high ceiling, with catwalks near the top of the machine or openings into a second floor. The machines are very complicated to operate and expensive to build, so the resultant fabrics are costly. As in the dobby weave, Jacquard designs combine two or more of the basic weaves. They are used for decorating fabrics, table coverings, and apparel. (See Plate 1.)

Examples of fabrics woven by Jacquard techniques are damask, tapestry, brocade, brocatelle, matelassé, and home furnishing materials. Jacquard mechanisms have been adapted for use on knitting machines in order to produce very elaborate designs in knit fabrics.

Leno Weaves

The leno weave is also referred to as *doup weave* or *gauze weave*. In the most correct usage doup is the name for the attachment on the loom that controls the warp threads. This attachment moves both horizontally and vertically, permitting the warp yarns to be interlaced and crossed between the picks. When a distinction is made between leno and gauze, the term gauze indicates only an open-mesh type of fabric, while leno applies to all fabrics made by this special interlacing process. It is important to note that a "gauze" fabric may be a plain-weave fabric and need not always be constructed by a leno weave.

The leno weave produces open-textured fabric that may be sheer or heavy. The unusual warp interlacing prevents slippage of the filling. This increases wear, stability, strength, and durability of sheer fabrics. Some patterned fabrics combine one or more of the basic weaves with a leno construction.

Examples of the leno weave are found in curtain and dress marquisettes, mosquito nets, laundry bags, and food bags.

Surface Figure Weaves

Extra warp and filling yarns can be employed to produce many different designs. When extra warp yarns are used, they are wound on an additional warp beam and threaded into separate heddles so they can be controlled—depending upon the complexity of the pattern—either by the dobby attachment or by the Jacquard mechanisms. Extra filling yarns are inserted by special shuttles, using either a box loom or a regular shuttle loom. The box loom permits greater flexibility of design. The three main design

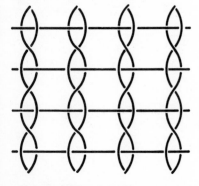

above: Figure 22.26 Diagram of the leno weave.

below: Figure 22.27 Casement fabric of a leno weave. (*Kagan-Dreyfus*)

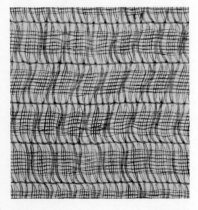

varieties that involve the use of additional yarns are lappet, swivel, and spot or dot.

Lappet Weave   Lappet is a form of weaving in which extra warp threads are introduced in a manner that creates designs over predetermined portions of the base fabric. Patterns are woven by means of an attachment to the loom, and the resultant designs resemble hand embroidery. If long floats are left on the back of the fabric, they are cut away. Short floats are usually left, but this can be a disadvantage because they may be easily snagged.

The lappet weave is considered strong and durable, but because of high production costs, it is expensive. It is not made in the United States at the present time but it may be found in Europe.

Swivel Weave   The swivel weave is made with extra filling threads. The yarns to be used in each pattern are wound on quills and placed in small shuttles located strategically at each point where the design occurs. The pattern mechanism produces a shed, and the shuttle carries the yarn through the shed the distance of the pattern. This is repeated for each row of the design. Between repeats the extra filling floats on the back of the fabric and is cut away after weaving is completed.

The swivel process permits the weaving of different colors in the same row, because each figure has its own shuttle. This method fastens the yarn securely as each figure is completed, and it cannot pull out. There is almost no fabric made by this process in the United States, but several Swiss manufacturers utilize it. Swivel weaves can be recognized by the fact that the designing yarn is usually the same on face and back. It appears to go around a group of warp yarns several times.

Spot Weave   Spot or dot designs can be fabricated with extra warp or filling yarns. The yarns are inserted the entire length or width of the fabric in predetermined areas. If small, widely spaced dots or spots are made, the long floats on the reverse side are cut away, leaving dots that can be pulled out with little effort. Design yarns usually differ in color from the base fabric; they may differ also in diameter and twist. Designs in which the back floats have been clipped away are called *clipped spot patterns*.

The durability of a spot design depends on the compactness of the background yarns that hold the design yarns in place. Spots in compact weaves are quite stable, while in loose weaves they can be pulled out rather easily. Dotted swiss (Fig. 22.29), made in domestic fabric mills, is a typical clipped spot weave. "Eyelash" designs are also clipped spot, with sufficient yarn ends left to produce fringe effects.

Spot designs in which floating yarns have not been cut are referred to as *uncut spot patterns*. These are frequently border designs, and the repeat patterns are often close together. In some cases these fabrics are reversible, with one side forming a mirror image of the other. Uncut spot designs can be made with either a dobby or a Jacquard attachment on the loom to control the yarns in the design area. In both cut and uncut spot fabrics the yarns forming the design can be removed without disintegration of the background construction.

Pile Weaving

Woven-pile fabrics have an extra set of warp or filling yarns interlaced with the ground warp and filling in such a manner that loops or cut ends are produced on the surface of the fabric. The base or ground fabric may be either plain or twill weave.

Filling Pile   Filling pile fabrics have two sets of filling yarns and one set of warp. Although the ground may be of twill or plain weave, twill is generally preferred for durability. The extra set of filling yarns floats over a planned number of warp yarns—three or more, usually. After weaving is completed, the floats are cut and brushed up to form the pile. Velveteen and corduroy fabrics are manufactured by this method. Corduroy differs from velveteen in that the floats are interlaced in such a manner that rows are formed, and when the pile is cut, it produces a ribbed effect.

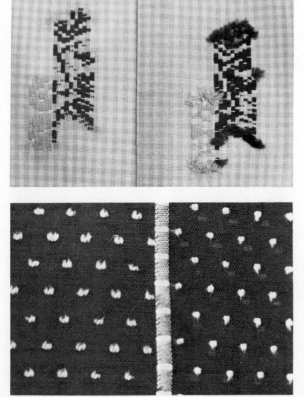

left: Figure 22.28   Face and back of fabric with clipped spot design.

below left: Figure 22.29   Face and back of dotted swiss fabric.

below right: Figure 22.30   Face (left) and back (right) of uncut spot design.

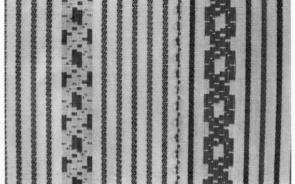

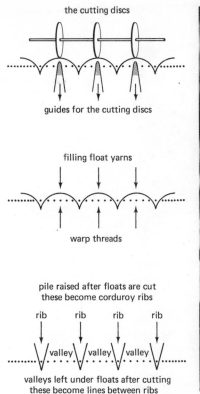

the cutting discs

guides for the cutting discs

filling float yarns

warp threads

pile raised after floats are cut
these become corduroy ribs

rib   rib   rib   rib

valley   valley   valley

valleys left under floats after cutting
these become lines between ribs

far left: **Figure 22.31**   Diagram illustrating the cutting of yarn to form corduroy. (*Cone Mills*)

left: **Figure 22.32**   A dress of corduroy. (*Crompton-Richmond Company, Inc.*)

below: **Figure 22.33**   Corduroy fabrics.

Velveteen floats are interlaced to produce an allover effect when cut. The depth of the pile is controlled by the length of the floats: the longer the float, the deeper the pile. Pile yarns may interlace in either a V or a W form; the W is more durable, since the pile is held down by two ground yarns instead of one.

Corduroys and velveteens are prepared for cutting in the same manner. The floats are treated to give them cutting surface, and the fabric is stiffened so it will remain smooth and firm. The pile may be cut by hand with a thin steel blade, but because this is tedious and time consuming, it is seldom done, except in countries where skilled labor is inexpensive. Most filling pile fabric is cut by machine. The fabric, held under tension, moves under sharp knife blades, which carefully cut the floats without damage to the base fabric. For corduroy, circular knives revolve and cut the rows of floats. There may be a knife for each row, or, for narrow-wale (rib) corduroy, there are knives for every other row and the fabric is fed through the cutting machine twice, with the knives set to cut the alternate rows on the second run. Tandem cutters also may be used. Novel effects result from cutting the floats to produce tufts of different lengths or by cutting only certain sections to form interesting and intricate designs. Both corduroy and velveteen are usually made of spun yarns.

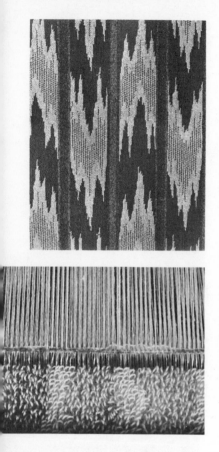

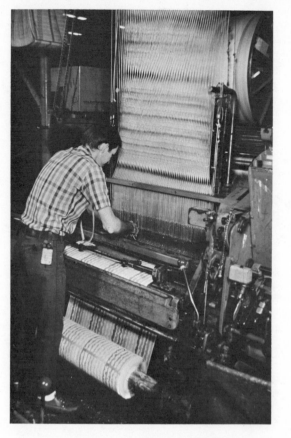

above left: Figure 22.34 Wilton carpet of a warp pile wool fabric. (*Jack Lenor Larsen, Inc.*)

above right: Figure 22.35 Loom with two warp beams for weaving terry cloth, an uncut pile fabric. (*Springs Mills*)

above: Figure 22.36 Formation of loops in a terry cloth pile construction. (*Springs Mills*)

Warp Pile In warp-pile fabrics the pile is formed by extra warp yarns. Velvet, velour, rug velvet, and Wilton rugs are examples of warp pile. They are usually made from filament yarns by three general methods: double cloth, wire-cut pile, and looped pile.

The *double cloth* technique is one of the most common methods in manufacturing cut warp-pile fabrics. In this construction five sets of yarns are necessary: two sets of warp and two sets of filling form the ground fabrics, and a third set of warp yarns makes the pile.

The pile yarns are interlaced with one set of ground ends and picks and then passed to the other ground set, where they interlace with those yarns. When the weaving is completed, a cut is made through the center of the pile yarns to produce two separate fabrics. The pile can be sheared to make it even if necessary.

In the past, carpeting was often made by the *wire-cut* method. The manufacture of Wilton rugs depends on the wire technique with a Jacquard attachment. Today very little fabric or carpeting is produced in this way.

Terry-pile fabric (loop) construction is best known and most easily recognized in terry-cloth toweling. It is constructed with uncut loops of warp yarn on both sides of the cloth. These loops are formed by holding the ground warp yarns taut and leaving the pile warp yarns slack. The shed is made, picks are placed, and this is repeated for a specified number of picks, usually three, without any beating in. After the picks have been placed, they are battened into position. This causes the slack warp yarns to be pushed into loops between the picks. Loops are formed generally on both sides of the fabric. The taut warp holds its position and remains smooth. Ply yarns work better for the ground warp because they are strong. The warp yarns that form the loops are soft, fluffy, and absorbent. Two low-twist yarns treated as one frequently serve for the pile to provide these desirable characteristics. Loop or uncut pile is found in such items as turkish toweling, terry cloth for robes, some types of carpeting, and upholstery fabrics.

Double Weaves

Double weaves are most accurately defined as those in which at least two sets of filling and at least two sets of warp yarns are interlaced. The most common types of double cloth have two sets of warp and two sets of filling, with or without a binder set. Warp-pile weaves that employ five sets of yarn are considered double cloth during the weaving, but once cut apart they become single fabrics. True double weaves are not severed. They exhibit good strength, a variety of design detail, and extra weight.

At times, the term *double weave* is used to indicate fabrics in which two sets of filling and one set of warp yarns, or two sets of warp and one set of filling yarns have been interlaced. These are more accurately called *backed fabrics*.

Double cloths woven from four or five sets of yarns can create heavy, unusual, and highly patterned fabrics. They may be designed to be reversible, with compatible colors or patterns on the two sides. (See Plate 2.)

Fabrics requiring additional bulk or those with unusual design effects can be produced with three sets of yarn, such as one warp and two filling. The warp yarn is not easily visible, for the filling threads predominate on both face and back. A common fabric of this type occurs in blankets that have a different color on each side.

Yarns with varied amounts of twist and different fibers, combined by the several weaving techniques, permit the manufacture of many elaborate and attractive fabrics. Double or backed fabrics are used for design, weight, strength, and warmth. The most important double fabrics appear in coatings, blankets, and elaborate creations such as matelassé, double brocade, and brocatelle.

23 Other Fabric Construction Processes

The fabrics discussed in this chapter are characterized, for the most part, by unusual design or manufacture. They include new products about which little has been written and those confined to rather specific uses.

Braided Fabrics

Braided fabrics have a diagonal surface effect. They are made by plaiting three or more yarns that originate from a single location and lie parallel before the interlacing occurs. The yarns intercross from one side to the other, resulting in a column of horizontal Vs. Narrow braids can be joined together to form wide fabrics or large articles, such as carpets. They are made either in flat rectangular or in circular formations.

Circular braids appear in such everyday items as shoelaces and insulation for wires. Flat braids serve for trimming. All braided fabrics have considerable stretch in the length and some in the width. This property may create problems in the application of braided trim, because it is difficult to keep even. However, the stretchiness enables a skilled person to apply braid so it lies smooth at corners and curved areas as well as straight edges.

Fabrics made by braiding are not limited to yarn forms. Cut strips of fabric, leaves, leather, straw, or any other flexible product can be braided to create attractive and distinctive fabrics.

Nets

Nets are open-mesh fabrics with large geometric interstices between the yarns (Fig. 23.2). Early nets were made by knotting the yarns at each point of intersection, and to some extent this is still done. Knotted nets have a comparatively large mesh and will not slip or spread. All net fabrics before 1800 were knotted by hand. In 1809 a machine was developed that duplicated the net construction so accurately that only an expert could distinguish the handmade from the machine-made product.

In recent years nets have been constructed on tricot and raschel knitting machines. They still have the open-mesh effect, but since knitting only interloops the yarns, these fabrics are not as durable as those formed by the old knotting technique.

Nets appear in such items as evening apparel, curtains, millinery veils, window screens, and hammocks.

Laces

Lace has been defined in many ways, and authorities differ about what really constitutes lace. However, most people agree that lace is an open-work fabric consisting of a network of threads or yarns formed into intricate designs (Fig. 23.3). No one knows when lace was first made, but specimens in museums have been dated as early as 2500 B.C. However, regardless of its origin, we can assume that lace was developed for beauty and adornment.

Lace is truly the aristocrat of textile fabrics. No other material is so difficult to make yet so delicate, requires so much skill in manufacturing, or demands so much creative ability. Everything about lace is different. It is a product of yarn twisting, and the machinery for lacemaking is among the most complicated known.

The Leavers lacemaking machine—developed by John Leavers and his brothers after decades of research and experimentation—was launched commercially in 1837. The equipment in use today is essentially the same machine. It remains the most complex piece of textile machinery in the world. Of course, the complexity of production contributes to the high cost of true lace. That is why in recent years there has been a tremendous increase in the output of knitted laces. These are much easier to produce; they are, therefore, less expensive; yet they have good durability.

Yarns used in making lace are stronger and more firmly twisted than those for other types of fabrics. The adaptation of man-made fibers, such as nylon with its inherent high strength, has added durability to lace.

Figure 23.1   Braid trimming.

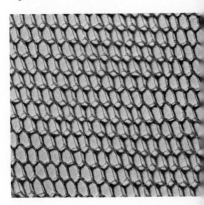

Figure 23.2   Net fabric.

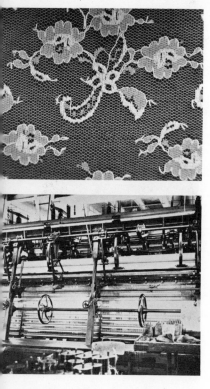

Laces can be manufactured in many widths and shapes with a practically limitless variety of patterns.

While many lace fabrics are fragile and require careful handling, those made of strong fibers are quite durable. Nevertheless, lace is treasured for its decorative appearance; its major function is to adorn.

Tapa Cloth

One of the earliest fabrics known was created from the bark of the paper mulberry tree by natives in the South Sea Islands. This fabric, called *tapa,* is still made by hand in the South Pacific. The bark is cut into thin layers, soaked for a period of time, and then pounded into a thin, filmy layer. The layers are combined to produce the desired weight of the final product. Tapa cloth is generally printed by hand with native designs, using colors in the tan and brown range with touches of black. The natural color of the tapa is light tan. The Islanders make tapa into clothing and indoor matting. Tapa is a frequent purchase of tourists in Polynesia.

Recently a series of printed cotton fabrics inspired by the original tapa designs have been placed on the market.

Film Fabrics

Films are not true textiles in that they are not composed of fibers. However, because they are used today for such a wide variety of products, it seems advisable to mention them. Films may be clear and transparent, colored and transparent, translucent, or opaque (Fig. 23.6). A frequent application is protective clothing, such as rainwear. These films derive from the same chemicals as some of the man-made fibers, but they are extruded in sheets instead of filaments. This difference can be visualized if one

top: Figure 23.3 Lace fabric.

above: Figure 23.4 Section of a Leavers lacemaking machine. (*Thomas Wilson & Co., Inc.*)

below: Figure 23.5 Tapa fabric from Polynesia.

compares Saran Wrap®, a film, with Saran fiber, which is used in rugs and furniture webbing.

The films vary in thickness from thin layers such as those in rainwear to heavy vinyl films for upholstery. Many films are supported or laminated; that is, they are sealed onto a knitted or a woven fabric base. This lamination adds resistance to tearing and increases durability. Nonsupported films are not considered "long-life" fabrics. Films may be cleaned easily by wiping with a damp cloth or by gentle laundering.

Multicomponent Fabrics

Multicomponents include *bonded fabrics, laminated fabrics,* and *foam-backed fabrics.* Some authorities group all these products under the heading of bonded fabrics, while others classify them as laminates. Inasmuch as there are differences among them, they will be discussed as subtypes of multicomponent fabrics.

A multicomponent fabric is one in which at least two layers of material are sealed together by some effective adhesive. Many of these structures frequently use tricot knit as the backing fabric in order to provide a self lining. Bonded fabrics have good stability, resistance to stretch or deformation, and a low incidence of raveling. However, the quality of the bond varies considerably, and consumers may encounter difficulties ranging from separation, to bubble effect, to uneven shrinkage. Recent products have been much improved, but they still require careful analysis before purchase.

Another type of multicomponent has a layer of fabric bonded to a layer of foam, which adds warmth and stability. In sandwich construction a layer of fabric is bonded to a second fabric by means of a thin layer of foam in the center. Besides providing stability and warmth, the sandwich laminate shows a finished appearance on both sides.

Figure 23.6 Clear vinyl printed with opaque enamel, for drapery or a wall panel. (*Jack Lenor Larsen, Inc.*)

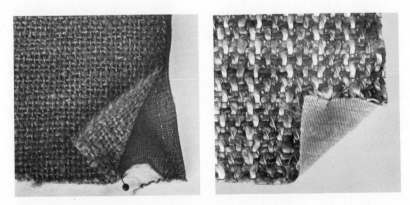

left: Figure 23.7 Fabric-to-fabric laminate.

right: Figure 23.8 Fabric-to-foam-to-fabric laminate.

Among the other multicomponent products are the following:

1. Film laminated to fabric. This creates an attractive plastic-effect fabric with the durability of a woven or knit structure.
2. Film laminated to foam. These fabrics are relatively durable and have good insulative properties.
3. Two fabrics sealed together with heat and/or adhesives by the chemstitch method. This technique provides for the crinkling or rippling of one of the fabrics to achieve a quilted effect.
4. A layer of fabric bonded to a layer of fibers. This results in an interesting material for special end-uses, with the added advantage of warmth, insulation, and bulk.

Multicomponent fabrics are gaining popularity. In addition to the built-in lining effect, they offer easy construction into end-use items by both manufacturers and home sewers; greater comfort than single-layer fabrics because of the smooth inner surface; and easy-care properties if the fabrics are adaptable to laundering. (See Plate 3.)

The consumer should examine multicomponent fabrics to determine that

- the fabric layers are sealed together firmly
- the grain lines are held in their proper relationship
- adequate care instructions are included
- there is no unusual odor
- there is no undesirable stiffness
- the adhesive is not visible
- the foam, if used, is not discolored

Tufted Fabrics

Handmade tufted fabrics originated in the American Colonial period. At that time hand tufting, practiced as an art, was limited to making fabrics for special uses. About 1900 the craft was revived, and machines were developed to produce tufted fabrics at rapid speeds.

Tufting is a process of manufacturing pile fabrics by inserting loops into an already woven ground fabric. This ground fabric may be of any type and composed of any fiber, but most tufted materials use a base of cotton, linen, or jute in a close or tight weave. The tuft yarns may also be of any fiber.

Yarn loops are inserted into the ground with needles and held in place either by a special coating applied to the back, or by untwisting the tufted yarn and shrinking the base fabric. Tufted fabrics cost less than their woven counterparts.

Tufted carpets and rugs first came on the market in 1950. Their success and popularity was immediate and has remained phenomenal. Approximately 90 percent of all carpets and rugs produced in the United States are

far left: Figure 23.9 Tufted carpeting, face.

left: Figure 23.10 Tufted carpeting, back. Backing fabric, usually added for stability, has been removed to show tufting yarns.

below: Figure 23.11 Close-up of the tufting process. Yarns are punched through a base cloth to form loops on the face of the fabric. (*Springs Mills*)

made by the tufting process. (Another 5 to 6 percent are needle punched, leaving a very small amount produced by weaving methods.) This predominance of tufted carpets derives from the fact that a great variety of fibers can be used successfully, and durable floor coverings can be made for lower cost than by other construction methods. Tufted fabrics are utilized also in furnishing fabrics and for some apparel.

By controlling the amount of yarn being fed to each needle, the size of the loop can be determined, and this in turn produces variations in texture and design. Tufts can be cut or uncut, and combinations of both create interesting effects. Color depends upon the arrangement of colored yarns, the use of space dyed yarns, or the choice of dye method.

Poromeric Structure

DuPont introduced a poromeric structure to the public in the early 1960s. Trademarked Corfam, it served primarily for shoe uppers. Corfam resembles leather in appearance, but unlike leather it permits the free passage of air and moisture. Thus, it may be more comfortable. The product wears well, is easy to clean, and does not scuff. In late 1971 DuPont sold the rights to Corfam. At the present time plans for the material's production are uncertain.

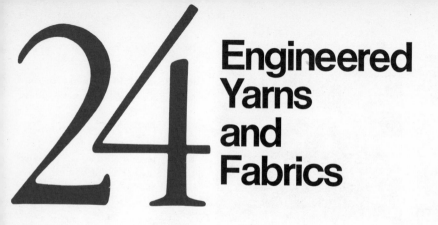

24

Engineered Yarns and Fabrics

Engineered yarns and fabrics are those that combine two or more textile fibers. The fibers can be blended in various yarn and fabric structures:

1. Different fiber types can be blended in single yarns.
2. Yarns of different fiber content (that is, single yarns each of one specific fiber) can be woven or knitted into fabric.
3. Single yarns of different fibers can be plied together and then formed into fabrics.

Fiber Blends

The accepted definition of a *blend,* as stated by the American Society for Testing Materials is

a single yarn spun from a blend or mixture of different fiber species.

According to this definition, only the first type of fiber mixture listed above would qualify as a true blend. Unfortunately, many consumers have come to associate the term *blend* with any fabric containing two or more fibers, regardless of how they are used. As a rule, woven fabrics designated as blends by fabric producers employ blended yarns throughout the construction. Exceptions to this might occur when the warp yarn is a blend and the filling a single yarn, or the reverse. Fabrics in which blended yarns are used throughout more likely will give better performance characteristics. Knit fabrics that are true blends generally have blended yarns throughout the construction. Nonwoven fabrics are blends when two or more species of fiber are made into the fiber mat.

Blends consist of various percentages of the fibers involved. Thus, a blend of 65 percent polyester and 35 percent cotton utilizes yarns in which each single yarn strand has approximately two polyester fibers for each cotton fiber.

For most blends on the textile market, optimum percentages have been established for at least one of the fibers involved. For example, it has been fairly well agreed among textile manufacturers that in blends of polyester and cotton, the percentage of polyester should be 50 percent or more. A blend of 55 percent acrylic with 45 percent wool results in a fabric with satisfactory washability, and 15 percent nylon fiber is frequently added to wool that has been finished by chlorination to produce "washable" wools. The nylon increases abrasion resistance and helps prevent damage to the wool from the chlorination process.

In manufacturing blend fabrics the fibers may be intimately mixed before yarn manufacturing, or the blending may occur during the drawing operations. For nonwovens the fibers are intimately mixed before entering the felting or bonding machinery. Unless a thorough blending occurs, the end product will not be uniform.

Engineered textile fabrics result from considerable research, development, and testing. Instead of concentrating on new fiber development, manufacturers are trying various combinations of existing fibers to achieve yarns and fabrics with desired qualities. A blend that is properly engineered exhibits the most desirable properties.

Blends can be developed to provide the consumer with special performance qualities or to meet predetermined end-use requirements. They may be designed strictly for appearance; to combine appearance and performance; to include small quantities of a luxury fiber for prestige effects; or as a means of reducing cost. Blends of polyester and cotton are usually sought for their performance. Rayon and acetate may be blended for appearance, particularly if a subtle cross-dye effect is desired, and for performance, especially if a fabric with appealing drape and hand is the goal. Silk, vicuña, or cashmere is sometimes blended with a less costly fiber to lend prestige to the fabric. These fibers do have many desirable properties and, if used in sufficient amounts, contribute pleasing characteristics to the final fabric. Blends that contain relatively low-cost fibers—such as rayon, acetate, or cotton—with more expensive fibers—acrylics, polyesters, or nylons—will be somewhat less costly than fabrics composed entirely of the higher-cost fiber. Properties of these fabrics will, in general, be superior to properties of fabrics from a single fiber.

Combination Fiber Fabrics

Combination fabrics are also composed of two or more fibers. However, instead of each single strand of yarn being an intimate blend of the fibers involved, each yarn is made from a single species of fiber, and the combination is developed by using some yarns of one fiber and some of another. Many combination fabrics have yarns of one fiber in the warp and yarns of a second fiber in the filling. When more than two fiber species are included, the yarns are arranged in a manner that creates special design effects, special color effects by cross dyeing or yarn dyeing, or desired performance properties. Checks can be produced in combination fiber fabrics by skillful arrangement of the yarns so they can be cross dyed to create the desired pattern. Some stripes are obtained in the same manner.

Strength is introduced into combination fiber fabrics by using yarns of high breaking load in the direction that requires extra resistance to force, or by spacing strong yarns among yarns of low-tenacity fibers so that the strong yarns increase resistance to breaking force. Nylon yarns in the warp direction, with a low-tenacity fiber in yarns for the filling, would produce such a product.

Some fabrics are neither true blends nor true combinations. For example, a fabric common in lingerie has a nylon yarn in the warp and an intimate blend yarn of cotton and polyester in the filling. Other fabrics employing fibers in this manner appear on the market from time to time.

Engineered fabrics usually are developed for predetermined end-uses, and they perform best under these circumstances. However, the product manufacturer may select engineered fabrics for end-use items to which they are not suitable. In such instances the consumer may not be satisfied with the item.

It is particularly important for the fiber content of a blend or combination fabric to be labeled properly. Unfortunately, the law does not require identification regarding fiber arrangement. For example, if an item is labeled 50 percent rayon and 50 percent polyester, the consumer cannot be sure the fibers have been intimately blended. Should the fabric be a combination, with warp threads of rayon and filling of polyester, it would not exhibit the wrinkle resistance of a blend of these two fibers.

Combinations of this type can often be verified by applying the burning test to the yarns. Unfortunately, this test is not always appropriate, nor do all combination fabrics respond with adequate individuality to provide a definitive result. Moreover, few consumers have sufficient knowledge of testing procedures to make the proper analysis. It is important, therefore, to use the products of reliable manufacturers who do provide the consumer with adequate information to make the right selection.

Finish and Color Application

"The finishing of a fabric marks the occasion of its birth."[1] This statement is not meant to be amusing; it is a fundamental fact. A modern fabric, as the average consumer knows it, does not exist until it has been subjected to various finishing procedures. Most fabrics that reach the consumer market have received one or more finishing treatments, and, except for white fabrics, color in some form has been applied. The textile industry tends to consider the application of dye as a finishing step, but for convenience dyestuffs are discussed in separate chapters in this text.

The history of finishes (excluding color) is sketchy. Smoothing fabrics on flat stone surfaces was the forerunner of calendering; application of white clay was a rudimentary sizing. The first written information concerning finishes dates from the mid-19th century. We assume that, before that time, routine finishes were anything but routine. Mercerization is one of the oldest finishes. John Mercer discovered the effect of caustic soda on cotton in 1853, but it was H. A. Lowe who perfected the process

[1] "Modern Finishes," *American Fabrics,* No. 28 (Reporter Publications, Inc.), p. 56.

in 1889. Shrinkage control by finishes such as sanforization was developed, for the most part, in the 20th century.

This text has divided finishes into two major groups: (1) routine or general, and (2) functional (including those that influence final appearance). Each of these can be either mechanical or chemical and durable or renewable.

Stretch fabrics are, in a sense, a summation of textile science. They could, with some justification, be included in any of the main subdivisions of this book, for they can be created by fiber technology, by methods of yarn production, by fabric-construction techniques, or by the application of special finishes. Because these fabrics do encompass the entire range of textile technology, they have been placed in Part V at the end of the discussion on finishes.

Routine or General Finishes

25

The application of finishes is the province of the converting industry. Manufacturers in this group devote their research and production to finishes that will change, improve, or develop the appearance or desired behavior characteristics of a fabric. For the consumer this part of textile processing may well be the most important. It is the finish that determines the degree of satisfaction or dissatisfaction that consumers experience with a specific fabric.

Finishes can be classified into various groups—mechanical or chemical; permanent or nonpermanent (more properly called *durable* and renewable); general or functional. Some of these finishes do and some do not alter appearance.

In the following section finishes are discussed in terms of the care procedures required for retention of durability. Their effect on hand and appearance will be discussed also, for it may influence a consumer when making a purchase.

Finishes are said to be durable if they can withstand a "normal" amount of wear. Normal is, obviously, a relative term, and one person's interpretation may be very different from another's. The industry measures

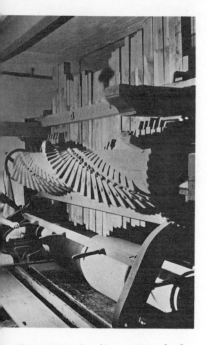

Figure 25.1   Beetling machine for flax fabrics. (*Irish Linen Guild*)

the durability or permanence of a finish by its ability to withstand tests designed to simulate average use and care. Renewable finishes are those that rub off or are removed easily by washing or dry cleaning.

Routine or general finishes are discussed in this chapter in alphabetical order. Since many of these processes produce a standard fabric, care procedures are not explained in detail except in special instances.

Beetling

Beetling is a mechanical finish applied to cotton and linen fabrics. It increases the luster of fabrics by flattening the yarns to provide more area for light reflection. The fabric is fed over rolls that rotate in a machine where large hammers rise and fall on the surface of the fabric. Continued pounding flattens the yarns and closes the weave. The beetled finish will withstand wear and maintenance if the fabric is laundered carefully and ironed with pressure to restore the flat appearance. Fabrics for table coverings are often beetled to add luster and to make them lie flat.

Bleaching

Fabrics, yarns, or fibers can be bleached to make them white or to prepare them for dyeing or printing. Bleaching is a chemical finish. It is relatively durable when the bleaching method is appropriate to the fiber or fibers involved. Whiteness retention of textile products is important to the consumer and may require frequent bleaching during the life of the article.

The consumer seldom considers the effect of preliminary bleaching on colored fabrics. However, if a textile has not been properly bleached during routine finishing, it may return to its natural color, thus causing a change in the color applied to the fabric. For example, if wool is bleached

Figure 25.2   Overall view of the open-width finishing frame for scouring and bleaching. (*Springs Mills*)

by a reduction process, it will reoxidize in the presence of the oxygen in the air and return to its natural yellowish color. When this happens, a light blue wool could become green-blue.

The particular chemical used for bleaching depends on the textile fiber. Chlorine or perborate bleaches are those available to the consumer on the retail market. The products used commercially are generally stronger. Chlorine bleaches are safe for such natural fibers as cotton and linen, as well as for many synthetics. However, it is essential to follow all directions for care, both on the labels that may accompany the textile products and on the containers of the bleaches themselves. Chlorine bleaches usually result in loss of color and fiber strength and eventual deterioration of the fabric.

Perborate bleaches are satisfactory for some products, but they will not remove deep stains or soil. They have the advantage of doing little or no damage to the textile.

A current trend in bleaching is the use of optical brighteners, which are included in the formulations of a large number of soaps and synthetic detergents on the market. These substances react rather like dyes and are applied from a solution. They alter the reflectance characteristics of the surface of the fabric, producing a visual effect of whiteness.

Brushing

Brushing is a mechanical finish. It involves the removal of short, loose fibers from the surface of the fabric. Cylinders covered with fine bristles rotate over the fabric, pick up loose fibers, and pull them away by either gravity or a vacuum. This finish is usually applied to fabrics of staple fiber content to give a smooth and uniform appearance.

Calendering (Pressing)

Calendering is applied to cottons, linens, and silk, as well as to rayons and other man-made fiber fabrics. *Pressing* is the term used for wool fabrics. Basic calendering and pressing are mechanical processes and must be renewed after each laundering or cleaning.

The finish is similar to ironing but is done with much greater pressure. It gives a smooth surface to fabrics. More complicated calendering processes include moiréing, embossing, and schreinerizing. Because these add design to fabrics and can be combined with other finishes, they are discussed with functional finishes in Chapter 26. (See Fig. 25.3.)

Carbonizing

Carbonizing is a chemical finish applied to wool fabrics. Wool yarns and fabrics frequently contain vegetable matter that was not completely removed during carding. To eliminate this, the wool fabric is immersed in a solution of sulfuric acid; it is then subjected to high temperatures for a

Figure 25.3 Calender machine. (*Pepperell Manufacturing Company*)

brief time. The acid and heat react to convert the vegetable matter to carbon, which is easily removed by a final scouring and, if necessary, brushing. The process must be carefully controlled to prevent fiber damage, which would result in weakened fabrics.

Crabbing

A mechanical finish applied to wool fabrics, crabbing permanently sets the weave. The fabric is immersed in first hot then cold water, and passed between rollers. If properly fed into the rollers, the warp and filling yarns are set at a true 90-degree angle to each other. Improper crabbing contributes to "off-grain" fabric. Crabbing may reduce or eliminate shrinkage in wool fabrics. It generally prevents uneven shrinkage.

Decating

Decating is a mechanical finish. On wool it is used to set the luster and develop a permanent sheen. On rayons, silks, and blends it softens the hand of the fabric and helps to set the grain in its proper relationship in the woven structure.

Fulling

Fulling is a mechanical finish applied to wool to produce a compact fabric. When wool is removed from the loom, it bears little resemblance to the fabric that the consumer purchases, being loose and hard in texture. To make the fabric compact and soft it is fulled by applying the proper amount of moisture, heat, and friction. The fabric yarns shrink together and the fabric softens to the desired texture. Fabrics that have not been adequately fulled will tend to shrink badly during use and care by the consumer.

Heat Setting

Heat sensitive (thermoplastic) fibers are generally given a heat-setting finish to produce a special shape or to ensure a stable fabric. While the process is mechanical, the heat changes the physical characteristics of the polymer.

A major reason for heat setting is to introduce dimensional stability, and the degree of dimensional stability is determined by the temperature, the period of exposure, and the amount of force used to hold the fabric in the desired shape and size during setting. Other characteristics introduced by heat setting include resiliency, which contributes to wrinkle resistance; elastic recovery, which aids in size retention; and relatively permanent design details, such as pleats, planned creases, or surface embossing. Fabrics can be heat-set in a smooth, flat shape or with pleats and creases pressed in. They can even be made to assume an end-use shape, such as nylon hosiery.

If at any later time the fabric is exposed to temperatures higher than the heat-setting temperature, or if it is subjected to heat for an extended period of time (longer than the heat-setting period), it may take on a new shape. For example, if the fabric is wrinkled or folded where it should not be, these undesirable conditions may be permanently set into the material. To prevent this, certain maintenance requirements must be satisfied. Laundering, drying, and smoothing temperatures must be safely below the softening or the stabilizing temperatures of the fiber.

Inspection

Fabric inspection involves three possible steps. Originally, only wool fabrics received detailed inspection, but today nearly every fabric is examined before it leaves the manufacturing plant. The process is obviously somewhat subjective.

Perching

Perching is a visual inspection. The name derives from the frame, called a *perch,* of frosted glass with lights behind and above it. The fabric passes over the perch and is inspected visually. Flaws, stains, or spots, yarn knots, and other imperfections are marked.

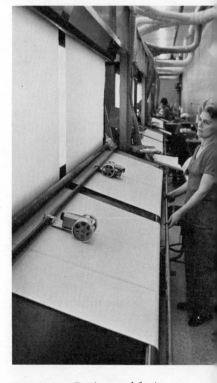

Figure 25.4 Perches used for inspection of fabric. (*Springs Mills*)

Figure 25.5 Mercerization. Fabric leaves mercerizing bath and passes over timing cans that control length of saturation. (*Springs Mills*)

Figure 25.6 Shearing blades used to smooth fabric surfaces. (*Springs Mills*)

Burling

While burling is generally applied to wool, it, too, is being used now in relation to other fibers. Burling is the removal of yarn knots or other imperfections that can be repaired without producing inferior fabrics.

Mending

Mending is, obviously, the actual repair of imperfections. It may leave marks that result in a fabric being classified as "second quality," or it may be done so the repair is not visible.

Mercerization

Mercerization is a chemical finish applied to cellulosic fibers, especially cotton. It adds luster to fabric, improves dyeing characteristics, and increases strength. In mercerizing, yarns or fabrics are immersed in a solution of 18 to 27 percent sodium hydroxide. For conventional mercerization the yarns or fabrics are held under tension during the finishing procedures. Slack mercerization is one method of introducing stretch properties into fabrics (see Chap. 28).

The finish swells the fibers, giving them a round cross section that reflects light to create a gloss or sheen. The natural twist of cotton fiber is largely removed. Mercerization under tension produces fibers with increased strength and increased affinity for dyestuffs, which is due to the rounding of the fiber and the increased space between the fiber molecules.

Scouring

Scouring procedures vary depending upon the fibers involved. Some fabrics are sold as they come from the loom, while others must be scoured to remove foreign materials that might be present. The latter include natural waxes, dirt, processing oils, and sizing compounds used on yarns during weaving. Fugitive colors introduced for yarn identification are removed during the scouring.

Soaps or synthetic detergents with alkaline builders constitute the common scouring agents. For protein fibers a neutral or slightly acidic synthetic detergent is often used. Fibers with natural impurities or fabrics with noticeable amounts of sizing are the most frequent candidates for scouring.

Shearing

Shearing is a mechanical process applied to some fabrics constructed from staple-length fibers. It involves cutting or shearing off undesirable surface fibers or evening nap or pile.

After singeing and subsequent processing, fiber ends or loose fibers may protrude from the fabric surface. Shearing cuts off these ends and permits a clear view of the weave. For pile or napped fabrics, shearing evens the surface to give a uniform appearance. By manipulating the shearing it is possible, also, to cut designs into pile fabrics.

The shearing machine has a wide, spiral cylinder to which cutting blades are attached. It resembles a lawn mower in action. The fabric passes over brushes that raise the fiber ends or the fabric nap, then it moves over the cutting blades.

Singeing

Singeing consists of burning off the fuzz or fiber ends on fabric in order to obtain a smooth surface. Fabrics of natural fibers and staple-length man-made fibers can be singed to produce a clear, smooth appearance.

Before singeing, the cloth is brushed to remove loose fibers, lint, and dust. The fabrics are singed in full width, under tension to keep the surface flat and free of wrinkles, creases, and curled selvages. In the most common method the fabric is passed directly under an open gas flame. The fabric moves rapidly, 230 to 270 yards per minute, and enters a water bath as soon as it leaves the singeing area. The water bath extinguishes any sparks or afterglow and prevents damage. Another system has the fabric pass over two or more heated plates or rollers; the second plate or roller is red hot and singes the surface. A water bath is involved in this technique to prevent damage and cool the fabric.

Figure 25.7   Open flame singeing. (*Springs Mills*)

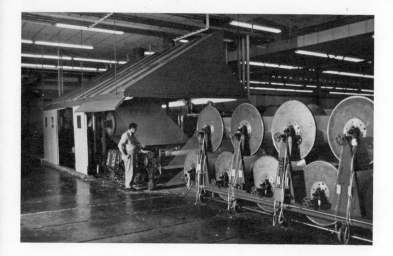

Figure 25.8 Application of sizing to yarns before weaving. (*Springs Mills*)

Singeing combines chemical and physical processes; the singeing is an oxidation reaction, while brushing is mechanical. However, the process of oxidation does not affect the final fabric, since only surface fiber ends are removed.

Sizing

Sizing is the application of various materials to a fabric to produce stiffness or firmness. It is a chemical process in that substances are added to the fabric. Cellulose fabrics are sized with starch or resins. Starch gives weight to a fabric and can make an inferior product look attractive until laundered. It also prevents fabrics from soiling quickly. Resins have the same function as starch in the sizing process. The consumer should be aware that sizing is temporary unless it is part of a permanent or durable finish. It will thus be lost the first time the fabric is laundered.

Tentering

Tentering is the mechanical straightening and drying of fabrics. A tenter frame holds the fabric between two parallel chains, with either clips or special pins. The chains spread apart to the desired fabric width, move with the fabric through finishing or drying units, and release the fabric to be rolled or folded onto cylinders.

If the fabric is picked up by the tenter chains in such a manner that the filling yarns are not absolutely perpendicular to the warp yarns, the fabric is finished off grain and exhibits *skew*. This poses many problems to the consumer, since the fabrics will not hang properly and may change shape after care. Grain cannot be corrected if it was incorrectly set following the application of resin finishes. The product will then be unattractive and the fabric shape will increasingly distort as the other finishes are gradually removed during use and care.

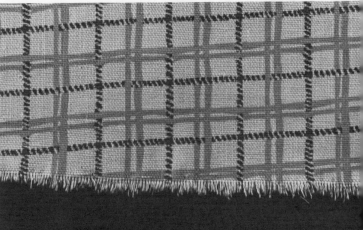

There are a number of devices that help to set the fabric on true grain. A tenter with a variable chain drive enables the operator to slow down one chain and keep the filling threads in their proper location. The same variable mechanism can be controlled by "electronic-eye" sensors that adjust the speed of the individual chains. The controls stop the tenter if the grain becomes too crooked and provide for readjustment of the fabric. The marks of the clips or pins used to hold the fabric are often seen on the selvage edge. Some fabrics are made with heavy selvages to reduce tenter damage.

Heat setting of man-made fabrics is frequently combined with tentering. Products thus processed tend to keep their shape during use and care, and shrinkage becomes minimal.

Weighting

Weighting is a sizing technique applied to silk fabrics. After complete degumming, silk fibers are very soft. To make heavy or stiff materials, manufacturers resort to weighting the fabrics with metallic salts, such as stannous chloride. The absorbency characteristics of silk protein make this a feasible procedure. However, weighting, if overdone, causes silk fabrics to crack and split. Weighted silk has body and density, but the fabrics are not as durable, since they are more sensitive to sunlight, air, and perspiration damage.

left: Figure 25.9 Tenter frame, to maintain fabric dimensions. (*Pepperell Manufacturing Company*)

right: Figure 25.10 Fabric printed off grain.

26 Special Finishes

Despite their name, many "special" finishes have come to be regarded as essential by the consumer. They can be divided into two major categories: finishes that change or modify the *appearance* and/or *hand* of the completed fabric, and *functional finishes,* which improve or otherwise alter the *behavior* or service characteristics of the fabric and produce certain properties. In the discussion that follows no attempt has been made to establish the relative significance of finishes, and their order in the text should not be interpreted as an indication of importance. Finishes that affect appearance are grouped by similarity of process; functional finishes are discussed alphabetically, except for related groups.

Finishes That Alter Appearance or Hand

Special Calendering

The preparation of some fabrics involves special calendering—smoothing under pressure—which imparts design to the fabric surface. Permanence or durability of appearance depends on several factors: if fibers are thermo-

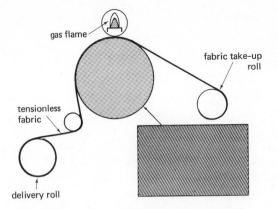

Figure 26.1   Diagram of a Schreiner calender. Insert shows lines on the face of the calender roll.

plastic, the calendering can actually soften them and impart a permanent design effect; if a resin is applied to the fabric, a durable calender design can be produced; if pressure alone is used on nonthermoplastic fibers, the design will probably be lost during the first laundering. The consumer should request data on care and verify durability of special calendering. If no information or warranties are available, it would be wise not to purchase the product.

Schreinering   Schreinering is produced on a special calender. The metal roll has a series of fine lines, about 250 per inch, engraved so they form an angle of roughly 20 degrees to the construction of the cloth. The angle is usually such that the lines are parallel to the twist in the yarns. This finish produces a soft luster and is used frequently on cellulosic fibers such as cotton and linen. In addition, the rolls flatten the yarns and create a smooth and compact fabric. During the last several years schreinering has been employed on tricot-knit lingerie fabric of nylon and polyester fibers to produce an opaque fabric. If properly done, the process does not affect care procedures.

Moiré   In the days before man-made fibers moiré was known as "watered silk," and the finish was applied only to silk fabrics. Today, moiré is used on many fibers. A moiré finish is characterized by a soft luster and a design created by differences in light reflection. Rib fabrics, such as failles, taffetas, and bengalines, work best in producing moiré effects.

   The ribbed fabric is doubled and fed between rollers that exert pressure and add heat. Two rollers are involved—a large one covered with cloth and a smaller one that is heated and often includes a design. The ribs in one thickness impress images on the other thickness by flattening the ribs. If there is an etched pattern on the heated metal roll, the design is transferred to the fabric. Without the etching there is a bar (irregular or broken) effect. A moiré finish on thermoplastic fibers, such as acetate or nylon, is durable. When applied to nonthermoplastic fibers, rayon or

Figure 26.2   Moiré fabric.

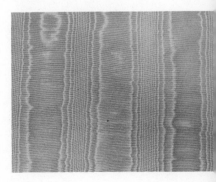

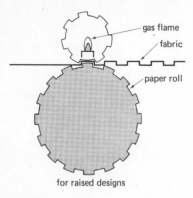

Figure 26.3 Diagram of embossing rolls.

cotton, for example, a resin finish is required to provide even minimal durability.

Embossed Surfaces   Embossed fabrics have three-dimensional designs. Before the introduction of resin finishes, embossing lacked durability, but now resins aid in making embossed patterns relatively permanent. Thermoplastic fibers produce fabrics that hold embossed designs.

The calenders used for embossing may consist of two or three rolls. One roll is of cotton or paper, and the second roll, which is metal, has the engraved design. In the three-roll method, the center roll is engraved metal, while the outer two rolls are cotton or paper. After the design has been engraved on the steel roll, the paper or cotton rolls are dampened, and the machine is turned on but the fabric is not passed through. The pattern on the steel roll will be deeply impressed in the soft roll. After the impression is sufficiently deep, the machine is run until the soft roll has dried. The fabric is then fed through the calender, and the design is transferred to the fabric. Any type of design can be adapted to embossing. Embossed finishes frequently are of the "no-iron" variety. The consumer can expect good performance with minimum care.

Polished Surfaces

Modified calenders with special chemicals produce fabric with a degree of permanent polish.

Glazed Surfaces   A friction calender produces glazed surfaces such as those found on glazed chintz or polished cottons. The process involves three rolls, the center one of cotton or paper, the other two metal. One of the metal rolls operates at a high speed, developing a polish on the fabric

Figure 26.4   Glazed fabric.

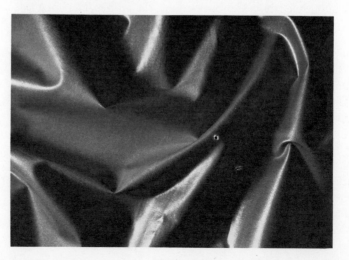

by friction. To make the glazed finish permanent, the fabric is impregnated with resins before calendering.

Ciré   Ciré is a high-polish finish often applied to silk or blends including silk. It is accomplished by impregnating the fabric with wax or with a thermoplastic substance and passing it through a friction calender. This finish is not considered permanent, although it may be rather durable if handled carefully. Ciré is a fashion finish. During the 1960s it was sometimes called "the wet look."

Raised Surfaces

Gigging and napping are the two principal methods for raising the fiber ends to the surface. Staple or short fibers in spun yarns are essential in fabrics that are to be napped. The nap hides the yarns and weave and produces a soft, hairy appearance. Flocking creates a raised effect by adding short fibers to the surface of the fabric.

Gigging   Gigging is a napping process used for wool, rayon and other fibers where a short lustrous nap is desired. Teasels obtained from a special variety of thistle plant are attached to a cylinder. The fabric is then fed into the machine, and the teasels gently tease or pull the fiber ends to the surface to produce the nap. The nap obtained by gigging is soft. The process is gentle and does little damage to the fabric. The nap is sometimes pressed flat, as for wool broadcloth, or it may be left full and fluffy as in soft blankets.

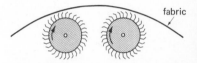

Figure 26.5 Diagram of napping rolls. The bent wires nap the surface of the fabric.

Napping   Napping is applied to cotton, rayon, wool, and any other staple fiber yarns to produce a deep nap or when fibers will not respond to the teasels. The process utilizes cylinders on which there are fine metal wires with small hooks. These hooks pull fiber ends to the surface and create the nap. Napping can be done either on one or on both sides of the fabric.

Fabrics used for napping should contain soft-spun yarns with low twist and comparatively loose fibers. Plain-weave soft-filled sheeting fabrics and soft-filled twill-weave fabrics are preferred for napping or gigging. In these fabrics the warp yarns are strong enough to provide adequate strength to the fabric, and the soft filling yarns are easily roughened so they permit pulling the fiber ends to the surface.

Fabrics with napped surfaces include flannels, flannelettes, blankets, and some coating and suiting materials. Suede cloth and duvetyns are made by napping the fabric and shearing the nap to produce a smooth, compact, and uniform surface. Napped fabrics should not be confused with pile surfaces produced by fabric construction.

Fabrics with napped surfaces are difficult to work because the nap causes light reflections to vary, which, in turn, alters the appearance of the fabric as its direction changes. Consequently, when this fabric is used in a

Figure 26.6 A napped fabric. Note that the weave is obscured by the surface finish. (*Collins & Aikman*)

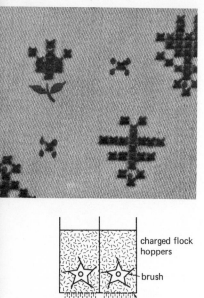

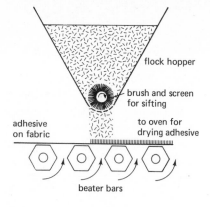

left: **Figure 26.7** Fabric with flocked design.

right: **Figure 26.8** Diagram of mechanical flocking.

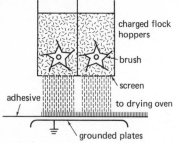

Figure 26.9 Diagram of electrostatic flocking.

construction process, the patterns should face and be cut in the same direction to ensure uniform appearance.

Flocking   Flocking is sometimes considered a printing method, but because of its similarity to raised surface finishes, it is included with finishes in this text.

Flocking consists of attaching very short fibers to the surface of the fabric by means of an adhesive. The result is a textured or a pile appearance. Frequently, some areas of the fabric are flocked while others are left smooth to produce a pattern. The flock is usually of rayon fibers and is cut so that the ends are square. The flock length varies, but the average is about $\frac{1}{8}$ inch.

The adhesive is printed onto the fabric in the desired pattern, after which the flock is applied by one of two methods. The vibration or mechanical method can apply flock to one or both sides of the fabric. The flock is circulated in a container through which the fabric passes. As the fabric moves, it vibrates and builds up static that attracts the flock. The latter adheres to the areas where the adhesive has been applied. The fabric then moves into a drying chamber where the adhesive dries with the flock firmly embedded. Finally, the fabric is brushed to remove flock in areas where there is no adhesive.

The second method, the electrostatic or electrocoating technique, depends on electrical charge of fibers and the presence of an electrical field above and below the fabric. The fabric, printed with the adhesive, passes over an electric field, which establishes an atmosphere that forces the loose fibers in the area away from one of the electrical fields and toward the second. With the fabric moving, the loose fibers strike the adhesive, and the electrical field orients the fibers and pulls them into the adhesive. The fabric moves into a drying area where the adhesive is dried to hold the flock fibers in place.

Flocking is comparatively permanent to laundering as long as high temperatures are avoided. Dry cleaning, however, may cause damage by softening or dissolving the adhesive. The consumer should check for loose fibers by rubbing a flocked fabric. If such a condition exists, the fabric should be avoided.

Acid Finishes

To produce transparent or parchmentlike cottons with permanent stiffness, such as organdy, cotton fabric is treated with sulfuric acid. The fabric is immersed in the acid under carefully controlled conditions for a very brief time and then quickly neutralized. One finish, developed in Switzerland, is called the *Heberlein process*. Together with *Bellmanized* and *Ice organdy*, these are the terms common in the United States. This type of acid finish can be applied to the entire fabric to produce a clear organdy. By printing an acid-resistant substance on the fabric before treatment, designs can be developed with both opaque (frosted) areas and transparent areas.

The durability of stiffness and transparency characteristic of organdy depends on the quality of the finish. A well-applied finish will be long lasting and not weaken the cloth. Fabric with this finish wrinkles badly during laundering and requires considerable ironing.

A second acid finish produces "burned-out" designs. It employs a fabric composed of two properly selected fibers—one that is easily destroyed by acid, such as rayon or acetate, and another that is acid resistant, such as wool, acrylic, or polyester. The fabric is exposed to an acid, which burns away the first fiber to leave sheer areas. Careful planning of the fiber content and arrangement is essential for satisfactory results.

Burned-out designs can also be made with chemicals other than acids. Acetone is used on fabrics composed of acetate and a second fiber not affected by acetone. The acetate is destroyed in the treated areas, leaving the second fiber and an interesting design. Phenol is effective on fabrics made partly of nylon. These fabrics may require ironing.

Figure 26.10 Organdy with flocked design.

Basic Finishes

The application of chemical bases or alkalies—frequently called caustics because of their corrosive action—produces certain finishes.

Plissé crepe, a crinkled or crepelike cotton, results from the action of sodium hydroxide on cotton fabric. Caustic soda in a paste form is printed onto the fabric in a predetermined pattern. This causes the coated areas to shrink and the untreated areas to pucker. The crinkled finish is quite durable, but it may be removed by heavy or prolonged ironing, which will stretch out the fabric and result in dimensional change. Ironing is, therefore, not recommended, and it is not really necessary. The appearance of this type of fabric is generally retained with minimum care.

Crinkled, embossed, or plissé effects in irregular designs can be obtained with phenol on nylon fabrics. But not all crinkled effects are the result of finishing. In seersucker fabrics an effect similar to plissé is achieved by weaving modifications or the use of fibers with different shrinkage characteristics. During final fabric processing one group of yarns will shrink while the second group will not, and, thus, the desired crinkled effect will be achieved. These fabrics will have good stability.

above: Figure 26.11 Plissé, a fabric puckered by finishing.

below: Figure 26.12 Seersucker, a fabric design created by weaving.

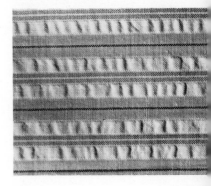

Stiffening Finishes

Sizings discussed in the previous chapter contribute stiffness to fabrics, but they are relatively temporary. Recently, thermosetting resins or plastic compounds of various types have been used with success in producing fabrics with quite durable stiffness. They keep sheer fabrics crisp and attractive, prevent sagging and slipping of yarns and wilting of fabric, reduce the formation of lint, and help maintain a smooth surface that is resistant to snags and abrasion. Resin finishes also contribute to dimensional stability.

Softening Finishes

Softening finishes improve the hand and drape of a fabric. They may add body, facilitate application of other finishes, subdue the coarseness imparted during processing, and increase the life and utility of the fabric. Batiste is an example of a fabric treated with a softener.

Softening finishes have gained new importance with the acceptance of durable-press fabrics. Durable press stiffens fabrics considerably, and, to maintain a pleasant hand, softeners are included in the finishing procedure. A wide selection of fabric softeners are available to the consumer for home care. These products not only maintain or restore fabric softness, but they also help to reduce static electricity.

Optical Finishes

Delusterants Man-made fibers often have a high degree of luster, since their relative transparency and their shape reflect light. A few long light rays reflected from a surface give more luster than many short rays, because the latter are diffused as they cross and blend. Luster can be diminished by intelligent selection of fibers or yarn-construction techniques. Conversely, luster can be enhanced by the same methods. A common system to reduce luster is to introduce pigments into the spinning solution. A white pigment will reduce luster by the breakup of light reflection, thus creating an opaque fiber. The finishing techniques include special heat treatments that soften yarn and fabric surface to change light reflection.

External delusterants in the form of a solution can be applied directly to the fabric. The solution is deposited on the fiber as a coating that reduces the light reflection. The coating is easily removed during care, whereas the delusterants introduced directly into the spinning solution provide durable delustering.

Optical Brighteners Many fabrics lose their brightness, whiteness, and clearness during processing and maintenance. In an attempt to prevent this and to maintain white and bright fabrics, optical brighteners have been introduced. These are sometimes called "optical bleaches," but the term in this case is inappropriate, since no bleaching occurs. Optical brighteners are used by fabric converters in finishing, and they are added to many home laundering agents, so the consumer can restore brightness each time a product is laundered. The substances attach themselves to the fabric and create an appearance of whiteness and/or brightness by the way in which they reflect light.

Other Finishes That Affect Appearance and Hand

Several finishes discussed as routine or general techniques produce changes in appearance. These include calendering, mercerizing, fulling, singeing, and beetling. Finishes such as sizing, fulling, and heat setting influence the hand of fabrics. (See Chap. 25 for a discussion of these techniques.)

If properly applied by reliable converters, finishes resulting in changed appearance or hand do not reduce fabric durability in the end-use for which the fabrics are typically selected. Nondurable finishes will be destroyed by laundry or cleaning. Some, such as optical brighteners, are easily replaced. However, if such finishes as glazing, ciré, plissé, and flocking are not permanent, they disappear during maintenance, and the fabrics will never look as attractive as when new. Permanent or durable finishes will retain their appearance with proper care.

The appearance, hand, and behavior of finishes should be considered in the selection of fabrics and fabric items. This information should be available to the consumer on attached labels.

Functional Finishes

To provide the public with fabrics that have special service qualities, the finishing industry has been called upon to develop many new techniques. Finishes in this category are of two basic types: (1) external finishes, and (2) internal finishes or chemical modifiers.

External finishes are applied to the surface of fibers, yarns, and/or fabrics and do not combine chemically with the fiber. They include softening agents; film-forming finishes, such as starches, thermosetting resins, and thermoplastic resins; surface deposits, such as delusterants, slip-resistant finishes, and hygroscopic agents; and corrective finishes, such as water repellents, fire inhibitors, moth repellents, and bacteriostatic agents. External finishes sometimes alter the appearance and hand of the fabric.

Internal finishes are deposited within the fiber. They combine chemically with the fibers and modify or inhibit some inherent fault or weakness in the actual fiber structure. In some cases internal finishes produce cross-linking of fiber molecules. This can be compared to parallel chains of paper clips that are held together at intervals by clips perpendicular to the long chains. Internal finishes are applied to fibers with porous surfaces. They do not alter the appearance of fabric, but they frequently modify the hand to some degree.

Abrasion-Resistant Finishes

Many of the newer manufactured fibers, particularly nylons, have inherent resistance to abrasion. However, natural fibers and some man-made fibers may be damaged by rubbing. To reduce this type of fabric damage, manufacturers do one of two things. They can blend fibers of high abrasion resistance with those of low resistance, or they can apply soft thermoplastic resins, which appear to increase the fabric's resistance to abrasion damage.

The problem of abrasion is extremely complicated, but it is believed a substantial part of the resistance produced by these resins results from the fact that the resin binds the fibers more firmly into the yarns, and, thus, increases the time and amount of abrasion required to roughen the surface by fiber breakage.

Recent evidence indicates that abrasion-resistant finishes may increase the wet soiling of fabrics. Therefore, their use is decreasing. They are still popular for trouser pockets, carpet backings, and hat bands.

Absorbent Finishes

Absorbent finishes increase the moisture-holding power and speed up the drying action of fibers, yarns, and fabrics. While fabrics treated with these finishes can absorb more moisture than they normally would, the drying is delayed an amount of time commensurate with the additional moisture that must be given off. Consumers may well appreciate more absorbent towels, but they must realize that these will take longer to dry either in the air or in a dryer due to the increased amount of moisture absorbed.

The use of absorbent finishes has declined in recent years. They are still applied to such items as towels, diapers, underwear, and sport shirts under trade names such as Hysorb, Nylonized, Telezorbant, and Sorbtex.

Antislip Finishes

Finishes applied to a fabric to reduce or eliminate yarn slippage are called antislip, slip resistant, or nonslip finishes. They help keep yarns in their proper position in the fabric and reduce seam fraying. Many of these finishes are not durable. Some chemicals with other functional properties such as crease resistance and durable press will also heighten resistance to yarn slippage. While the presence or absence of an antislip finish is, undoubtedly, of importance to many consumers, it is seldom included in the available textile information.

Antistatic Finishes

Static buildup in fabrics has long been recognized as a problem by textile scientists and consumers alike. Besides causing difficulties in the production of fabrics, static buildup also increases soiling. Above all, however, static is annoying. It is evident to the consumer when garments cling to the body or to other fabrics; when sparks with sufficient force to be seen or felt jump from the wearer to metal after the person has walked across floor coverings or slid across upholstery; when crackling sounds are heard as a person walks or takes off a garment; or when a visible spark is produced by rubbing the fabric.

Antistatic finishes work by one or more of three basic methods. First, the finish may improve the surface conductivity and thereby help the electrons to move either to the ground or to the atmosphere. Second, the finish may attract molecules of water to the surface, which, in turn, increase the conductivity and carry away the static charges. Third, chemical finishes may develop an electric charge opposite from the one of the fiber, which will neutralize the electrostatic charges. The most effective finishes work in all three ways. However, because fibers differ in the type of static charge they generate, there must be different finishing agents for different fibers.

Most antistatic finishes are not durable and must be replaced after each laundering. The addition of fabric softeners such as Nusoft, Sta-Puf and Downy to the final rinse cycle does help to control static. But the finishing industry continues to work on the development of durable antistatic agents. The most successful of these are incorporated into the fiber, including Fybrite, a polyester, and 22N, a static-free nylon. Until static-free fibers become more widespread, however, the consumer can solve the static problem in the home by adding a softener to the rinse cycle or using the type that can be applied in the dryer.

Bacteriostats

Bacteriostatic agents or antiseptic finishes are added to fabrics for three reasons. They may control the spread of disease and reduce the danger of infection following injury; they help to inhibit the development of unpleasant odors from perspiration and other soil on fibrous structures; and they reduce damage to fabrics from mildew-producing fungi and rot-producing bacteria.

Evidence indicates that substances to prevent fabric deterioration from microorganisms were known in ancient Egypt. Mummy wrappings were preserved by applying spices and herbs, which protected them from rot. The current interest in antimicrobial finishes dates from about 1900. However, during World War II the importance of these finishes was emphasized. The German army treated soldiers' uniforms with special compounds, and records indicate that men wearing the treated fabrics suffered considerably less infection from wounds.

Bacteriostatic finishes may be either durable or renewable. The renewable ones are external finishes that produce a "climate" unfavorable to the microorganisms. Some durable finishes are surface coatings that have been made insoluble so they remain on the yarns and fabrics during care, while others are internal in that they are insolubilized within the fiber structure. It is possible to include bacteriostats with other finishes, such as water repellents.

Finishes to prevent the growth of microorganisms appear on fabrics for a wide variety of apparel, home-furnishing, commercial, and industrial products. Apparel items include socks, shoe linings, foundation garments, sportswear, and babies' clothing, especially diapers. Sheets, pillowcases, mattress padding and covering, carpet underpadding, carpeting, blankets, and towels are among the many items in the home that are treated. Fabrics for tents, tarpaulins, and auto convertible tops have a longer life when treated with finishes that reduce rot and mildew damage.

A number of research projects have proved the value of bacteriostatic finishes. A lower incidence of reinfection from athlete's foot was noted when shoe linings were treated. A reduction in diaper rash was evident in a group of babies who were clothed in treated diapers. Homemakers have remarked on the absence of musty odors that accompany mildew in hot, humid climates when floor coverings are protected with mildew-resistant finishes.

Renewable bacteriostatic finishes are recognized by such trademarks as Sanitone, Sanitized, and Dowicide. These can be reapplied by the consumer during care procedures.

Durable-Press and Minimum-Care Finishes

Wrinkle recovery is an expression used in technical literature to indicate the ability of a fabric to recover from folding deformation while the fabric is dry. *Crush resistance* is similar, but this term usually describes the recovery from crushing of a pile fabric. *Durable press* refers to the ability of a fabric to retain an attractive appearance during wear and to return to its original smooth surface and shape after laundering. These characteristics can be imparted to fabrics by finishing processes and by fiber choice. The following discussion is limited to finishes.

A recognized defect of cellulose fibers is their tendency to wrinkle badly during wear and maintenance. This results in unattractive products that require considerable ironing to restore a neat appearance. Before the 1920s the only method known to minimize wrinkling of cellulosic fiber fabrics was to apply starch, and this was only a temporary solution. In 1919 textile scientists made the first measurements of fabric creasing and recovery. In the following decade finishes to reduce wrinkling were developed and applied to cotton and linen. These early finishes had one undesirable side effect: they caused considerable loss of strength and fabric deterioration. Linen fabrics had strength to spare, and the finish made the fabric look so much better that the processing was accepted by consumers with little awareness that a strength loss had occurred. Cotton fabrics, on the other hand, did not stand up well under processing, and in 1948 less than 1 percent of all cotton was treated. The consumer, however, was impressed with the few examples and did not seem to realize that such fabrics were less durable.

The introduction of man-made thermoplastic fibers, which could be heat-set to build in optimum appearance values, made the easy-care concept a major goal of the textile industry. Manufacturers of cellulosic fiber fabrics, as well as the United States Department of Agriculture, expended considerable time and money in research to find techniques that would produce satisfactory easy-care products. Rapid strides were made during the 1950s, and in 1964 durable- or permanent-press fabrics were introduced to the consumer.

Early examples of durable press were not an unqualified success. They had low abrasion resistance and tearing strength and exhibited wear after very little use. Manufacturers then began to blend polyester fibers with the cellulosic fibers to produce truly durable-press fabrics. Blend fabrics are popular. The strong thermoplastic fibers offset any reduction in strength of the cellulose fibers, which makes it possible to construct lightweight as well as durable fabrics. Blends are comfortable and easy to care for, and, in general, they are the most common durable-press fabrics on today's market.

Despite their tremendous acceptance, these fabrics pose problems for the consumer. Precured fabrics are difficult to press into new shapes, and it is almost impossible to alter garments made from them. However, most people are so pleased with the easy-care properties that problems are overlooked.

Durable-press fabrics appear in all types of apparel and in a wide selection of home furnishings. Most of the fabrics composed of cellulosic fibers now incorporate polyester in a blend and have received a durable-press finish.

Fabrics with durable press can be laundered in washers and dried in dryers, and they require little or no ironing. Including fabric softeners in the final rinse may help to maintain a smooth surface and reduce static cling.

Flame Inhibitors

Finishes that reduce the flaming, charring, or afterglow of fibers and fabrics are important for safety. Most finishes in this group produce fabrics that *will* burn in the direct path of flame; they self-extinguish, however, when the source of flame is removed. A truly fireproof fabric will not burn even in the path of direct flame, but actually, only asbestos and fiberglass have this property. Finishes cannot provide completely safe products. They can, however, reduce the danger of complete destruction of the treated fabric (though they do not eliminate damage altogether) and provide a margin of safety that may prevent serious harm to individuals.

Flame inhibitors are not new. Their history can be traced back at least three hundred years. In 1821 J. L. Gay-Lussac produced some flame retardants for Louis XVIII of France. Versmann and Oppenheim did comparative studies of flame inhibitors in 1859 and found ammonium phosphate and tungsten salts to be effective. These substances are still used in renewable finishes. In 1922 Kling and Florentin studied borax and boric acid and arrived at a workable mixture of the two. Ramsbottom and Snoad tested the same compound in 1947. Renewable finishes applied in the home on cellulosic fibers still employ the two chemicals.

There are many recorded incidents of serious fires caused by the flash burning of brushed rayon negligees or sweaters ignited by cigarette ashes. More notorious were the group disasters—the Coconut Grove nightclub fire in Boston and the circus-tent fire in Hartford. As a result of these tragedies, the federal government enacted a bill to control the interstate sale of highly flammable fabrics. This legislation, passed in 1953, applied to all textile fabrics sold for use or contained in wearing apparel. In 1967 the law was amended to prohibit interstate commerce of articles of wearing apparel and fabrics that are so highly flammable as to be danger-ous. The definitions now include fabrics that may *reasonably be expected* to be used in wearing apparel or interior furnishings. The legislation also established guidelines for identifying situations where fabrics must meet rigid safety standards, as well as special test procedures for fabrics, and regulations for their sale. Specific controls were established for carpetings, mattresses, and children's sleepwear, sizes 0 to 6x. Since then, the federal law has been further amended to cover all children's sleepwear, sizes 0 to 6x and 7 to 14, and some states are now considering legislation that will control the entire range of children's clothes, sizes 0 to 14, and the fabrics sold for making them.

Flame-resistant finishes are of two general types. One group is water soluble and must be replaced after each laundering or, in many cases, dry cleaning. The second group is considered durable. The latter will with-stand dry cleaning, laundering, and weather. However, the durability of these finishes is quite variable, so it is important to study the label detailing what they will withstand and their approximate life. Finishes on children's sleepwear, for example, are required to withstand fifty launder-ings.

The consumer should be aware also of the fact that some detergents may adversely affect some finishes; thus, selection of the proper detergent is critical in maintaining their effectiveness.

The finish should be linked or bound to the fibers in such a way that it will release flame-retardant chemicals at the time flaming temperatures are reached. It is essential that the release does not occur under ordinary conditions. Improperly applied finishes or improperly chosen chemicals can result in fabric degradation. The most desirable finishes do not change the hand or appearance of the fabric. In practice, however, many finishes used to inhibit flaming do affect certain colors and tend to produce harsh and somewhat stiff fabrics. Where safety is important, these side effects are overlooked.

Flame-retardant finishes are classified in one of the following groups: (1) water-soluble compounds that must be reapplied after exposure to moisture such as laundering; (2) insoluble salts applied by dissolving in a suitable solvent; (3) oils, waxes, or resins that incorporate chlorinated substances, bromines, or other flame retardants; (4) substances that react with the fiber to produce molecular change to create flame resistance.

Not all types of finishes are suitable for all fabrics. The selection of finish for the particular fiber and fabric is determined by such factors as planned end-use, appearance, hand, and, to some degree, normal care for the product.

The individual who wishes to treat fabrics at home can apply a rinse of borax and boric acid (2 quarts of water, 7 ounces of borax, and 3 ounces of boric acid). Other finish formulas can be obtained by requesting USDA Bulletin L454 from the Superintendent of Documents, Washington, D.C.

Flame inhibitors are sometimes applied in conjunction with other finishes, such as water repellents and durable press. Trade names of flame inhibitors include Banfire, CM Flame Retardant, Fi-Retard, Firegard, Firemaster, Pyropel, Pyroset, Pyrovatex, and X-12.

The application of fire-retardant finishes usually increases the cost of textiles, so the consumer must decide whether the finish is important enough to warrant the extra expense. There are other problems with flame inhibitors that the consumer should be aware of. During a fire some melting may occur, which is a hazard in itself. In addition, the fumes from charring may be toxic. The finish on the fabric can also cause an allergic reaction in some individuals.

While finishes are supposed to withstand fifty launderings, many detergents reduce the finish performance after fifteen to twenty washings; soap reacts negatively in three to five washings. Recent research has shown that phosphate detergents are the most effective in cleaning flame-resistant fabrics while retaining the effectiveness of the finish. Citrate detergents can be employed without damage to the finish, and nonionic detergents,

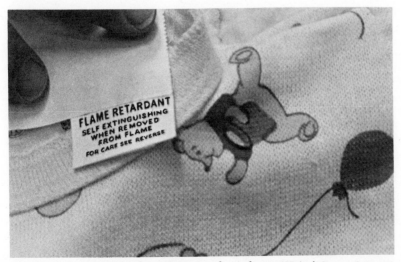

Figure 26.13 Flame-retardant sleepwear for infants. (*United States Consumer Product Safety Commission*)

available in some areas as heavy-duty liquids, are safe also. But the following products must never be used in the care of flame-resistant fabrics: soap, because it coats the finish and increases the flammability of the fabric; chlorine bleaches, because they destroy the finish; and fabric softeners, which create a coating that burns readily.

Before laundering or otherwise caring for flame-resistant items, the consumer should read carefully any information on the labels attached to the product as well as the instructions on the detergent package.

Fume-Fading Resistant Finishes

Certain dyestuffs on particular fibers are subject to color loss or change by atmospheric fumes. These gases in the atmosphere are oxides of nitrogen compounds and prevail in areas where gas for heating is improperly vented, and where incomplete combustion of fuels produces by-products other than water vapor and carbon dioxide. One of the conditions where irritants are present is smog. Dyes applied to acetate fibers are particularly susceptible to fume fading, and the same dye-stuffs may cause problems on nylon or polyester fabrics.

A major step in efforts to reduce color breakdown was taken when pigments were introduced into the solution of the fiber polymer before extrusion. Unfortunately, not all fabrics subject to fume fading can be dyed economically by solution coloration. For items colored after the yarns or fabrics have been made, finishes can be added to reduce or prevent fume damage. Simple alkaline substances, such as borax, may be used, but these are not permanent and require renewing after laundering. Trademarks for finishes that reduce or eliminate fume fading include Antifume, Crestofume, Emkafume, Permafume, and Protex.

The consumer should be aware that the most durable colors for acetate are applied to the solution and are identified as solution- or dope-dyed. Chromspun and Celaperm are the trade names of two such products. Both fumes and pollution may affect the color of nylon and of the newer nylon variants somewhat. Polyesters are less susceptible to fume fading, but they may be subject to fading in areas of excess pollution.

Metallic and Plastic Coatings

In an effort to produce fabrics that reflect heat, fabric converters have developed a finish in which aluminum coating can increase warmth or coolness, depending upon the situation. An important use of aluminum-coated fabrics has been for lining coats or jackets. It was originally hoped that the metallic finish would help retain body heat and reflect heat lost from the body by radiation. However, several research studies have determined that these finishes are not effective and do not keep the body warm. The insulative value is related to fabric construction rather than finish and to a psychological feeling of protection.

A popular use for reflective fabrics is in drapery linings. The fabric helps maintain a constant room temperature: it reflects sunlight in summer and retains heat in winter. It is especially helpful when entire walls of glass have these drapery covers.

Aluminum finishes with adhesives that resist solvents will dry clean fairly well, but others are lost during cleaning. In general, they have low resistance to washing. A metallic coating will not compensate for inferior fabric construction nor will it make a loose-weave fabric really warmer.

Plastic coatings decrease heat loss by reducing air circulation. Fabrics coated with a plastic (similar to coated fabrics like oilcloth) are used as drapery linings. They not only help prevent temperature change but reduce the amount of soil that can penetrate the draperies. In garment manufacturing, imitation leather fabrics made by applying a coating of plastic to a fabric base have been successful. Because they have low air permeability, they resist wind penetration. Therefore, the fabrics will be warmer on a windy day than a fabric without the plastic coating that is comparable in weight and thickness. Some plastic-coated fabrics tend to stiffen at low temperatures and may become uncomfortable to wear. It is difficult to identify fabrics that will become stiff. This information should be supplied by the manufacturer.

Mothproofing Finishes

Fibers containing protein, such as wool and silk, are especially susceptible to damage by moths and carpet beetles. The protein keratin, which is found in wool and other hair fibers, is believed to be what the moths prefer, and this explains why they will eat hair fibers containing it rather than the fibroin of silk. Carpet beetles, however, are likely to eat all protein substances including keratin and fibroin.

Fibers other than the protein type may be damaged by insects trying to escape confinement and reach desirable food. The same situation arises when other fibers are blended with protein fibers. For example, a blend of acrylic and wool may show damage to the acrylic, which was inflicted by the moth larvae when it consumed the wool fibers. Wool is the most susceptible and most frequently damaged fiber. Recent United States Department of Agriculture figures indicate that damage to wool and other protein fibers by moths and carpet beetles results in an annual loss valued between $200 million and $500 million.

While consumers may blame the holes they find in wool or wool blends upon the "clothes moth," the damage may have been caused by any one of thirteen species of moths and carpet beetles. The term "moth" will be used here to indicate the entire group. The larva of the moth is the culprit in fiber damage. During the eating period the larva increases its weight approximately three hundred times.

Finishes to reduce or prevent damage by moths can be renewable or durable. The substances may be effective because

1. They give off an odor that repels the mature moth and prevents the deposit of eggs. Naphthalene crystals or moth balls are examples. These are comparatively unsuccessful in preventing damage. They do

not last for any great length of time, nor do they destroy any eggs that might have been deposited before the crystals were used.

2. The agent gives off a gas (which may or may not be noticeable to human beings) that is toxic to the mature moth and the destructive larvae.

Products such as Crestocide, Hartocide, Mitin, Neocide, and Repel-o-Tac are usually added to the fiber during dyeing or fulling operations. These are considered durable. Most mothproof agents that have fluorine as the active ingredient are water soluble; any exposure to water will remove the finish, and it will have to be renewed. Larvex and Eulan are in this latter category.

Good practices in the care of silk, wool, wool-blend or other hair fiber fabrics should be observed by the consumer regardless of mothproofing finishes present. Soiled fabrics should never be stored, for they are highly subject to attack by larvae. Closets should be kept clean, and spraying of the closet is an extra precaution. Carpets must also be kept clean.

Stabilization Finishes

A question frequently asked by the consumer when purchasing a textile item is, "Will it shrink?" The problem of fabric shrinkage is not new, and some solutions were developed years ago. However, before the 1930s fabric shrinkage was generally left to the consumers, who would preshrink the fabric themselves or buy garments large enough so that they would fit after laundering. Stabilization also controls stretch, for a fabric may shrink in one direction and stretch in the other.

Fabric converters and processors recognize two distinct types of shrinkage: relaxation or residual shrinkage and felting shrinkage. *Residual shrinkage* is relaxation shrinkage remaining in the fabric when it is purchased. *Relaxation shrinkage* occurs when some factor causes a release of stress imposed during fabric manufacturing and finishing. *Felting shrinkage* is caused by certain fiber characteristics and may continue over a long period of time.

Relaxation shrinkage is rather complex. It is the most common type and occurs when some operation such as laundering releases the tensions imposed during fabric manufacture, so the yarns return to their original length. This type of shrinkage is sometimes progressive, in that all the potential shrinkage may not take place during the first laundering. The delay may be caused by the presence of various finishing agents, and, as they are gradually removed, the additional relaxation shrinkage occurs. Dry cleaning can also cause relaxation shrinkage, especially if a wet cleaning process is used.

A second problem with relaxation shrinkage is that, while shrinkage occurs during laundering, ironing will often restretch or strain the fabric. This may continue for the life of the garment, so the size will vary with each laundering period.

Some fabrics shrink or stretch with changes in humidity. This is a fiber property, but it is reflected in the fabrics. It occurs when a fiber is more easily stretched or elongated when humidity is high, and the weight of the fabric causes some fibers to extend. As humidity decreases, the fiber returns to position. This type of shrinkage is visible in some drapery fabrics, where an actual variation in length can be noticed on damp and dry days. The chain weighting in draperies increases the effect.

Fabrics occasionally exhibit shrinkage in one direction and stretch in the other. This occurs when the fabric has been held under high tension during the drying period following other finishing processes.

Nearly all fabrics containing natural fibers and many fabrics of man-made fibers exhibit relaxation shrinkage. The amount will vary, but if left uncontrolled it will result in unsatisfactory products.

Residual shrinkage occurs over a long period of time. It can be the result of changes in yarn or fiber shape stemming from the laundering process, other care procedures including storage, or environmental conditions.

Felting shrinkage is primarily a characteristic of hair fibers. It occurs when fibers entangle as a result of heat, moisture, and pressure. Consumers most often confront this condition in wool products.

The techniques employed to control shrinkage vary with fiber content. In recent years fabric stabilization has been included with other finishes, such as wrinkle resistance and water repellency. Durable-press finishes also help to control fabric dimensions. The use of fiber blends tends to increase fabric stability, but it does not ensure it.

The primary methods for eliminating residual or relaxation shrinkage in cotton and linen fabrics are mechanical. The simple method, frequently employed by the consumer as well as the fabric converter, is to wet the fabric thoroughly, dry it in a tensionless state—as in a dryer—then smooth it out by calendering or ironing. A second method involves feeding the cloth into the tenter frame in a slack condition and applying stretch to the filling. This is not as desirable, since the fabric will frequently return to its original size upon exposure to moisture.

The third method is the most common and will produce fabrics that have less than 1- to 2-percent shrinkage. This system is called *compressive shrinkage.* Fabric is fed over a feed roll that stretches the surface and then under a heated drum, where the stretch surface is compressed as it is dried. Fabrics carrying trade names such as Sanforized and Rigmel are examples of compressive shrinkage (Fig. 26.14).

Rayon fabrics are highly subject to shrinkage. The method most frequently used for controlling this shrinkage has been resin impregnation to produce a finish such as durable press. The technique forms the resin within the fiber, not on the surface.

One of the most successful methods to control shrinkage of fabrics —including rayon, cotton, and linen—is to blend man-made fibers with cellulosic fibers. Polyester or nylon fibers are particularly effective in contributing shrinkage control if they are sufficiently plentiful in the

Figure 26.14 Compressive shrinkage equipment. (*Springs Mills*)

blend and if the fabrics have been properly heat-set during finishing. Even then, however, it is still possible for shrinkage to occur. Therefore, if label information does not indicate either the probable amount of shrinkage or the fact that shrinkage is controlled, the consumer would be wise to consider an alternative purchase, unless shrinkage is not important in the end-use of the item.

Wool has always posed many problems in relation to shrinkage. In addition to relaxation shrinkage, wool also has a high degree of felting shrinkage. Current finishing procedures that have produced fabrics identified as washable wools do contribute to a reduction in dimensional change. But if no data are available to indicate that the wool product is washable, the consumer can expect the fabric to change size, since shrinkage during laundering is almost certain. Thus, these fabrics should be dry cleaned.

The advantages of shrink-resistant finishes are obvious. A product that shrinks or stretches and changes size results in poorly fitting, uncomfortable items and general discontent with the product.

Consumers should be cautioned about stabilization finishes, however. They often pose problems for home sewing in that it is difficult to shrink out fullness during construction. Loose weaves, in which yarns can be packed more closely, present no serious difficulty, but firmly woven fabrics may require pattern modification to obtain neat, even seams.

Fabrics of manufactured fibers that require heat-setting as a part of the normal finishing process will usually give good service—except for polyester knits, which tend to shrink considerably during the first and second laundering. Therefore, it is generally advisable to preshrink these fabrics before cutting a pattern. They should be laundered once or twice as well as dried in a dryer.

Despite the many advances in the finishing of fabrics, dimensional change is one of the most frequent causes of consumer dissatisfaction. Thus, consumers should be alert and request information concerning fabric performance during use and care.

Water-Repellent and Waterproof Finishes

Waterproof finishes are those that coat or seal a fabric so water does not pass through it. Such fabrics are nonpermeable to air, and, thus, are not comfortable in wearing apparel. Water-repellent finishes result in a fabric that *resists* wetting and is relatively porous.

Early methods used to produce waterproof fabrics coated the fabric with rubber, oxidized oil, or varnish. While they prevented water from passing through, most were heavy, bulky, and uncomfortable. Oiled silks were light in weight, but they were not so durable as rubber or varnish-coated fabrics. There are some plastic-coated waterproof fabrics on today's market, but because they are very heavy, the only apparel items they are found in is rainwear. This group does include the many imitation leather fabrics used so successfully as upholstery for furniture and automobiles.

Water-resistant or water-repellent finishes are popular in consumer goods, because the fabrics are comfortable and the finish does not alter the original appearance. At the present time there are durable, semidurable, and renewable water-repellent finishes on consumer goods. Durable finishes, such as Aquagard, Impregnole, Norane, Ranedare, Zepel, Scotchgard, and durable Cravanette will withstand considerable use and care. They will take laundering better than dry cleaning, but the latter process may be employed if the cleaner knows that the fabric has a durable water-repellent finish.

Semidurable finishes, including some types of Cravanette and Durane, will withstand several launderings but not dry cleaning. However, a dry cleaner can renew this type of finish easily enough. It is essential that the consumer be informed of the type of finish on the product, so proper cleaning methods can be used.

Renewable water-repellent finishes are designed for one-time use. They are removed during laundering and dry cleaning but can be renewed, as the name implies. Water-repellent finishes such as Scotchgard also come in spray cans and may be applied by the consumer. If the directions are followed carefully, the result is quite effective.

Stain- and Soil-Resistant Finishes

Removal of stains from fabrics has been, and is, a constant problem for consumers, so finishes that reduce staining and soiling are always welcome. These finishes reduce the rate of soil deposition on fabrics and help prevent spot staining—a real aid to the consumer. In this category, Zepel and Scotchgard are the names most frequently encountered.

Although the presence of these finishes delays the penetration of stains and soil into fabrics, it is important to remove them as quickly as possible to prevent their setting. Once soil or stains have become embedded, they are nearly impossible to remove. Frequent cleaning will maintain the finishes of these products.

Soil-Release Finishes

With the proliferation of synthetic fibers and durable-press finishes, the difficulty of removing soil has increased. In an effort to alleviate the problem, manufacturers have incorporated soil-release properties with durable-press finishes or have supplied soil-release alone. These finishes operate on one of two principles: they provide a hydrophilic surface that attracts the water and permits it to lift off soil, or they coat the fibers so the soil never penetrates.

Many soil-release finishes are nearly identical to soil-repellent finishes. They often provide several side benefits, such as preventing soil redeposition, introducing anti-static qualities, and improving the softness and

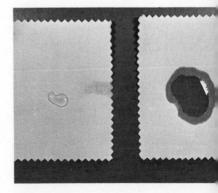

Figure 26.15 Fabric with stain-resistant finish (left) and same fabric without finish (right). Finish causes stain to "bead up" and roll off.

hand of fabrics. Trade names for the better-known processes include Dual-action Scotchgard, Fybrite, Visa, Cirrasol, and X-it.

A growing trend in finishing techniques is to incorporate several finishes into one fabric. Functional characteristics such as durable press, soil release, water repellency, softening, and fire retardancy are now often built into fabrics by means of chemical finishing processes.

Evaluation of Finishes 27

Finishes add many desirable qualities to a fabric. Unfortunately, they also add to the cost of production, and this increase is passed on to the consumer. In some instances, properties such as durability or the requirements for care may be affected, but, in general, the advantages far outweigh the disadvantages.

Standard test procedures for evaluating durability, performance, and maintenance of finishes are prepared by several organizations. They include test methods for qualitative and quantitative analysis of selected finishes and a number of tests for determining specific fabric properties that are the result of finishing materials.

Organizations involved in testing and test development include the American Society for Testing and Materials (ASTM), the American Association of Textile Chemists and Colorists (AATCC), and the American National Standards Institute (ANSI). The Federal Specifications Test Methods CCC-t-1916 from the federal government include procedures to

above left: Figure 27.1 Conditioning room in a quality-control testing laboratory. (*J. C. Penney Company, Inc.*)

above right: Figure 27.2 Testing for abrasion resistance. (*J. C. Penney Company, Inc.*)

left: Figure 27.3 Testing for strength and elongation of fabrics. (*J. C. Penney Company, Inc.*)

test fabrics for various performance characteristics to determine if they meet specifications established for government purchases.

Examples of selected test instruments used in evaluating fabric and finish performance are illustrated in Figures 27.1–27.3.

The average consumer does not have access to testing equipment used for laboratory analysis. However, many simple procedures can be followed in the home to provide helpful information about fabric finishes. Before identifying these tests, it is necessary to emphasize several points:

1. At no time should a consumer or student who uses home tests substitute results from those tests for regular tests completed by research and development laboratories.
2. The tests give limited information about fabric and finish behavior. However, the consumer may gain valuable insight into care problems, so that he can more readily formulate procedures for maintaining fabric appearance and behavior.

Home Tests for Fabric Properties

Dimensional Stability (Shrinkage or Stretch)

The possibility of shrinkage or stretch in a fabric is very important to the consumer. Even if a maximum percent is stated on the label, consumers may wish to verify this. It may be interesting to see if this technique results in more or less shrinkage or stretch than cited on labels.

Test #1   If a 12-inch sample can be obtained,

1. Mark a 10-inch square on the sample, with the warp clearly identified.
2. Launder the sample with a regular wash load.
3. Dry and press, then measure to determine the shrinkage or stretch.

If the consumer is interested in learning the effect of a dryer upon dimensional stability of the fabric, two samples can be prepared. One will be laundered and air dried, and the second sample will be laundered and dryer dried. The percent of change in dimension can be calculated by the following formula:

$$\% \text{ stretch or shrinkage} = \left(\frac{\substack{\text{original} \qquad \text{final} \\ \text{measurement} - \text{measurement}}}{\text{original measurement}} \right) \times 100.$$

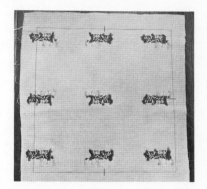

Figure 27.4 Fabric sample marked for determination of dimensional change, shrinkage, or stretch.

Determine change in warp and filling of woven fabrics and in lengthwise and crosswise dimensions of other fabric structures. A shrinkage or stretch of more than 3 percent is said to cause a full size change in wearing apparel. A 2-percent shrinkage or stretch is usually considered a maximum for consumer satisfaction.

If there is inadequate material available, a consumer can obtain some idea of potential fabric shrinkage or stretch with method #2.

Test #2

1. Trim a sample so the cut edges are parallel to lengthwise and crosswise structural lines of the fabric. Clearly identify the lengthwise dimen-

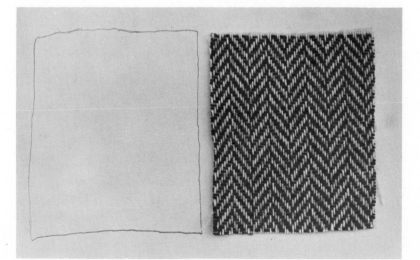

Figure 27.5 Small sample to test for shrinkage by comparison with marked outline of original before laundering.

sion. For practical results the scrap of fabric should be approximately 4 to 5 inches square.

2. Place the test sample on paper and draw around it so there is a clear record of the original sample.
3. Wash the sample by hand (or in a washing machine if secured in a laundry bag) using recommended detergent and water temperature.
4. Rinse, dry, press if needed, and compare with the original size.

This method does not provide for change in size caused by raveling, and a fabric in which raveling of yarns does occur will give misleading results. This might be controlled to a degree by edge stitching the sample before the test.

Dimensional Stability to Dry Cleaning

Shrinkage in dry cleaning is usually caused by water added to the cleaning solvent to remove water-borne soil and stains, by agitation in the presence of water, or by steam pressing. The consumer can obtain some idea of the potential shrinkage of a fabric in cleaning by subjecting a marked sample to the following steps:

1. Wet the sample in water and remove all excess moisture.
2. Place the sample in cleaning solvent and agitate frequently by stirring, shaking, or rubbing. Continue this procedure for 8 to 10 minutes.
3. Remove from the solvent, squeeze out excess fluid, and dry.
4. Measure the percent of shrinkage or stretch.

It is important that anyone using cleaning solvents in a test observe all necessary precautions.

The consumer can also note the degree of retention of such finishes as glazing and embossing. Subjective observation after laundering or soaking in cleaning solvents will give an idea of the durability of appearance finishes.

Durable Press

Test samples similar to those described for dimensional stability tests can be used to evaluate the quality of durable-press finishes.

1. Launder the sample according to recommended procedures.
2. Dry.
3. Evaluate by visual inspection, before pressing, to determine the need, if any, for touch-up ironing.

Unless standard test equipment is available, this method of evaluation is completely subjective. However, since the final decision on ironing is

Figure 27.6 Testing durable press finishes for appearance. (*Springs Mills*)

made by the consumer, the information gained by this home test can be helpful in the care of the finished garment.

Water Repellency

With a clothes sprinkler or eye dropper, drop or shake water onto fabric that has been placed on a smooth surface or in an embroidery hoop and held at a 45-degree angle. If the water forms tiny beads and rolls off without penetrating, the fabric is considered water repellent.

Oil Repellency

Place a drop of salad oil on a scrap of fabric. If the drop of oil forms a bead and can be removed easily with a blotter or a piece of absorbent tissue leaving no stain, the fabric has repellency to oil-borne stains and oily liquids.

Flame Resistance

1. Hold a small piece of fabric in a pair of tongs.
2. Place a lighted match, candle, or burner at the lower edge until the fabric appears to flame. Time this step.
3. Remove the source of flame, and observe the behavior of the fabric. Time the movement of flame from one end to the opposite end of the sample.

Figure 27.7 Testing for flame resistance. (*Springs Mills*)

If the flame extinguishes itself, the fabric is flame resistant to some degree. The time involved in any flaming of the fabric is another important gauge. It is essential to observe extreme caution in doing this test to prevent damage to person and property.

As with the other methods, this cannot be considered in any way as the equivalent of standard tests. However, it will provide a cursory idea of potential flammability.

Summary

Some finishes are destroyed by the first laundering or dry cleaning; others last for more than fifty washings or cleanings. When purchasing fabrics with various finishes, the consumer should make careful note of labeling information and observe any recommended care procedures. The purchase of any textile fabric or product is a matter of personal choice and decision-making, but to be an intelligent consumer, one must know how to evaluate a product.

The testing techniques given in this chapter require fabric scraps. They are, therefore, impossible to use on ready-made articles. For these the consumer must depend entirely on available label information. If such data are meager, consumers will find out the hard way—generally after the first laundering—that a product is unsatisfactory.

When merchandise is defective, it should be returned and the manufacturer notified. Reliable manufacturers want to know about problems involving their products; otherwise, they cannot begin to solve them. Comments or reports from consumers are important in the development of quality merchandise.

Stretch Fabrics 28

The concept of stretch originated in 1589, when the first knitted fabrics were introduced. Since that time knits have been prized for their comfort and appearance, and many other methods of imparting stretch to fabric have been attempted. In the early 1960s textile manufacturers began using the principle in new and dramatic ways, and the stretch revolution was launched.

The word *stretch* has now acquired a more specific meaning. In modern terminology, a true stretch fabric has the ability to extend or stretch under tension, *plus* the equally important capacity to return to its original size after release of strain. The degree of potential stretch, sometimes referred to as *elongation,* varies from as little as 5 percent to as much as 500 percent. Most fabrics fall within either the 10- to 25-percent category or the 30- to 50-percent range. In stretch fabrics this amount of elongation occurs at low amounts of pull or stress. Suggested standards from various testing organizations specify a load of 4 pounds per 2-inch-wide strip or 2 pounds per 1-inch-wide strip as the force to be used in determining the percent of stretch. It is generally held that any test

 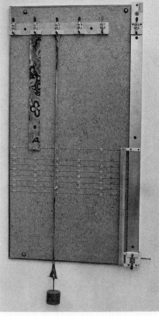

Figure 28.1 Samples in static tension tester ready for testing.

Figure 28.2 Sample with weight to measure stretch.

specimen that fails to stretch 20 percent or more under the load or pull applied should not be called a stretch fabric.

Stretch fabrics are classified into two categories: comfort stretch and power stretch. *Comfort stretch* describes stretch fabrics that go into clothing for everyday use with a stretch factor of up to 30 percent. It can also apply to fabrics for home furnishing. *Power stretch* or *action stretch* describes stretch fabrics that have more snap and muscle power, more extensibility, and quick recovery. The stretch factor generally ranges from 30 to 50 percent and is best adapted to ski wear, foundation garments, swimwear, athletic clothing, and the more professional types of active sportswear.

There is a nebulous area between these types where the amount of stretch may reach 40 percent and still provide comfort, or a viable action stretch may extend slightly below 30 percent. In general, however, comfort stretch is designed for use under low loads such as 2 pounds per inch, while power stretch usually is designed for higher loads.

Stretch fabrics as a group defy classification. The property of stretch can, under certain conditions, be introduced at any stage of fabric manufacture. For convenience, the following discussion has been divided into four categories:

1. fiber stretch—elastomeric fibers and fiber modification
2. yarn stretch—including heat setting and other techniques
3. fabric stretch—knitting and similar processes

4. finishing stretch—the application of special finishes to impart stretch after the fabric has been completed

Fiber Stretch

Stretch has been produced through the use of elastomeric rubber fibers since about 1920. Fine filaments of rubber were covered with cotton, rayon, or silk, and then woven, knitted, or braided into fabrics with combinations of other yarns. Narrow elastic fabric is a good example of one type of construction. Rubber core yarns were early examples of elasticity and stretch. These yarns are still used in such items as elastic banding, elastic bandages, and some yard goods. However, spandex fibers have now replaced rubber in a large percentage of fabric construction.

Spandex, described fully in Chapter 14, owes its stretchability to its chemical molecular configuration, not to a mechanically imparted property. Spandex fibers can be used in several ways in stretch fabrics. Uncovered or bare, spandex filaments are combined with other fibers, staple or filament. These power stretch fabrics appear in items such as foundation garments, swimsuits, and surgical hose. In small amounts, bare spandex may be included in fabrics for comfort stretch, but the trend in these fabrics is to core-spun yarns.

Core-spinning is a procedure by which an elastic spandex filament is fed directly into the twisting zone of the spinning frame (Fig. 28.3). The tension under which the elastomeric filament is held is carefully controlled and predetermined in relation to the end-use of the fabric. The resulting yarn has variable degrees of stretch, depending upon manufacturing controls. Spandex filament forms the core of the yarn and is surrounded by staple fibers of one or more types, which provide a flexible outer sheath. Core-spun yarns have two significant advantages. Only 3 to 10 percent spandex is required to produce a high-quality stretch yarn. Furthermore, the percent of stretch can be controlled from as little as 3 percent to as much as 200 percent. Most core-spun yarns take on the hand and appearance of the fibers that form the outer sheath. Thus, depending upon the fiber used as covering, the fabric may have good moisture absorbency or it may be resistant to moisture; it may be comfortable or harsh and stiff. The care of core-spun yarns is, basically, the same as that required of the covering fibers. However, the presence of spandex, even in small amounts, makes it advisable to know those procedures that will prolong the life of the product.

Spandex yarns are also employed in *intimate-blend spinning*. At present, the technique is still relatively new and experimental, but it shows promise of excellent success. This procedure involves the cutting of spandex into staple lengths to match the length of one or more types of rigid fibers. These are spun to produce a true blended yarn, with the amount of stretch dependent upon the amount of spandex fiber used. It has been suggested that such blends be formulated at the fiber-producer level and then sold to the yarn and fabric manufacturer.

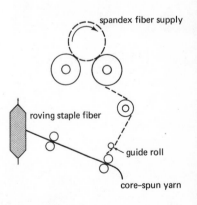

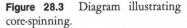

Figure 28.3 Diagram illustrating core-spinning.

Figure 28.4 Sheer support panty-hose; Monvelle nylon/spandex blend. (*Monsanto Company*)

Stretch through modification of fiber structure is also relatively new. Probably the best-known product of this type on the consumer market is Cantrece nylon. This fiber is found in women's hosiery and in certain other apparel items. Cantrece is a bicomponent nylon and is discussed in Chapter 10. Other bicomponent nylons and modified polyesters exist that may impart some stretch because of the fiber structure.

Bicomponent stretch occurs when the filaments are subjected to processing: one component shrinks and causes the other component to coil. The resulting filaments and yarns have a high degree of coil and, as a result, of stretch. The stretch will vary according to the amount of coiling and natural "give" in the fibers.

Yarn Stretch

Of the techniques for producing stretch fabrics, heat-set stretch yarns are considered the original. The first stretch yarn of this type was developed by the Swiss firm of Heberlein and Company, A.G. The original goal was to impart a crimp to man-made fibers so that they would resemble wool. After initial work on viscose fibers, Heberlein adapted the process to nylon and developed the first nylon stretch yarns, which were introduced in 1947 as *Helanca*. This yarn is used in hosiery, leotards, and other figure conforming apparel.

The current techniques for producing stretch yarns by heat-setting include the false-twist method, the twist-heat-set-untwist method, and the knife-edge method. These are discussed in some detail in Chapter 19. Though the stuffer-box method is not generally known for its stretch-producing ability, some authorities include it in the list. Depending on the method employed, stretch can be obtained from either continuous filament or staple fibers.

Two methods similar to those used in producing stretch yarns from thermoplastic fibers were developed by the research laboratories of the United States Department of Agriculture and were called *back-twisting* and *crimping*.

In the back-twisting method cotton yarn is treated with cellulose cross-linking chemicals or resins similar to those used for durable press. The yarn is twisted, the twist is set by curing the finish, and then the yarn is untwisted and retwisted in the opposite direction. The resultant yarns are kinky and springy and have good stretch properties.

In making crimped cotton the cotton yarn is treated with one of several chemicals that react with the cellulose to form a cellulose ester or cellulose ether that is thermoplastic. The modified cotton is then processed by one of the methods employed with other thermoplastic fibers.

Stretch yarns made by the heat-set technique are satisfactory in both knitted and woven fabric construction. Cured yarns, also, can be used in both types of fabrics, but it should be remembered that these yarns are not yet proven in use and care.

Fabric Stretch

The most common method for introducing stretch in the fabric-construction stage is by knitting. Hand-knit fabrics have been popular since the 16th century, and the products of modern knitting machines are now equally sought after for every conceivable article of wearing apparel. Knits are discussed in Chapter 21.

Finishing Stretch

The process of imparting stretch to a fabric after it has been constructed is called variously *piece-goods stretch, mechanical stretch,* and *chemical stretch.* The first of these terms is probably the most convenient. The actual finishing procedure involves the use of chemicals and results in some molecular change, so, theoretically, the term "chemical" is appropriate. However, chemical change of the molecular structure of the fiber does not occur at all times. Instead, a physical or "mechanical" change takes place. On the other hand, due to the fact that chemicals are required to bring this change about, the word "mechanical" can be somewhat misleading. Thus of the three terms, *piece-goods stretch* appears to be the least confusing.

As this phrase indicates, stretch is introduced into the fabric after it has been woven. Cotton, cotton blend, and some wool fabrics are treated in this manner. The procedure used on cotton and cotton blends is called *slack mercerization.*

Slack mercerization utilizes the same principles as those applied in standard mercerization, except that the fabric is not held under tension; hence the term *slack*. For horizontal or "filling" stretch, the fabric is held under lengthwise tension; or it may be processed completely slack, then restretched, and set for length at a later step in finishing. If both horizontal and longitudinal stretch are desired, the fabric is treated without tension and not restretched.

Production of stretch fabrics by slack mercerization requires carefully controlled conditions. Reliable manufacturers have tried to maintain quality in the goods they put on the market. Still, the durability of these fabrics is at present less than satisfactory. Stretch by slack mercerization works better when it is incorporated into a minimum-care finishing process, since the resins used in the latter also help maintain stretch. In general, however, consumers will get better stretch performance from elastomeric fibers such as spandex.

Stretch Fabrics in Use

Stretch can be produced in the horizontal or filling direction of fabrics, in the vertical or warp direction, or in both directions (two-way stretch). The latter is found primarily in action stretch, while horizontal or vertical stretch fabrics are common in comfort stretch items.

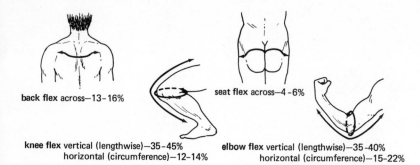

back flex across—13-16%

knee flex vertical (lengthwise)—35-45%
horizontal (circumference)—12-14%

seat flex across—4-6%

elbow flex vertical (lengthwise)—35-40%
horizontal (circumference)—15-22%

Figure 28.5 Measuring body stretch. (American Fabrics)

Considerable research has been conducted to determine how much stretch is required in fabrics and where and how it should be used. Studies to determine the amount of stretch required have been conducted by the DuPont Company and J. P. Stevens, Inc. Both studies analyzed how much the body's skin stretches in various locations. Results indicate that the elbow, when bent, flexes from 35 to 40 percent in the vertical or lengthwise direction and from 15 to 22 percent in the horizontal or circumference direction; the knee flex is 35 to 45 percent in the lengthwise direction and from 12 to 14 percent in the circumference; the hip area stretches 4 to 6 percent in the horizontal direction when seated and as much as 60 percent in the vertical direction; the amount of stretch across the shoulders is from 13 to 16 percent.

Further studies by the J. P. Stevens Company recommended that the following amounts of stretch be used:

Tailored clothing: 15 to 25 percent stretch; no more than 5 percent unrecovered stretch.

Spectator sportswear: 20 to 25 percent stretch; no more than 5 percent unrecovered stretch.

Form-fit garments: 30 to 40 percent stretch; no more than 5 percent unrecovered stretch.

Active skiwear: 33 to 50 percent stretch; no more than 6 percent unrecovered stretch.

The optimum percentages suggested by another writer are somewhat different:[1]

Vertical stretch pants: stretch potential of 40 to 60 percent with a "growth" of less than 6 percent.

Tailored clothing: stretch of 25 to 35 percent with a growth of less than 6 percent.

Sportswear and dresses: stretch of 25 to 40 percent with a growth of less than 5 percent.

Standards developed by the Good Housekeeping Institute for stretch fabrics that may bear their seal require at least 35 percent stretch for active sportswear, 25 percent stretch for casual apparel, and 20 percent stretch for tailored clothes.[2] According to these standards, it was also determined that

[1] Marylou Luther, "Stretchology," *McCall's Piece Goods* (Summer 1964), p. 76.
[2] *Good Housekeeping* (May 1965), p. 6.

left: Figure 28.6 Tailored travel suit with comfort stretch; a blend of Antron nylon and Lycra spandex. (*E. I. DuPont de Nemours & Company*)

right: Figure 28.7 Swimsuit with power stretch; a blend of DuPont nylon and Lycra spandex. (*E. I. DuPont de Nemours & Company*)

more than 2 percent growth, or unrecovered stretch, in any fabric or product is unacceptable.

Most stretch fabrics do not return completely to their original measurements after elongation. The difference between the original size and that measured after elongation is referred to as *growth* or *unrecovered stretch*. Some growth may be eliminated in laundering, but it frequently leads to permanent deformation. A growth or increase in size of $2\frac{1}{2}$ to 3 percent would result in an unattractive garment. The maximum growth of 2 percent would appear to be a good standard.

The problem of where and how stretch should be used has caused considerable controversy. It is now generally accepted that power stretch is desirable for foundation garments, swimwear, and other items where a high degree of figure shaping and holding ability are required. The amount of potential stretch should be high, but the garment should stretch only under great force.

Comfort stretch garments should be sized in the same way as "rigid" fabric garments and should be purchased under regular size guidelines. Stretch is not meant to take the place of proper garment sizing; it is merely an added factor that puts comfort into movement.

Consumers need to understand the qualities of stretch in a product, and they must learn to decide when and whether these properties are of sufficient value to justify any added costs. In purchasing stretch products, the consumer must also learn to read manufacturer's labels regarding

Figure 28.8 Furniture covered with stretch fabric. (*Turner, Ltd.*)

proper care of the product. The type of stretch, fiber content, and finishes or explicit directions for care should be indicated on labels. Some stretch needs careful handling, while other kinds respond well to machine laundering and drying. Products without labels should be avoided.

Stretch products should always be selected on the basis of the need for and the value of this property in end use, and the care required should also be considered. Stretch items should provide the following qualities:

- comfort
- good fit
- shape retention
- design flexibility
- psychological appeal
- wrinkle resistance
- appearance appeal
- longer wear
- reduced seam puckering

In addition to apparel, stretch has considerable value in home-furnishing fabrics for such items as fitted sheets and slipcovers. It is also important in medical aids—bandages, special support items, and therapeutic devices.

Dyestuffs and Their Application 29

The importance of color in textile products cannot be overemphasized. Color speaks louder than words. Its appeal is universal, and it repeatedly serves as a common language. In the modern marketplace, consumers are usually more concerned with selecting the "just right" color than they are with other factors.

The textile industry is well aware of the consumer's desire for color. Manufacturers know that the consumer who selected an item because of its color will be extremely annoyed if the color is not maintained. Consequently, research by dyestuff manufacturers has produced coloring agents that will satisfy the aesthetic desires of consumers and meet their demands for durability if the color is properly applied. However, it is important to remember that the manufacturers cannot do the actual maintenance of the products. It is their responsibility to provide care instructions, but it is the responsibility of the consumer to follow those instructions.

Historical Review

Dyestuffs and dyeing are as old as textiles themselves and predate written history. Fabrics dating from 3500 B.C. have been found in Thebes that still possess the remains of blue indigo dye. Other fabrics, discovered in the ancient tombs of Egypt, were colored yellow with dye obtained from the safflower plant. Beautifully colored fabrics dating back several thousand years have been unearthed in China, Asia Minor, and some sections of Europe.

Prior to A.D. 1856 all dyestuffs were made from natural materials, mainly animal and vegetable matter. A bright red was obtained from a tiny insect native to Mexico. This insect was used by the Aztecs to color their fabrics, and when the Spaniards invaded Mexico in 1518, they called the insect and the dyestuff *cochineal*. A tiny mollusk found on the Phoenician coast near the city of Tyre produces a beautiful purple color. By 1500 B.C. Tyre became the center for the trading and manufacture of this purple dye. Some historians believe this was the first example of a "city" industry. The dye was tremendously expensive to produce because approximately 12,000 of these tiny shellfish were needed to obtain a single gram of dye. Thus, the expressions "royal purple" or "born to the purple" came into being as an indication that only the wealthy could afford the dye. Other ancient dyes included madder, a red dye from the roots of a

Figure 29.1 Woodcut from *The Plictho: Instructions in the art of the dyers . . .*, by Gioanventura Rosetti, 1548. (*Universität Bibliothek, Göttingen, West Germany*)

plant; blue indigo from the leaves of a plant; yellow from the stigmata of a plant; and logwood from the pulp of a tree.

Many of the early natural dyestuffs were prohibitively expensive. It is quite probable that the growth and development of the dye industry came about, in part, in an effort to find less costly methods and provide colorful fabrics for people of all economic levels.

Early efforts at coloring fabrics were hampered by the fact that few of the natural dyes formed colorfast combinations with fibers. Eventually, scientists found that this defect could be partially overcome by the use of *mordants*—compounds that render the dye insoluble on the fiber.

During the Dark Ages there was little advancement in fabric coloring, and most dyeing was done in the home. The beginning of the Italian Renaissance saw the art of dyeing revived, and the first books on the subject were published in Italy during the 15th century. Other books soon appeared in France, Germany, and England. Dyeing techniques were constantly being improved during the ensuing centuries, and written materials kept pace with these developments. Several interesting publications appeared in the United States during the late 18th and early 19th centuries. All these writings were devoted to the use of dyes from natural resources.

As long as people were dependent upon animals and vegetables for their dyestuffs, and on minerals for the mordanting agents, progress was limited by the skill of the operator in mixing the natural dyes and in perfecting the techniques used. As with many of nature's products, the quality of materials varied considerably, and, consequently, the results were rather unpredictable.

The year 1856 marked the turning point in the history of dyes. Sir William H. Perkin, while trying to make artificial quinine from coal tar, accidentally produced the first synthetic dyestuff—*mauve*. This discovery launched the modern dyestuff industry. Today, nearly all dyes are chemically compounded and, in most cases, are superior in every way to natural dyes.

Modern dye chemists are constantly challenged. Each new textile fiber requires either new dyestuffs or new methods of application. But the chemists have responded energetically and have met all industry demands successfully. They have produced a variety of interesting dyes with a good record of colorfastness.

The history of dyes is fascinating. Much of it is legend, and it is sometimes difficult to separate fact from fiction. The history in this text is necessarily brief. It has been included to provide insight into the chronicle of humanity's unceasing desire for a colorful life.

Seeing Color

Color is a visual sensation. It results from the reflectance of certain visible light rays that strike the retina and stimulate cells in the nerves of the eye. The nerves send a message to the brain, which in turn produces the sensation of a specific hue. Thus, we "see" color. When all the visible light rays are reflected, an object appears white; if none of the rays are reflected, it appears black. When one or more rays are reflected, the viewer senses the color produced by the specific reflected ray or combination of rays.

The purpose of a dye is to absorb light rays on a selective basis, causing the substrate (fabric) to reflect those rays that are not absorbed. In other words, if all the rays except those producing blue are absorbed, the viewer sees blue. The ability of an organic compound to create this desired color derives from the presence of chemical groups called *chromophores*. Substances that include chromophores in various arrangements will produce the sensation of different color hues.

While chromophores confer color upon a substance, the intensity or brilliance of the color depends on the presence of one or more chemical groups called *auxochromes*. The auxochrome also can give water solubility to the dye and provides the groups that form associative bonds with the fiber. Dyestuffs themselves or combinations of dyes and other additives contribute both chromophores and auxochromes.

The technical definition for a *dye* is a compound that can be fixed on a substance in a more or less permanent state and that evokes the visual sensation of a specific color.

Types of Dyes

Dyes can be classified in several ways: according to hue produced, according to chemical class, and according to the method of application and types of fibers to which they are successfully applied. The discussion in this section is designed to acquaint the consumer with dyes classified by method of application, and with the characteristics of these dyes on selected fibers, including their colorfastness properties.

Substantive or Direct Dyes

Substantive or direct dyes comprise the largest and most commercially significant group of dyestuffs. Direct dyes are water soluble; they are applied primarily to cellulosic fibers. When the dye is dissolved in water, a salt is added to control the absorption rate of the dye by the fiber. Then, either the fabric is immersed in the dye bath or it is covered with a paste. The amount of dye absorbed depends on two factors—the size of the dye molecule and the size of the pore opening in the fiber.

To improve the colorfastness of the dyes, finishing chemicals of various types may be added. Some of these will react chemically with dye to create a new insoluble compound; they are called *developed direct dyes*. There is a large market for direct dyes, because they are inexpensive, easy to apply, and producible in a wide range of colors. These dyes exhibit good colorfastness to sunlight, but unless they are treated with finishing chemicals or developed, their colorfastness to laundering is poor. The application of easy-care finishes has increased the colorfastness of direct dyes to some extent.

Direct dyes are used frequently for low- to medium-priced cellulosic fabrics. Their colorfastness to light makes them a good choice for drapery fabrics and other textiles that have to withstand extended exposure to light.

Azoic or Naphthol Dyes

Azoic dyes are employed for cellulosic fibers and to a limited extent for such manufactured fibers as nylon, acrylic, polyester, and polypropylene. These dyes produce color by an involved chemical action. They are sometimes called "ice" colors, because they are applied from a low-temperature bath.

Azoic dyestuffs produce brilliant and pastel colors at relatively low cost. They exhibit good colorfastness to laundering, bleaching, and light, so they often serve to color fabrics used for towels, sheets, pillowcases, and the like. The colors will withstand even the heaviest care procedures for soil and stain removal.

Acid Dyes

Acid dyes can be used on protein, acrylic, nylon, and certain modified polyester fibers, as well as on spandex and polypropylene fibers. The dyeing process involves a chemical reaction with the fiber molecules of an associative type—that is, the fibers attract the acid dye and an associative bond is established. Since the dyes are applied from an acid bath, their use on fibers subject to acid damage is not recommended. The colors achieved with these dyes range from very bright to light and dark.

Colorfastness properties of acid dyes vary widely. Some of these dyes fade very quickly in light, during care, or from perspiration. Labeling is of particular importance. Consumers should follow all care recommendations.

Cationic or Basic Dyes

Cationic dyes—often referred to as *basic dyes*—are among the oldest synthetic dyes. They are excellent for coloring acrylic fibers and are successful on modified nylons and polyesters. When properly selected for the right fibers, they produce brilliant colors and good colorfastness under most environmental and laundering conditions. The dyes are not colorfast on cellulosic or protein fibers. However, they occasionally serve as "topping" colors to increase the brilliance or brightness of a fabric.

Disperse Dyes

Disperse dyes, formerly called *acetate dyes,* were originally developed for acetate fibers. They are used now for coloring acetate, polyester, acrylic, and nylon fibers. Such dyes are dispersed, not dissolved, in the dyebath and attach themselves to the fiber. This quality of adherence to fibers differs widely, depending on the dye and the fiber. Thus, it is extremely important that the dyer match the proper dye with the proper fiber.

If disperse dyes are applied to polyester fibers at low temperatures, carriers are required to bring about penetration of the dye into the fiber. The combination of high temperatures with high pressure eliminates the need for carriers; the *thermosol* process reduces the need. Thermosoling involves padding the dye into the fabric and then setting it in a heat zone.

Colorfastness of disperse dyes to light, laundering, and dry cleaning is excellent. However, on acetate and some nylons, the dyes are subject to fume fading—a reaction to nitrogen oxide fumes found in the atmosphere in smoggy areas or in large areas where large quantities of gas are burned. To prevent this type of color loss either the fabric can be treated with special finishes or the dye can be mixed directly with the chemicals forming the fiber. Disperse dyes are frequently used with direct or vat dyes in the coloring of polyester and cellulose blends.

Pigment Colors

Technically, pigments are not dyes, but they are employed in coloring some fabrics, so it is essential to include them in this discussion. Pigment colors have no affinity for fibers. Thus, they are attached to fibers or fabrics by means of some type of adhesive, resin, or bonding agent. The resultant colors are relatively permanent, but their durability is directly related to the durability of the binding agent. As the latter wears away, the color will also disappear.

It is also possible to mix pigments thoroughly with the fiber solution, and thus the fiber is already colored as it is extruded. When pigment colors are added to the fiber solution or molten polymer, the terms *dope* or *solution dye* are used. Fibers colored in this manner exhibit good colorfastness.

Vat Dyes

The dyestuffs frequently publicized as having the best colorfastness are the vat dyes. In general, these dyes do exhibit excellent colorfastness, although their lightfastness can be inferior to other dyes such as pigments or reactives. Furthermore, the dyes in this category exhibit some variation in colorfastness because of differences in chemical structure. If the dyeing procedure is not carefully controlled, the color may fade quickly. Actually, the textile industry today is advanced enough to be able to create excellent colorfastness with dyes other than vat dyes.

Vat dyes were developed originally in Europe about 1910 and took their name from the large vats used for applying the dye to yarns or fabrics. Today vat dyes can be applied in vats or in continuous-feed methods. Vat dyes are insoluble in water unless chemically modified, but they will dissolve in an alkaline solution. It is their insolubility in water that makes vat dyes colorfast in all processes that do not utilize alkaline substances. Vat dyes are adaptable to all cellulose fibers and some of the newer man-made fibers, and they are available in a wide choice of colors.

Reactive Dyes

The first practical reactive dyes were introduced in 1956. These dyes actually react chemically with the fiber molecule, thus producing a high degree of colorfastness. While they are used primarily on cotton, some types adapt to rayon, nylon, acrylic, and protein fibers such as silk and wool.

Bright colors with excellent washfastness are available by means of reactive dyes, and lightfastness is good to excellent depending on the dye. One of the major problems of reactive dyes is their susceptibility to damage from chlorine. Generally, however, the consumer can expect satisfaction from these dyes as long as recommended care procedures are followed.

Application of Color

Color can be applied to textile products at various stages—to fibers (or the chemical solution for man-made fibers), yarns, or fabrics. The equipment necessary will vary widely depending on the physical form of the product.

Fiber Dye

Dyeing is often done to the raw fiber stock in large kiers that may operate at atmospheric or increased pressure. This provides the possibility of deep penetration of the dye into the fiber, which gives uniform color and a tendency to greater colorfastness. Some fiber dye processes are continuous.

left: Figure 29.2 Pressure dye unit.

right: Figure 29.3 Vat dyeing equipment.

Figure 29.4 Dye kier with fiber. (*Morton Machine Works, Inc.*)

The fiber stock is carried by a conveyor system through the dye bath and directly to the rinsing area.

Solution or Dope Dye

In the manufacture of man-made fibers, color can be added to the chemical solution before it is forced through the spinnerettes. If the pigment is good, this method ensures not only even dyeing but colors that are an integral part of the fiber and, therefore, fast to most outside influences. Solution or dope dyeing has been especially important in coloring man-made fibers that resist many standard dyestuffs or tend to fade easily when dyed by other techniques.

Yarn Dye

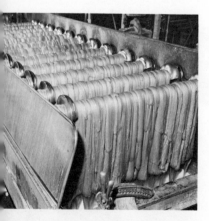

Figure 29.5 Yarn dyeing in skein form. (*Service Yarn Dyeing Corp.*)

One of the oldest systems of dyeing textiles is to color the yarns. Yarns can be dyed in a skein form, rolled on tubes (*package dyeing*), or rolled onto the warp beam (*beam dyeing*). In skein dyeing the yarn is moved through the dyebath while at the same time the dye is forced through the arms holding the skeins. Package dyeing involves placing many packages or tubes of yarn into a large vessel, whereupon the dye is forced through the yarn. Beam dyeing is similar to package dyeing except that large beams are placed in the dye vessel. (See Plates 4 and 5.)

Yarn dyeing provides good color absorption and adequate penetration. It permits the use of various colored yarns in one fabric and gives the fabric designer wide latitude in designing plaids, checks, stripes, muted color arrangements, and iridescent effects. In a variation of this process, called *space dyeing,* selected areas of the yarns are dyed different colors to produce pattern in the fabric. (See Plates 6 and 7.)

Piece Dye

Most solid-color fabrics are dyed after the fabric has been completed. This is the easiest and least expensive method for adding color. Fabrics can be dyed in a rope form or flat and under tension to maintain smoothness. Manufacturers can color fabrics as ordered and need not maintain a large stock of dyed fabrics that might become obsolete if the fashion changes. Piece dye does not always provide a thorough penetration of dyestuff, but for many uses it is quite satisfactory. Normally, piece-dyed fabrics are a single color. When a fabric contains more than one fiber, however, a pattern can result from the different absorption rates of the fibers. The most important variations are union-dye and cross-dye techniques. (See Plates 6, 8, 9, 10 and 11.)

Union Dyeing   The term *union dye* indicates that a fabric containing two or more fiber types has been dyed a single uniform color. Various dyestuffs are applicable only on certain fiber types, so when a fabric containing two or more types of fibers is to be colored a solid color, the dyes must be carefully selected and properly applied in order to ensure color uniformity. Dyes can be applied simultaneously to the fabric. However, in some cases the dyes must be introduced individually, each by its recommended procedure.

Cross Dyeing   Fabrics of two or more fiber types and two or more fiber variants of the same type can be dyed so that each fiber type accepts a different dyestuff and becomes a different color. Since the end product depends upon the fiber arrangement in the fabric, the designer must know dye technology. Checks, plaids, tweed effects, and stripes are just some of the design possibilities with this method. (See Plate 12.)

Polychromatic Dyeing   Polychromatic dyeing is a new technique that provides for pattern effects in an almost infinite variety. There are two basic techniques: the *flow-form* method and the *dye-weave* method. These differ mainly in the point at which the dye is actually applied.

The basic principle of the flow form consists of running streams of different colored dye solutions onto a moving fabric and then crossing these with other colors. The fabric may be moved horizontally and vertically as it goes through the machine, which increases the design potential. The pattern is fixed in place by the timing and padding of color. In other words, the timing, amount of color extruded onto the fabric, and fabric movement all determine the resulting pattern. (See Plate 13.)

In the dye weave process the patterns are developed by running streams of dye solution down an inclined plane onto the moving fabric. The dyes are fixed into the fabric by the method most appropriate to dye and fiber type. Here, too, the amount of dye and the movement of the fabric influence both color and design.

It is possible to make a completed product—for example, a dress—and then dye it. Some couture designers employ this technique, but it is not considered practical for general use by apparel manufacturers. If it is done, however, a procedure similar to piece dye is followed, with a paddle dye machine taking the place of the ordinary dye vessel. Other methods of dyeing, such as tie-dye and batik, are discussed in relation to applied design in the following chapter. (See Plate 14.)

above: **Plate 1** Fabric woven on a Jacquard loom. (*Springs Mills*)

right: **Plate 2** Double cloth.

below: **Plate 3** Pinsonic process to produce a quilted effect, a type of chemstitch.

left: **Plate 4** Package dyeing.

below: **Plate 5** Warp beam dyeing.

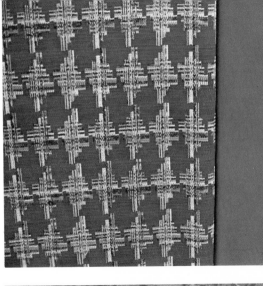

right: Plate 6 Coordinated yarn-dyed and piece-dyed fabrics.

below right: Plate 7 Yarn-dyed Jacquard fabric.

below: Plate 8 The equipment for jig dyeing, a variation of piece dyeing.

left: **Plate 9** Winch or dye beck for dyeing fabric.

below left: **Plate 10** Dyeing fabric in rope form.

below right: **Plate 11** Dyeing fabric in open-width flat form.

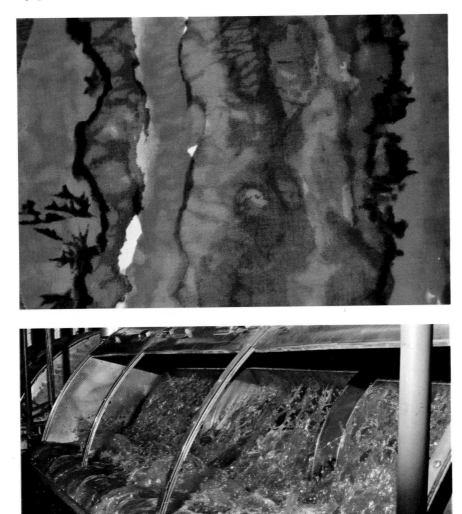

right: Plate 12 Cross-dyed fabric with two fiber variants of the same generic type.

below: Plate 13 Polychromatic dyed fabric.

bottom: Plate 14 Paddle dye equipment.

left: **Plate 15** Tritik; tie-dyed and discharge-dyed silk by Marian Clayden.

below: **Plate 16** Forcing dye through a silk screen to form part of the print pattern on fabric surface.

above: **Plate 17** Silk screen print design.

left: **Plate 18** Hand screen printing.

below: **Plate 19** Flat-bed screen printing. (*Allied Chemical*)

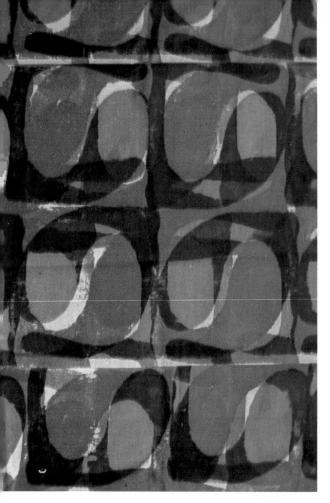

left: **Plate 20** Block printed fabric.

below: **Plate 21** Roller printing equipment.

Plate 22 Transfer printing. Left: paper before use; center: printed fabric; right: paper after printing.

Applied Design

Printed fabrics are defined as those that have been decorated by a motif, pattern, or design applied to the fabric after it has already been constructed. In general, printing refers to colored designs created by surface modifications through the application of dyes.

Printing

The art of printing color onto fabrics originated thousands of years ago—right after cloth fabrication itself. Primitive peoples decorated garments with paints as they did their bodies. However, since these colors were not "fixed," they were of temporary value. Pictures painted on the walls of some Egyptian tombs depict figures costumed in fabrics with printed motifs. Actual remnants of printed fabric found near Thebes have been dated about 1600 B.C.

   The oldest textile prints found in Europe date from about A.D. 600. In the Americas, examples of printed fabrics have been found in remains of the Inca civilization. However, it was during the latter part of the 16th century that textile printing attained general acceptance. Printing became

Figure 30.1 Painted linen textile fragment from Nazca, southern Peru, c. A.D. 300–500. (*Staatliche Museum für Völkerkunde, Munich*)

a fine art in France during the 18th century, when Christophe Phillipe Oberkampf opened his textile printing factory at Jouy and began production of the famous "Toiles de Jouy," considered by many to be the finest patterned fabrics in the world. Other quality printed fabrics were developed with individual decorating techniques by the peoples of India, Java, and Mexico.

Resist Printing

It is generally accepted that resist printing is one of the oldest methods of applying surface design. Early Javanese batiks, Japanese stencil prints, and Plangi tie-dyes are examples of this technique. The basic principle of resist printing is the protection of certain areas of the fabric by some device to prevent color (dye) penetration. Both early and modern methods of resist printing will be described here briefly.

Plangi Tie-Dye Plangi resist methods were used by primitive peoples in the Far East. Early designs were extremely delicate. In this technique, tiny puffs of fabric were pulled over a pointed object, tied tightly with waxed thread below the puff, and dipped in color. Where the fabric was to resist the color it was protected by the waxed thread. The cloth was always retied for each color in order to retain color clarity.

Plangi designs can also be made by folding the fabric so that certain areas are protected from the dye, or by knotting or plaiting the fabric itself to prevent dye penetration. A third method, called *tritik,* involves hand or machine stitching. The stitching is placed to follow designs, after which the thread is pulled tight, drawing the fabric together. The puffed area will accept the color, while the stitched area will resist it. Modern tie-dye prints are usually characterized by large irregular areas of color, but the principle for achieving the design is the same. Areas not to be colored are tied off with thread or cord. Tie-dye prints are popular as handcrafted products and machine-made imitations in both apparel and home decoration fabrics. (See Plate 15.)

Batik A resist method perfected by the Javanese, batik has recently been revived and adapted to modern fabrics by designers and handcraft artists in other areas of the world. An important part of producing batik prints is the preparation of the fabric. It must be thoroughly washed to remove any dirt, wax, oil, or processing residue such as starch or sizing. The cloth is then stiffened with a special tapioca starch to produce a smooth surface and prevent excessive penetration of wax. The batik design is produced by the following steps:

1. Melted wax is applied to all areas that are to remain unaffected by the color.
2. The cloth is dipped in dye, whereupon only the untreated areas absorb the color.

3. The fabric is dried carefully and then immersed in boiling water to remove the wax. As the water cools, the wax solidifies, floats on the surface, and is recovered for reuse.
4. Wax is reapplied in new areas in preparation for application of the second color. The process is repeated as many times as required for the design.

Sometimes the wax cracks or is deliberately cracked so that fine spider-web lines appear in the background areas.

Batik prints often are made with a block in which the design has been executed in copper wires and bands. The block is dipped in melted wax, then the wax is transferred to the cloth. The wax coats the fabric with the pattern embedded in the block. Although this technique speeds up the batik process, it does not produce designs of better quality.

Stencil Printing

Stencil printing, first developed by the Japanese, was the precursor of modern screen printing. Today, it is considered a handcraft. In stencil printing design areas are cut from sheets of paper coated with oil, wax, or varnish, or from thin sheets of metal. A separate stencil is generally prepared for each color. The stencils must be planned so they *register* or fit together properly to result in a perfect print. A difficulty with stencil printing is that the design areas must be connected to prevent parts of the stencil from falling out. To offset this problem, Japanese stencil artists developed a method of tying the various sections together with silk filament or human hair.

In producing stencil prints today, the color can be applied by hand brush, air brush, or spray gun. The technique is necessarily limited to small amounts of yardage or one-of-a-kind items.

Silk-Screen Printing

Screen printing is considered by many textile authorities to be the newest technique for decorating fabrics. It developed from stencil printing and is essentially a stencil process. The screen is made by covering a frame with a fine mesh fabric of silk, metal, nylon, or polyester filament. The fabric is covered with a film, and the design areas are cut out of the film, leaving the fine mesh fabric open for the dyestuff to pass through and print the fabric. Screens can be prepared by several methods, but the end result is always the same, because a permeable area through which the dye will pass is essential for screen printing. A squeegee is used to move the dye across the screen and force the color through the open areas and onto the fabric. One screen is prepared for each color, and the size must be large enough to include at least one repeat pattern. As with stencil printing, all screens necessary for a specific design are arranged to register or fit together accurately for reproduction.

Figure 30.2 Toile de Jouy. Early printed linen fabric from France, 1784–1785. (*Los Angeles County Museum of Art; gift of Mr. and Mrs. John Jewett Garland*)

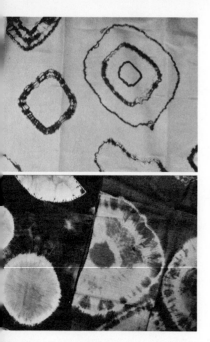

Screen printing is desirable for the production of large patterns and for fabrics that require considerable dye, such as uncut pile. The process is versatile. It is economical for limited yardage as well as for sample runs.

Before the introduction of automatic screen printing, the amount of yardage that could be printed at one time was limited by the length of the printing table, the speed of the operators, and the number of colors and screens used. Hand methods are still the same today. But during the past twenty years, most screen printing establishments have installed automatic equipment—flat-bed screen-printing machines, rotary screen printers, or models that combine both methods in one operation. Automatic screen printing is, of course, much faster than the hand-screen methods, and the process is continuous. The cloth moves slowly along the flat surface of the printing table, and the screens and color are applied to the fabric by mechanically controlled devices. Then the fabric is fed through drying equipment where the color is fixed. (See Plates 16, 17, 18 and 19.)

Rotary screen printers are relatively new. While the roll reduces the size of the repeat design—it can be no larger than the circumference of the roll—it increases printing speed. Furthermore, it is easier to add screens for additional colors and complexity of design. In rotary screen printing color is fed into the center of the roll, where a squeegee spreads the dye.

above left: Figure 30.3 Examples of modern tie-dyed fabric.

below left: Figure 30.4 Operator with Tjanting used to apply wax in batik printing. (*Royal Tropical Institute, Amsterdam; Photographic Archives*)

below right: Figure 30.5 Operator painting wax onto fabric. (*Royal Tropical Institute, Amsterdam; Photographic Archives*)

Although screen printing is a relatively slow process, it offers many advantages: designs can be large; small yardage lots can be produced economically; color changes can be made easily; a variety of dyes can be used; wide fabrics can be printed easily; cloth that would stretch on roller

above: **Figure 30.6** Batik design, fabric from Indonesia.

below: **Figure 30.7** Rotary screen printing.

right: **Figure 30.8** Color feed for rotary screens.

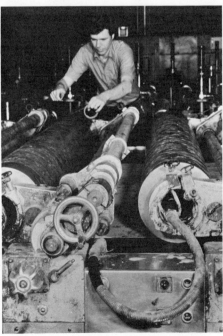

Figure 30.9   Silk-screen print.

Figure 30.10   Discharge printed design on handwoven Thai silk. (*Jack Lenor Larsen, Inc.*)

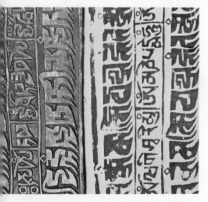

Figure 30.11   A block used for block printing (left) and fabric printed by it (right).

machinery can be printed without distortion; and a tremendous variety of patterns are feasible.

Discharge Printing

Discharge printing is used when print designs are to be applied to fabric that has previously been dyed a solid color. A design roll is coated with a reducing bleach that removes the base dye and leaves a white pattern on a colored ground. The printing machine may replace the color removed with a different color. This is done by a second design roll that applies dye to the discharged areas. More than one color can be added by means of additional rolls.

Discharge printing may reduce fabric strength if the chemical used to remove the dye is not promptly and completely removed from the fabric. However, if the proper procedures are followed, no damage should occur.

Direct Printing

Direct printing is the most common method of applying designs to fabric. Block printing, a type of direct color application, may be the oldest printing technique.

Block Printing   Actual samples of fabric stamped with block prints and dated about 1600 B.C. have been discovered by archaeologists. Wall paintings indicating the possible application of pattern by block stamping appear to have been made as far back as 2100 B.C. Some of the early blocks were up to 18 inches square and more than 3 inches thick.

In block printing, a separate block is required for each color. On the block the design area is raised, while the background area is carved away. The procedure for printing is more or less standard. The fabric is laid flat on a smooth, padded surface and anchored securely. Next, the dye is applied in a uniform layer to the raised portion of the block. Then the block is pressed onto the fabric so the dye is transferred·to the fabric. Extra pressure is exerted on the block to produce clear color.

Block printing is both a handcraft and an art form. It is done on paper as well as on fabric. (See Plate 20.)

Roller Printing   Many fabrics are printed by a direct roller method, where the equipment is completely automatic, requiring few operators. The process is fast and economical for large scale production. In roller printing the design, which can never have a repeat greater than the circumference of the printing roll, is reproduced to conform to the rolls, and the colors are clearly indicated. The design is actually etched into the roll. As the roll rotates in the dye solution, the design area picks up the color. A special blade removes dye from all the smooth areas of the roll. When the roll makes contact with the fabric, the dye from the etched areas is then transferred to the fabric. Each color is applied by its own roll. The

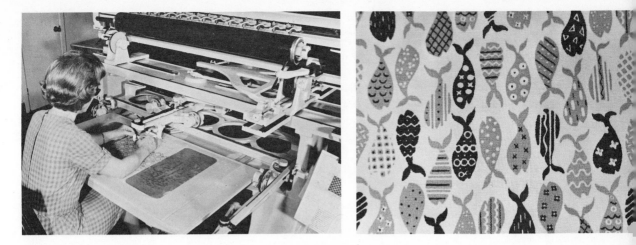

engraved rolls are arranged around or parallel to a main cylinder. As many as 16 rolls may be used for color application of complicated designs.

The quality of print fabrics has steadily increased during the past decades. Automatic controls assure accurate printing, while a willingness to experiment with unusual patterns and designs has resulted in beautiful and original print fabrics. (See Plate 21.)

Photographic Printing   Photographic prints are produced in a manner very similar to that used in making photographs. The fabric is treated with a light-reactive dye. A negative is placed on the fabric, light is transmitted to it, and the design is developed. After stabilization, the fabric is thoroughly washed, and the print becomes permanent. Either black and white or full-color designs can be made by this process.

above left: Figure 30.12 Etching a design into a copper roll for direct roller printing.

above right: Figure 30.13 Direct roller printed fabric.

below: Figure 30.14 Photographic print.

Figure 30.15 Embroidered fabric.

Sublistatic or Transfer Printing

A new process for printing fabrics is actually a modern adaptation of the old decalcomania technique. Called sublistatic or transfer printing, the process relies on the use of preprinted release papers that can transfer their prints to fabrics. The release papers are printed with disperse dyestuffs, which sublimate under heat and transfer their colors to the fabric.

The process is rapid and can be adapted to either yardage or garment parts. It can reproduce nearly any pattern in any size. Fabrics printed by the sublistatic method are attractive, and they have been found to give good service. (See Plate 22.)

Embroidery

The application of yarn or thread is a very old method of decorating fabric. Exquisite hand embroideries were made in Europe during the 14th, 15th, and 16th centuries, and some of these are now exhibited in museums. Embroidery is still practiced as a craft, and many years of training may be required to attain the skill necessary for intricate designs.

Today, most of the embroidered fabrics on the consumer market are produced by machines, much like those used in making lace, which duplicate the fine stitches in one or several colors. The machines can even create cutout patterns as part of the embroidery design.

Evaluation of Color

Standard test methods for evaluating colorfastness of fabrics are used by quality control and research laboratories and testing organizations. The consumer never has access to such test equipment. If products are well-labeled, consumers should know everything there is to know about expected performance and maintenance. In far too many cases, however, the product carries no information whatsoever about colorfastness. The following discussion will, therefore, include simple home tests for color-fastness.

Dyes still cause problems for consumers, despite the tremendous improvement of dyestuffs and coloring processes in the past thirty years. Dissatisfaction may be the result of improper fabric care, and the latter, in turn, may be due to inadequate labeling directions or neglect on the part of the consumer to follow instructions. Problems with color can also be caused by improper selection of dye or dye application method in the manufacturing stage. The consumer cannot always assume that fabric manufacturers have selected optimum methods of dye application or the

top left: Figure 31.1 Launderometer. (*Atlas Electric Devices Company*)

top right: Figure 31.2 Fadeometer. (*Atlas Electric Devices Company*)

center left: Figure 31.3 Crockmeter. (*Atlas Electric Devices Company*)

above left: Figure 31.4 Perspiration tester. (*Atlas Electric Devices Company*)

above right: Figure 31.5 Color difference meter. (*Gardner Laboratory, Inc.*)

best dyestuff. Manufacturers must adjust their costs to the prevailing selling price of the fabric, and to do this they may be forced to adopt dyes and dyeing methods that do not necessarily produce the most desirable product.

Label data regarding care and fiber content are mandated by legislation. Consumers should insist on receiving this information so they can determine proper use and care. However, since label data may be minimal, consumers may still wish to do their own home testing of color behavior under various environmental conditions. Several nontechnical tests are included here as guides.

Home Tests for Colorfastness of Fabrics

Dry Cleaning

Test #1   Sponge a sample of fabric (or the seam allowance at a point where it is hidden) with a dry cleaner or spot remover, using a clean white cloth. If the color is not fast to cleaning, it will discolor or stain the cloth. Color loss may also be visible in the fabric being tested, but color transference to the white cloth is a better guide because it will be more obvious. Dry cleaning solvents and spot removers should be used in well-ventilated areas and never near an open flame. It is important not to inhale the vapor of these substances.

Test #2   When a sample of sufficient size—approximately 2 by 4 inches—is available, it can be immersed in cleaning solution for ten to twenty minutes. Stir occasionally, or place in a jar, seal, and shake every two to three minutes, and observe whether any color has "bled" into the cleaning solution. Then dry the sample and compare it with the original fabric to determine any color change.

Laundering with Other Garments

Test #3   A small fabric sample is required. This can be clipped from the seam allowance, hem, or facing if a fabric scrap is not available. When yardage is used, a 2-by-2-inch swatch is adequate.

1. Use a pint jar and water at the temperature suggested for the fiber content.
2. Put one cup of water and one teaspoon of soap or detergent in the jar.
3. Add the sample.
4. Shake the jar frequently to simulate washing action, and allow the fabric to remain in solution for eight to ten minutes.
5. Observe the color of the solution.
6. Rinse the sample in warm water at least twice, and observe any loss of color into the rinse water.
7. Dry the sample and compare it with the original fabric to determine if any color change occurred.

Test #4   When dye is evident in the wash water, the consumer may wish to see if it will discolor other fabrics laundered at the same time.

1. Repeat test #3 with a new sample of fabric and include small samples of white fabrics of cotton, nylon, polyester, or any fabric typical of that frequently laundered with the sample.
2. Observe the white samples to see if they have picked up any color. If so, the colored product should be laundered separately.

Colorfastness to laundering, frequently called *washfastness,* is desirable in any textile item that requires frequent cleaning by water and detergents.

A product shedding color so it is picked up by other fabrics presents the consumer with special care requirements, which, at best, are time-consuming. Fabrics that merely lose their own color during care will eventually become unattractive.

It must be pointed out that label information can be misleading. Although a label states that a fabric is colorfast, it may not be colorfast to laundering. The term *washfast* is preferred and, when used properly, indicates that the product can be laundered without loss of color.

Sunlight

Test #5   Textile products that will be exposed to sunlight for many hours each day, such as curtains and draperies, should be colorfast to sunlight or *sunfast*. It is difficult and time-consuming for a consumer to execute accurate tests at home. However, it is possible to assess some degree of sunfastness.

1. Expose a sample of the fabric (directly or through glass) to sunlight between 10:00 A.M. and 4:00 P.M. Standard Time, during the period from May to September.
2. Keep a record of the number of hours of exposure.
3. Compare the sample with an original at frequent intervals.

Fabrics are not considered satisfactory for use at windows or in sunny areas unless they will resist fading for a minimum of 120 hours. A consumer wishing to pretest a fabric sample before purchase has the problem of time. Frequently, by the time sunfastness has been checked, the fabric is no longer available. Thus, in reality, the consumer must depend on label information and past experience. If the manufacturer guarantees sunfastness, the consumer should expect satisfaction.

Other conditions that can affect color include atmospheric fumes, perspiration, dry heat, and wet heat. These can be checked by the consumer with a little effort. Rubbing or abrasion of fabric by other fabrics or foreign substances can also cause color change. Some of these factors can be checked by the consumer, while others require special chemicals or special facilities.

Ironing

Test #6   While ironing or pressing may produce noticeable color change, the fabric will usually return to its normal color after cooling, especially when dry heat is used. The consumer can check this satisfactorily with an iron on either a sample of fabric or an inside seam allowance.

1. Press the fabric with an iron set at the recommended temperature. Observe any color change.

2. If color does change, watch the fabric as it cools to determine if it returns to its original shade.
3. If it does not, contact the retailer to find out if the product can be returned.

Pressing with steam or with a damp press cloth affects some dyes. Fabrics can be checked as for dry heat, using steam or a wet press cloth. If colors change with this test and not with the dry heat or the reverse, the consumer knows which ironing method is required.

Rubbing and Crocking

Test #7   Color may be lost by rubbing or friction, which can be especially disturbing if the color rubs off onto other fabrics. For example, upholstery fabrics could stain apparel fabrics; garment fabrics could stain slip fabrics under arms, belts, or other tight areas. A test to determine color loss from rubbing is simple.

1. Place a small square of white cotton fabric—preferably muslin or percale—over the forefinger.
2. With even pressure rub the white fabric at least ten times over the colored item.
3. Observe to see if the color rubs off onto the white fabric.
4. Repeat with a white piece of fabric that has been moistened thoroughly.

Label information, test results, experience, and knowledge are key elements in giving consumers a fairly solid basis for determining the use and care a product should receive.

The consumer who desires a special color or print design for limited usage does not need to pay special attention to color durability. But a textile product that is purchased for relative permanence should perform well during use and care, and the colors should be durable. Modern technology is advanced enough to be able to produce color that performs to the consumer's satisfaction. It is important, also, however, that consumers adhere to recommended care procedures, because color loss is often directly attributable to mishandling.

Fabric
End-Use

VI

Fabric Performance: Selection and Care

32

Fibers, yarns, fabrics, finishes, dyes—all are directed at one goal: the end-use of a product. Textiles are meant to be worn, sat upon, walked on. They protect and enhance the person and the environment. This chapter attempts to summarize and bring into perspective all of the factors involved in the making of textile products and determine how these factors figure in selection, use, and care.

Fiber content, yarn structure, fabric construction, color, and finish are the important factors to be considered regarding a textile product. They combine to determine the appearance, durability, maintenance, and comfort of a fabric. Each merits different degrees of emphasis, depending upon the desired end-use, and end-use depends upon the consumer.

The consumer must decide the order of priorities. Some choices will be obvious. For example: comfort will not be a consideration for draperies; maintenance or durability will have little relevance in the selection of an evening gown for a special occasion; comfort rather than appearance may be the overriding reason for choosing children's night clothes; the durability of a mattress pad may outweigh all other factors. However, since there will be individual differences among consumers in the evaluation process, this text will merely discuss the four factors without evaluating their relative importance.

Fabric Appearance

The *appearance* of a fabric can be described as its visual effect upon the consumers, who may use their sense of touch for greater comprehension of what they see. Fiber luster and texture influence the appearance of fabric. Yarn structure can produce different effects, such as a smooth or rough surface. Fabric structure is important. Color is an obvious property of appearance, and finish may alter the visual impact of a fabric. These elements have all been discussed in preceding chapters.

Depending upon the interaction of the various factors, fabrics may appear to be soft or stiff, rough or smooth, delicate or coarse, lustrous or dull, bulky or sheer, bright or gray, light or dark. A continuum can be established for each of these comparisons, and fabrics will rank at any one of the infinite number of positions on the scale. The potential for variety is used by the designer to provide the consumer with a multitude of choices.

Fabric Durability

Durability is defined as the ability to last or endure. Consumers, in general, do not wish to have fabrics last a lifetime. Thus, for purposes of this discussion, fabric durability is considered to be the ability to retain properties and characteristics for a *reasonable* period of time.

Although the factors examined below are related to appearance as well as to durability, the emphasis here is strictly on the latter. Generalizations concerning fabric durability might include the following:

1. Fiber content influences durability. Some fibers, such as acetate, are valued for their beauty of hand and drape more than for their wearing qualities. Others, such as nylon, are selected for their strength, abrasion resistance, and other properties that contribute directly to durability.
2. Yarn structure determines durability to a degree. For example, complex yarns with loops and similar surfaces are easily snagged, producing damage, altering appearance, and reducing fabric usefulness. Simple-ply yarns with medium twist will generally give good wear. Single yarns with even twist are less likely to show wear than those with slubs or irregular areas of very low twist, which may pull apart.
3. Fabric structure is an important factor in durability. Plain- and twill-weave fabrics are more durable than satin weave, for the floating surface yarns in satins are subject to snagging, breaking, and damage from abrasion. Decorative weaves that include long floats are easily damaged by rough or sharp objects, which may snag and break the floating yarn. Decorative weaves with short floats, high thread counts,

and strong yarns and fibers may be more durable than inferior plain weave fabrics.

Filling- or weft-knit fabrics of plain design are subject to the formation of runs when the yarn is broken. The run spreads more rapidly when fibers of a filament type are used in yarns. Nylon yarns in women's hosiery are an excellent example of smooth yarns that run rapidly in a plain-weft knit when a thread is broken or snagged. Yarns of rough fibers, such as wool, or of textured filaments tend to adhere to each other, and damage from runs is reduced. Mesh constructions are not as subject to runs, but holes will form if the yarns are broken. Warp-knit fabrics and double knits are comparatively run-resistant. They also have sufficient fabric give to resist damage from bending or extending.

Felt fabrics usually have good durability unless they are subjected to considerable pulling force or abrasion. Heavier felts give longer service than lightweight felt fabrics. Nonwovens may be durable or disposable depending on planned end-use. Nonwoven interfacings should be able to withstand various methods of maintenance to give satisfactory service in the final product. This may be difficult for consumers to determine, but labeling should be helpful.

Decorative fabrics, such as lace, are not usually purchased with durability in mind. Although they tend to be fragile, lace fabrics may last for many years with proper care.

In general, basic-weave constructions and plain-knit fabrics are more durable than complicated fabric constructions, which could show signs of wear as a result of surface distortion or damage. Fabrics with medium to high yarn count are usually considered more durable than fabrics with low count; however, this is greatly influenced by the type of yarn structure and fiber involved.

It should be evident that the properties of a fabric are determined by complicated interrelationships; therefore, it is not easy for consumers to predict ultimate durability. But an understanding of the interrelationships does aid, to some extent, in understanding performance or the lack of it.

4. Color selection and method of application influence durability. Choosing the proper dye for each fiber type is essential if the fabric color is to give good service. The consumer, however, should be aware of scientific, economic, and fashion effects on color. It is impossible to find all colors in all classes of dyestuff, and this may mean selection of a second-choice dye in order to obtain a current fashion color. Moreover, not all dyes within any one class are equally good, and it is difficult to find dyes in all colors that prove to be colorfast to all degrading environmental conditions.

Dyestuffs differ in cost and in the expense of application; thus, it is necessary to choose the dye that will be on a level with a reasonable competitive price. Dye selection should be based on the planned end-uses of the fabric, and this may mean a compromise. Fabrics intended for apparel may not be sunfast enough to serve as draperies, whereas fabrics intended for draperies may be sunfast but not washfast enough for apparel. In sum, both consumers and manufacturers must be cognizant of the interrelation between these factors. Loss of color during maintenance of any textile item generally results in consumer dissatisfaction and premature discard of the product. Thus, the durability of color is of considerable importance to appearance. In fact, color behavior emphasizes the importance of the interrelationship among appearance, durability, and care.

5. Finishes, whether applied for appearance or to alter certain properties, often affect fabric durability. Surface finishes such as glazing can be removed by improper care, so that the useful life of the product is reduced.

Most minimum-care and durable-press finishes reduce fabric tear strength and abrasion resistance—both desirable performance properties. The consumer, therefore, is usually willing to accept the reduced strength and durability that go with these finishes in order to have improved appearance and easy care.

It should be evident that durability is determined by many factors. Consumers hold the responsibility of deciding the relative importance of durability in terms of product end-use and of making their selections accordingly.

Fabric Comfort

The importance of fabric comfort will vary according to the predetermined end-use of the product and the personal preference of the consumer. Factors that will influence comfort include texture and tactile characteristics, heat retention, moisture absorbency, weight, wicking properties, air permeability, and the degree of softness or stiffness. While these qualities can be measured quite accurately by standard test procedures, the actual relationship between the properties and human comfort has not been clearly established. Ultimately, comfort is still a personal thing—part of a person's physical and psychological makeup. For example, color loss would hardly influence physical comfort, but it might help create a psychological atmosphere leading to an illusion of physical discomfort. This end result can be very real and should not be dismissed as irrelevant. Rather, both sensual and mental comfort should be assessed in the selection of textile products. Since no two people are identical, fabric comfort will be related to individual differences and will require careful decision-making on the part of each consumer based on his or her ideas and attitudes.

Fabric Maintenance

The care required for a textile product depends upon the fiber or fibers used, yarn structure or fiber arrangement, fabric construction, method of imparting color, types of dyestuffs, finishes, and the interaction of all of these. Considerable attention has been given to problems of maintenance in previous chapters. A few of the more important points to consider are cited here in an effort to aid the consumer in determining the most desirable fabric care methods.

Since care labeling is now required by law, the consumer can expect to obtain reasonably accurate maintenance directions. These will be detailed on a label accompanying fabric or product. Fiber identification must also be provided. This information should make it possible to identify products that normally require dry cleaning, those that need careful handling during laundering, and those that can be washed and dried in standard laundry equipment. In addition to the labeling information consumers should consider other important factors not included on labels.

The care-labeling legislation enacted in 1971 should help consumers. Examples of label information are shown in Figure 32.1 and Table 32.1.

Yarn structure may affect maintenance. Such characteristics as the amount of twist and the type of construction—simple, complex, ply, or cord—all play a part. For example, a yarn with a very high twist, such as a crepe, may relax when subjected to moisture and undergo excessive shrinkage. A complex yarn can be damaged by abrasion from equipment or other fabrics during the maintenance process. It is, therefore, important to consider the yarn in arriving at desirable methods of product care.

Blended yarns should receive the type of care recommended for the more easily damaged fiber. However, proper blending may result in easier care for *both* fibers. For example, a polyester and cotton blend produces a fabric that is easily laundered, dries quickly, and requires lower ironing temperatures than pure cotton. A blend of wool and acrylic can be home laundered, while wool itself must usually be dry cleaned.

Figure 32.1 Examples of care labels.

Table 32.1   Meaning of Labels*

Label Instruction	Washer Setting[1]	Dryer Setting	Line Dry
machine wash hot	regular[2] cycle, hot water	regular	yes
machine wash warm[3]	regular cycle, warm water	regular	yes
machine wash warm, line dry	regular cycle, warm water	no	yes
machine wash warm gentle, tumble dry low	gentle[4] cycle, warm water	low	yes
hand wash separately, line dry	no[5]	no	yes
hand wash separately, dry flat	no	no	no
dry clean only	no	no	no
wipe with damp cloth only	no	no	no

Other Commonly Used Labels

machine wash separately hot
machine wash separately warm
machine wash separately warm, line dry
machine wash separately warm gentle, tumble dry low
hand wash, line dry
hand wash, dry flat

Additional Terms

do not bleach	use cool iron
do not use chlorine bleach	furrier clean only
do not twist or wring	leather clean only
remove before fully dry	do not dry clean
wash inside out	wash separately
do not iron	remove trim

*Guide for Permanent Care Labeling, National Retail Merchants' Association, New York.

[1]Settings are based on typical home conditions. They approximate the following ranges: hot = 130° to 150°F; warm or hand = 90° to 110°F; cold = less than 75°F.

[2]The term "regular" encompasses other terms that may appear on some washers and dryers, such as automatic dry, timed dry, and special normal.

[3]The term "warm" encompasses other terms that may appear on some labels or washers, such as medium.

[4]Gentle or delicate cycle indicates low-speed agitation and shorter washing periods, or permanent press cycle on dryer.

[5]The word "no" indicates a prohibited procedure.

Fabric construction is closely related to maintenance. For example:

■ Woven fabrics of plain or twill weaves do not require special care, but fabrics with long floating yarns, such as satins or elaborate Jacquards, can be snagged during cleaning. This results in unattractive surfaces, destruction of appearance, and reduction of fabric durability.

■ Knitted fabrics may need only a minimum of ironing, but some require reblocking and reshaping to retain size and appearance after maintenance procedures. With knits it is important to consider fiber content. Polyester double knits are easy to care for; cotton knits may shrink; wool knits may require dry cleaning. Many polyester double knit fabrics currently on the market will shrink as much as 6 to 8 percent when laundered. Therefore, knits purchased by the yard for home sewing should be preshrunk unless a label indicates the fabric has been stabilized.

■ Sheer fabrics of leno-weave construction might require careful handling, but they are easier to maintain than sheer fabrics of a plain weave. The interlocking of the warp yarns reduces yarn slippage. However, other factors, such as fiber content, alter the care of sheer fabrics.

■ Nonwoven fabrics demand careful maintenance for incorrect care may result in loss of adhesive or in fiber separation.

■ Pile fabrics may require brushing to remove lint from the surface. Those that can be laundered look better if tumble dried, because the dryer action tends to raise the pile and to fluff the fabric.

■ Tufted fabrics can generally be laundered and tumble dried. If the product is too large for home equipment, many dry cleaners and commercial laundries will do the job satisfactorily. It is important to tumble dry such products in order to maintain the appearance of the tufts. Tufted floor coverings, which will not fit into tumble dryers, can be restored by cleaning and steaming, followed by vacuuming.

Proper laundering techniques should be observed for all washable fabrics. Excessively long wash cycles may cause redeposition of soil upon fabrics, which, in turn, produces a gray or dull appearance.

Color is an important aspect of care. Whether fabrics are dyed or printed, color may be lost during laundering or dry cleaning. Tests for evaluation of color were cited in the previous chapter. Proper care in relation to color results in continued good appearance.

The presence of finishes is of considerable importance in fabric care. Finishing substances may improve the behavior of fabric, but they may also cause new problems. A review of the discussion on finishes will be helpful.

The selection, use, and care of fabrics depends upon many factors. The importance of appearance, durability, comfort, and maintenance are relative. It is the responsibility of each consumer to evaluate the qualities of a fabric in terms of its ultimate end-use and then make the decisions required concerning its use and care.

Metric Conversion Tables

The student of textile science should be able to convert readily from the American system of measurement to the metric system, used in virtually every country outside the United States and increasingly used, especially in technical contexts, in the United States. The following tables provide multipliers for converting from metric to U.S. and the reverse; the multipliers have been rounded to the third decimal place and thus yield an approximate equivalent.

Metric to U.S.			U.S. to Metric		
to convert from:	to:	multiply the metric unit by:	to convert from:	to:	multiply the U.S. unit by:
length:					
meters	yards	1.093	yards	meters	.914
meters	feet	3.280	feet	meters	.305
meters	inches	39.370	inches	meters	.025
centimeters	inches	.394	inches	centimeters	2.540
millimeters	inches	.039	inches	millimeters	25.400
area and volume:					
square meters	square yards	1.196	square yards	square meters	.836
square meters	square feet	10.764	square feet	square meters	.093
square centimeters	square inches	.155	square inches	square centimeters	6.451
cubic centimeters	cubic inches	.061	cubic inches	cubic centimeters	16.387
liquid measure:					
liters	cubic inches	61.020	cubic inches	liters	.016
liters	cubic feet	.035	cubic feet	liters	28.339
liters	*U.S. gallons	.264	*U.S. gallons	liters	3.785
liters	*U.S. quarts	1.057	*U.S. quarts	liters	.946
weight and mass:					
kilograms	pounds	2.205	pounds	kilograms	.453
grams	ounces	.035	ounces	grams	28.349
grams	grains	15.430	grains	grams	.065
grams per meter	ounces per yard	.032	ounces per yard	grams per meter	31.250
grams per square meter	ounces per square yard	.030	ounces per square yard	grams per square meter	33.333

*The British imperial gallon equals approximately 1.2 U.S. gallons or 4.54 liters. Similarly, the British imperial quart equals 1.2 U.S. quarts, and so on.

Glossary
of Textile
Terms

absorption   The attraction and retention of gases or liquids within the pores of a fiber; also, the retention of moisture between fibers within yarns and between fibers or yarns within fabrics.

adsorption   The retention of gases, liquids, or solids on the surface areas of fibers, yarns, or fabrics.

antique satin   A satin-weave fabric made to resemble silk satin of an earlier century. It is used for home-furnishing fabrics.

art linen   A heavy plain-weave fabric used for tablecloths and as the basis for many types of embroidered household items.

balanced yarns   Yarns in which the twist is such that the yarn will hang in a loop without kinking, doubling, or twisting upon itself.

barathea   A closely woven dobby-weave fabric with a characteristic pebbly surface. It is generally made from silk or rayon, often combined with cotton or worsted.

The fabric is used for dresses, neckties, and lightweight suits.

batiste   A fabric named for Jean Baptiste, a French linen weaver. (1) In cotton, a sheer, fine *muslin*,[1] woven of combed yarns and given a mercerized finish. It is used for blouses, summer shirts, dresses, lingerie, infants' dresses, bonnets, and handkerchiefs. (2) A rayon, polyester, or cotton-blend fabric with the same characteristics. (3) A smooth, fine wool fabric that is lighter than *challis,* very similar to fine nun's veiling. It is used for dresses and negligées. (4) A sheer silk fabric, either plain or figured, very similar to silk mull. It is often called *batiste de soie* and is made into summer dresses.

Bedford cord   Lengthwise ribbed durable cloth for outer garments or sport clothes. The corded effect is secured by having two successive *warp* threads woven in plain-weave order. Heavier cords are created with wadding—a heavy,

[1] Italics denote a cross-reference within the Glossary.

289

bulky yarn with very little twist—covered by *filling* threads.

beetling A finish primarily applied to linen whereby the cloth is beaten with large wooden blocks in order to flatten the yarns.

bengaline A ribbed fabric similar to *faille,* but heavier, with a coarser rib in the *filling* direction. It may be silk, wool, acetate, or rayon *warp,* with wool or cotton *filling.* The fabric was first made in Bengal, India. It is used for dresses, coats, trimmings, and draperies.

bicomponent fibers Fibers in which two *filaments* of different composition have been extruded simultaneously.

bouclé A fabric woven with bouclé yarns, which have a looped appearance on the surface. In some bouclés only one side of the fabric is nubby; in others, both are rough. Sometimes the bouclé yarn is used as a *warp* rather than a *filling.* Bouclé yarn is very popular in the knitting trade; there are many varieties and weights.

breaking load The minimum force required to rupture a fiber, expressed in grams or pounds.

brins The two adjacent silk *filaments* extruded by the silkworm.

broadcloth A term used to describe several dissimilar fabrics made with different fibers, weaves, and finishes. (1) Originally, a silk shirting fabric so named because it was woven in widths exceeding the usual 29 inches. (2) a tightly woven, high-count cotton cloth with a fine crosswise rib. Fine broadcloths are woven of *combed* yarns, usually with high thread counts, such as 136 × 60 or 144 × 76. They are usually mercerized, Sanforized, and given a soft, lustrous finish. (3) A closely woven wool cloth with a smooth nap, velvety feel, and lustrous appearance. Wool broadcloth can be made with a two-up-and-two-down twill weave or plain weave. In setting up a loom to make the fabric, the loom is threaded very wide to allow for great shrinkage during the fulling process. The fabric takes its name from this wide threading. High-quality wool broadcloth is fine enough for garments that are to be closely molded to the figure or draped. Its high-luster finish makes it an elegant cloth. Wool broadcloth is 10 to 16 ounces per yard and is now being made in chiffon weights. (4) A fabric made from silk or man-made *filament fiber* yarns, woven in a plain weave with a fine crosswise rib obtained by using a heavier *filling* than *warp* yarn.

brocade Rich Jacquard-woven fabric with an allover interwoven design of raised figures or flowers. The name is derived from the French word meaning "to ornament." The brocade pattern is emphasized with contrasting surfaces or colors and often has gold or silver threads running through it. The background may be either satin or twill weave. It is used for dresses, draperies, and upholstery.

brocatelle Supposedly an imitation of Italian tooled leather, in which the background is pressed and the figures embossed. Both the background and the figures are tightly woven, generally with a *warp* effect in the figure and a *filling* effect in the background. Brocatelle is employed mainly in upholstery and draperies.

cambric A closely woven white cotton fabric finished with a slight gloss on one side.

Canton flannel A heavy, warm cotton material with a twilled surface and a long soft nap on the back, produced by napping the heavy soft-twist yarn. It is named for Canton, China, where it was first made. The fabric is strong and absorbent; it is used for interlinings and sleeping garments.

card sliver A ropelike strand of fibers about $\frac{3}{4}$ inch to 1 inch in diameter; the form in which fibers emerge from the *carding* machine.

carding A process by which natural fibers are sorted, separated, and partially aligned.

cavalry twill A sturdy twill-weave fabric with a pronounced diagonal cord. It is used for sportswear, uniforms, and riding habits.

challis or challie One of the softest fabrics made, named from the Anglo-Indian term *shalee,* meaning soft. It is a fine, lightweight, plain-weave fabric, usually made of worsted yarns. Challis was formerly manufactured with a small flower design, but now it is made in darker tones of allover prints and solid colors, in the finest quality fabrics.

chambray (1) A plain-woven fabric with an almost square count (80 × 76), a colored *warp,* and a white *filling,* which gives a mottled, colored surface. It is used for shirts, children's clothing, and dresses. The fabric is named for Cambrai, France, where it was first made for sunbonnets. (2) A similar but heavier carded-yarn fabric used for work clothes and children's play clothes.

cheesecloth A very loosely woven plain-weave cotton fabric. The yarn width is called tobacco cloth. It is used for curtains, costumes, and cleaning cloths.

chiffon A term used to describe many light, gossamer, sheer, plain-weave fabrics. Chiffon can be made of silk, wool, or man-made fibers. It is an open weave with tightly twisted yarns.

china silk A lightweight, soft, plain-weave silk fabric used for lingerie, dress linings, and soft suits.

chino A type of army twill made of combed, two-ply, mercerized yarns in a vat-dyed khaki color. It is now available in a variety of colors.

chintz A highly lustrous, plain-woven cotton with a bright, glazed surface, generally made by finishing a print cloth construction.

cohesiveness The ability of fibers to adhere to one another in yarn-manufacturing processes.

combing A process by which natural fibers are sorted and straightened; a more refined treatment than *carding.*

co-polymer A *polymer* composed of two or more different *monomers.*

corduroy A ribbed, high-luster, cut-pile fabric with extra filling threads that form lengthwise ribs or wales. The thread count varies from 46 × 116 to 70 × 250.

core yarn A yarn in which a base or foundation yarn is completely wrapped by a second yarn.

cotton linters Cotton fibers that are too short for yarn or fabric manufacturing.

course A series of successive loops lying crosswise in a knitted fabric.

covert Generally called covert cloth; a closely woven *warp*-face twill. Its characteristically flecked appearance is produced by using a two-ply yarn so that one dark thread alternates with a light thread. Covert is generally made of wool or cotton, but man-made fibers and blends can also be used.

crepe A lightweight fabric of silk, rayon, cotton, wool, man-made, or blended fibers, characterized by a crinkled surface that is produced by hard-twist yarns, chemical treatment, weave, or embossing.

cretonne A plain-weave fabric similar to unglazed *chintz,* usually printed with large designs.

crimp The waviness of a fiber, usually visible only under magnification.

crystallinity The degree to which fiber molecules are parallel to each other, though not necessarily to the longitudinal fiber axis.

damask A firm-textured fabric with raised patterns, similar to *brocade,* but lighter and reversible. Table damasks are Jacquard woven in lustrous designs.

denier A unit of yarn number equal to the weight in grams of 9000 meters of the yarn.

denim A twilled fabric made of hard-twist yarns, with the *warp yarns* dyed blue and the *filling yarns* undyed. Sports denim is softer and lighter in weight. It is now available in many colors and in plaids and stripes.

dimensional stability The degree to which a fiber, yarn, or fabric retains its shape and size after having been subjected to wear and maintenance.

dimity Literally, double thread; a fine checked or corded cotton sheer made by bunching and weaving two or more threads together.

dotted swiss A sheer, crisp cotton fabric with either clipped spot or swivel dots.

doupion Silk yarns made from two cocoons that have been formed in an interlocked manner. The yarn is uneven, irregular, and larger than regular *filaments.* It is used in making *shantung* and doupioni.

drawing The process by which slivers of natural fibers are pulled out or extended after *carding* or *combing.*

drill A strong cotton material similar to *denim,* which has a diagonal 2 × 1 weave running up to the left *selvage.*

duck A durable plain-weave, closely woven cotton, generally made of *ply yarns,* in a variety of weights and thread counts. Often called canvas, it is used for belting, awnings, tents, and sails.

duvetyn A very high quality cloth that resembles a compact velvet. It has a velvety *hand* resulting from the short nap that covers its surface completely, concealing its twill weave. It is used for suits and coats.

elastic recovery The ability of a fiber, yarn, or fabric to return to its original length after the tension that produced *elongation* has been released.

elongation The amount of stretch or extension that a fiber, yarn, or fabric will accept.

faille A soft, slightly glossy silk, rayon, or cotton fabric in a rib weave, with a light, flat, crossgrain rib or cord made by using heavier yarns in the *filling* than in the *warp.*

felt A nonwoven fabric in which the fibers develop a tight bond and will not ravel. It is used for coats, hats, and many industrial purposes.

fiber morphology The form and structure of a fiber, including its biological structure, shape, cross section, and microscopic appearance.

fibrils Bundles of fiber cells.

filament fibers Long, continuous fibers that can be measured in meters or yards, or in the case of man-made fibers, in kilometers or miles.

filling yarns Yarns that run perpendicular to the longer dimension or *selvage* of a fabric.

flannel A catch-all designation for a great many otherwise unnamed fabrics in the woolen industry. Flannel is woven in various weights of worsted, woolen, or a mixture of both. It can even be made of man-made fibers. The surface is slightly napped in finish. A wide range of weights is available: an 11-ounce flannel is made for suits, and there are tissue-weight flannels for dresses.

flannelette A soft, plain- or twill-weave cotton fabric lightly napped on one side. The fabric can be dyed solid colors or printed. It is popular for lounging and sleeping garments.

fleece Wool sheared from a living lamb.

flexibility The property of bending without breaking.

foulard A lightweight silk, rayon, cotton, or wool fabric characterized by its twill weave. Foulard has a high luster on the face and is dull on the reverse side. It is usually printed, the patterns ranging from simple polka dots to elaborate designs. It is also made in plain or solid colors. Foulard has a characteristic *hand* that can be described as light, firm, and supple.

gabardine A hard-finished, clear-surfaced, twill-weave fabric made of either natural or synthetic fibers. The diagonal lines are fine, close, and steep and are more pronounced than in serge. The lines cannot be seen on the wrong side of the fabric.

gauze A plain-weave fabric with widely spaced yarns, used for such things as bandages. Some weights of gauze can be stiffened for curtains or other decorative or apparel purposes.

gingham A light- to medium-weight plain-weave cotton fabric. It is usually yarn-died and woven to create stripes, checks, or plaids. The fabric is mercerized to produce a soft, lustrous appearance; it is sized and calendered to a firm and lustrous finish. Gingham is used for dresses, shirts, robes, curtains, draperies, and bedspreads. The thread count varies from about 48 × 44 to 106 × 94.

greige The state of a fabric before a finish has been applied.

grenadine A tightly twisted *ply yarn* composed of two or three *singles*.

grosgrain A closely woven firm corded fabric often made with a cotton filling. The cords are heavier than in *poplin,* rounder than in *faille.*

habutai A soft, lightweight silk dress fabric originally woven in the gum on hand looms in Japan. It is sometimes confused with china silk, which is technically lighter in weight.

hackling A *combing* process that separates short fibers from long fibers.

hand The "feel" of a fabric; the qualities that can be ascertained by touching it.

herringbone A fabric in which the pattern of weave resembles the skeletal structure of the herring. It is made with a broken twill weave that produces a balanced, zigzag effect and is used for sportswear, suits, and coats.

homespun A coarse, plain-weave fabric, loosely woven with irregular, tightly twisted, and unevenly spun yarns. It has a hand-woven appearance and is used for coats, suits, sportswear, draperies, and slipcovers.

homopolymer A *polymer* composed of one substance or one type of molecule.

honan Originally, a fabric of the best Chinese silk, sometimes woven with blue edges. It is now made to resemble a heavy *pongee,* with slub yarns in both *warp* and *filling.* Honan is manufactured from silk or from man-made fibers. It is used for women's dresses.

hopsacking An open-basket-weave *ply-yarn* fabric of cotton, linen, or rayon. The weave is similar to the sacking

used to gather hops, hence the name. It is used for dresses, jackets, skirts, and blouses.

huck or huckaback A toweling fabric with a honeycombed surface made by using heavy filling yarns in a dobby weave. It has excellent absorbent qualities. Huck is made in linen, cotton, or a mixture of the two. In a mixture it is called a "union" fabric.

hydrophilic Water-loving; having a high degree of moisture absorption or attraction.

hydrophobic Water-repelling; having a low degree of moisture absorption or attraction.

jean A sturdy cotton fabric, softer and finer than *drill,* made in solid colors or stripes. It is used for sport blouses, work shirts, women's slacks, and children's playclothes.

jersey Elastic knitted fabric in a stockinette stitch. It was first made on the Island of Jersey off the English coast and used for fishermen's clothing. Jersey can be made from wool, cotton, rayon, nylon, other man-made fibers, or a combination of any of these. The term is frequently applied to tricot-knitted fabrics used for dresses.

kersey A thick, heavy, pure wool and cotton twill-weave similar to *melton.* It is well fulled, with a nap and a close-sheared surface. Kersey is used for uniforms and overcoats.

lace An open-work cloth with a design formed by a network of threads made by hand or on special lace machinery, with bobbins, needles, or hooks.

lamb's wool Wool clipped from sheep less than eight months old.

lawn A lightweight, sheer, fine cotton or linen fabric, which can be given a soft or crisp finish. It is sized and calendered to produce a soft, lustrous appearance. Lawn is used for dresses, blouses, curtains, lingerie, and as a base for embroidered items.

linear polymer A *polymer* formed by end-to-end linking of molecular units. The resulting polymer is very long and narrow. It is typical of fibrous forms.

loft The springiness or fluffiness of a fiber.

longcloth A fine, soft cotton cloth woven of softly twisted yarns. It is similar to *nainsook* but slightly heavier, with a duller surface. Longcloth is so called because it was one of the first fabrics to be woven in long rolls. It is also a synonym for *muslin* sheeting of good quality. The fabric is used for underwear and linings.

luster The gloss, sheen, or shine of a fiber, yarn, or fabric.

macromolecule A large molecule formed by hooking together many small molecule units. The term can be used synonymously with polymolecule or *polymer.*

madras (1) A finely woven, soft, plain- or Jacquard-weave fabric with a stripe in the lengthwise direction and Jacquard or dobby patterns woven in the background. Some madras is made with woven checks and cords. It can be used for blouses, dresses, and shirts. (2) A fabric handwoven in India from cotton yarns dyed with native vegetable colorings. The designs are usually rather large, bold plaids that soften in color as the dyes fade and bleed.

marquisette   A light, strong, sheer, open-textured curtain fabric, often with dots woven into the surface. The thread count varies from 48 × 22 to 60 × 40.

matelassé   A soft double or compound fabric with a quilted appearance. The heavier type is used in draperies and upholstery, while crepe matelassé is popular in dresses, semiformal and formal suits and wraps, and trimmings.

melton   A thick, heavily felted or fulled wool fabric in a twill or satin weave, with a smooth, lustrous, napped surface. In less expensive meltons the *warp yarn* may be cotton instead of wool.

micronaire fineness   The weight in micrograms of 1 inch of fiber.

moisture regain   The moisture in a material determined under prescribed conditions and expressed as a percentage of the weight of the moisture-free specimen.

molecular orientation   The degree to which fiber molecules are parallel to each other and to the longitudinal axis of the fiber.

monk's cloth   A heavy, loosely woven basket-weave fabric in solid colors or with stripes or plaids woven into the fabric. It is used chiefly for draperies and slipcovers.

monofilament yarn   Yarn composed of only one fiber *filament.*

monomer   A single unit or molecule from which *polymers* are formed.

mousseline de soie   Literally, "muslin of silk"; silk organdy, a plain-weave silk chiffon-weight fabric with a slight stiffness.

multicomponent fabric   A fabric in which at least two layers of material are sealed together by an adhesive.

multifilament yarn   Yarn composed of several fiber *filaments.*

multilobal   A fiber with a modified cross section exhibiting several lobes.

muslin   A large group of plain-weave cotton fabrics ranging from lightweight to heavyweight. The sizing may also be light or heavy. Muslin can be solid colored or printed. It is used for dresses, shirts, sheets, and other domestic items.

nainsook   A fine, soft cotton fabric in a plain weave. Better grades have a polished finish on one side. When it is highly polished, nainsook may be sold as polished cotton. In low-priced white goods *cambric, longcloth,* and nainsook are often identical before converting; the

finishing process gives them their characteristic texture, but even so it is often difficult to distinguish one from the other. Nainsook is heavier and coarser than *lawn.* It is usually found in white, pastel colors, and prints and is used chiefly for infants' wear, lingerie, and blouses.

ninon   A smooth, transparent, closely woven *voile,* with the *warp yarns* grouped in pairs. It is available in plain or novelty weaves. Man-made fibers are generally used for glass curtains and dress fabrics.

nonthermoplastic   Not capable of being softened by heat.

oleophilic   Tending to absorb and retain oily materials.

oleophobic   Tending to repel oily materials.

organdy   A thin, transparent, stiff, wiry cotton *muslin* used for dresses, neckwear, and trimmings. Organdy, when chemically treated, keeps its crispness through many launderings and does not require restarching. It crushes readily but is easily pressed. Shadow organdy has a faint printed design in self-color.

organzine   A yarn of two or more plies with a medium twist.

orientation   See *molecular orientation.*

Osnaburg   Named for the town in Germany where it was first made, a coarse cotton or blended fiber fabric in a plain weave that resembles crash. It is finished for use in upholstery, slacks, and sportswear. It was originally used unbleached for grain and cement sacks.

ottoman   A heavy corded silk or synthetic fabric with larger and rounder ribs than *faille,* used for coats, skirts, and trimmings. *Fillings* of the cloth are usually cotton or wool, and they should be completely covered by the silk or man-made fiber *warp.*

outing flannel   A soft, lightweight, plain- or twill-weave fabric usually napped on both sides. Most outing flannels have colored yarn stripes. Outing flannel soils easily, and the nap washes and wears off. It is used chiefly for sleeping garments.

Oxford shirting   A cotton or blended fabric in a basket weave first made in Oxford, England, and used for shirts, blouses, and sportswear.

percale   A medium-weight, plain-woven printed cotton, such as 80 × 80; a staple of dress goods. Percale sheets are high quality, with a count of at least 180 threads per square inch. Most percales are made of combed yarns with a count of 84 × 96 or 180 threads per inch. Some fine percale sheets count over 200 threads per inch, such as 96 × 104 or 96 × 108.

picks   See *filling yarns.*

pilling   The formation of tiny balls of fiber in the surface of a fabric.

piqué   Strictly, a ribbed or corded cotton with wales running across the fabric, formed by *warp* ends. The term is often used in the trade to refer to Bedford cord or warp piqué, in which the cords run lengthwise.

plissé Usually a print cloth treated with chemicals that cause parts of the cloth to shrink, creating a permanently crinkled surface.

ply yarn A yarn in which two or more single strands are twisted together.

polymer A large molecule produced by linking together many *monomers.*

polymerization The conversion of *monomers* into large molecules or *polymers.*

pongee (1) A thin, natural tan-colored silk fabric originally made of wild Chinese silk with a knotty rough weave, named for the Chinese *Pun-ki,* meaning "woven at home on one's own loom." It is used primarily for summer suits and dresses, and both plain fabrics and prints are used for decorative purposes. (2) A staple fine-combed cotton fabric finished with a high luster and used for underclothing. (3) A man-made fiber fabric simulating pongee.

poplin A tightly woven, high-count cotton with fine cross ribs formed by heavy *filling yarns* and fewer, finer *warp yarns.* Poplin has heavier ribs, heavier threads, and a slightly lower count than broadcloth, ranging from 80 × 40 to 116 × 56.

pulled wool Wool pulled from the hide of a slaughtered animal.

raw silk Silk that has not been degummed.

reeling The process of winding silk filaments onto a wheel.

reprocessed wool Wool fibers reclaimed from scraps of fabric that have never been used.

resiliency The ability of a fabric to return to its original shape after compressing, bending, or other deformation.

retting The removal, usually by soaking, of the outer woody portion of the flax plant to gain access to the fibers.

reused wool Wool fibers reclaimed from fabrics that have been worn or used.

roving The process by which a sliver of natural fiber is attenuated to between $\frac{1}{4}$ and $\frac{1}{8}$ of its original size; also, the product of this operation.

sailcloth A very heavy, strong, plain-weave fabric made of cotton, linen, or jute. There are many qualities and weights. Sailcloth can be used for sportswear, slipcovers, curtains, and other heavy-duty items.

sateen A cotton or spun-yarn fabric characterized by floats running in the *filling* direction. It is usually mercerized and used for linings, draperies, and comforters.

saturation regain The moisture in a material at 95 or 100 percent relative humidity.

scroop A characteristic rustling or crunching sound acquired by silk that has been immersed in solutions of acetic or tartaric acid and dried without rinsing. It is probably caused by acid microcrystals in the fiber rubbing across each other.

scutching The separation of the outer covering of the flax stalk from the usable fibers.

seersucker A lightweight cotton or cotton blend with crinkled stripes woven in by setting some of the *warp yarns* tight and others slack.

selvage The long, finished edges of a bolt of fabric.

sericulture The raising of silkworms and production of silk.

shantung Originally, a hand-loomed plain-weave fabric made in China. Made of *wild silk,* the fabric had an irregular surface. Today the term shantung is applied to a plain-weave fabric with heavier, rougher yarns running in the crosswise direction of the fabric. These are single complex yarns of the slub type. The fabric can be made of cotton, silk, or man-made fibers.

sharkskin (1) A cotton, linen, silk, or man-made fiber fabric with a sleek, hard-finished, crisp, and pebbly surface and a chalky luster. *Filament yarns,* when used, are twisted and woven tightly in either a plain-weave or a basket-weave construction, depending upon the effect desired. *Staple fiber yarns* are handled in the same manner, except for wool. (2) A wool fabric characterized by its twill weave. The yarns in both *warp* and *filling* alternate white with a color, such as black, brown, or blue. The diagonal lines of the twill weave run from left to right; the colored yarns from right to left.

shed The opening between *warp yarns* through which *filling yarns* are passed.

shoddy See *reused wool.*

silk noil Short ends of silk fibers used in making rough, textured, spun yarns or in blends with cotton or wool; sometimes called *waste silk.*

singles A strand of several filaments held together by twist.

specific gravity The density of a fiber relative to that of water at 4°C.

spinning quality The ease with which fibers lend themselves to yarn-manufacturing processes; cohesiveness.

spun silk Yarns made from short fibers of pierced cocoons or from short ends at the outside and inside edges of the cocoons.

spun yarns Yarns composed of *staple fibers.*

staple fibers Short fibers that are measured in inches or fractions of inches.

suede fabric A woven or knitted fabric of cotton, man-made fibers, wool, or blends, finished to resemble suede leather. It is used in sport coats, gloves, linings, and cleaning cloths.

surah A soft, usually twilled fabric often of silk or man-made fibers, woven in plaids, stripes, or prints. It is used for ties, mufflers, blouses, and dresses.

swiss See *dotted swiss*

synthetic fiber A fiber made from chemicals that were never fibrous in form; more frequently referred to as "man-made synthesized fiber."

taffeta A fine, plain-weave fabric, smooth on both sides, usually with a sheen on its surface. It is named for the Persian fabric "taftan." Taffeta may be a solid color or printed or woven so that the colors appear iridescent. It is often constructed with a fine rib; this fabric is correctly called *faille taffeta.*

tapestry A fabric in which the pattern is woven with colored *weft* threads. It is used extensively for wall hangings and table covers.

tenacity The tensile strength of a fiber, expressed as force per unit of linear density of an unstrained specimen. It is usually expressed in grams per *denier* or grams per *tex.*

tensile strength The maximum tensile stress required to rupture a fiber, expressed as pounds per square inch or grams per square centimeter.

terry cloth A heavy, absorbent cotton made with extra heavy *warp* threads woven into loops on one or both sides.

tex A system of yarn numbering that measures the weight in grams of one kilometer of yarn.

textile Any product made from fibers.

thermoplastic Tending to become soft and/or moldable upon application of heat.

thermosetting A procedure in which a substance is softened by heat, whereupon the substance undergoes chemical change, becomes firm, and assumes a completely different structure and different properties. The substance cannot be softened by reapplication of heat.

three-dimensional polymer A *polymer* formed when molecules unite in both length and width, producing a relatively rigid structure. This is typical of polymers used in processing.

ticking A heavy twill made with a colored yarn stripe in the *warp.* It is used for mattress covers, home-furnishings, and sportswear.

trademark A word, letter, device, or symbol used in connection with merchandise and alluding distinctly to the origin or ownership of the product to which it is applied.

trade name A name given by manufacturers or merchants to a product to distinguish it as one produced or sold by them. It is called, more accurately, a trademark name and may be protected as a trademark.

tram silk A low-twist, ply silk yarn formed by combining two or three single strands.

trilobal A fiber with a modified cross section having three lobes.

tropical suiting A lightweight plain-weave suiting for men's and women's summer wear. It has various weaves and is made of a variety of fibers. If called *tropical worsted,* it must be an all wool worsted fabric.

tweed A term derived from the river Tweed in Scotland, where the fabrics were first woven. It is now used to describe a wide range of light to heavy, rough-textured, sturdy fabrics characterized by their mixed color effect. Tweeds can be made of plain, twill, or herringbone weave, in practically any fiber or mixture of fibers.

Tussah silk See *wild silk.*

unbalanced yarns Yarns in which there is sufficient twist to set up a torque effect, so that the yarn will untwist and retwist in the opposite direction.

velour A soft, closely woven, smooth fabric with a short, thick pile. It is named for the French word for velvet. Velour is often made of cotton, wool, or mohair.

velvet A fabric with a short, soft, thick, warp-pile surface, usually made of silk or man-made pile fiber with a cotton back. It is sometimes made of all silk or all cotton. The fabric is often woven double, face to face, and then, while still on the loom, it is cut apart by a small shuttle knife. There are several varieties of velvet, which differ in weight, closeness of pile, and transparency.

virgin wool New wool that is made into yarns and fabrics for the first time.

voile A sheer, transparent, soft, lightweight plain-weave fabric made of highly twisted yarns. It can be composed of wool, cotton, silk, or a man-made fiber. Voile is used for blouses, dresses, curtains, and similar items.

waffle cloth A fabric with a characteristic honeycomb weave. When made in cotton it is called waffle piqué. It is used for coatings, draperies, dresses, and toweling.

wale A column of loops that are parallel to the loop axis and to the long measurement of a knit fabric.

warp yarns Yarns that run parallel to the *selvage* or long dimension of a fabric.

waste silk See *silk noil.*

weft yarns See *filling yarns.*

whipcord A twill-weave fabric similar to *gabardine* but with a more pronounced diagonal rib on the right side. It is so named because it simulates the lash of a whip. Cotton whipcords are often four-harness warp-twill weaves.

wickability The property of a fiber that allows moisture to move rapidly along the fiber surface and pass quickly through the fabric.

wild silk   Silk produced by moths of species other than *Bombyx mori*. It is tan to brown in color and is coarser and more uneven than ordinary silk. It is usually called *Tussah silk*.

woof yarns   See *filling yarns*.

zibeline   A fabric made of wool, cotton, camel hair, mohair, or man-made fibers. It is characterized by a long, sleek nap brushed, steamed, and pressed in one direction, thus hiding the underlying satin weave.

Bibliography

Books

Alexander, Peter, Robert Hudson, and Christopher Earland. *Wool, Its Chemistry and Physics.* New York: Reinhold Publishing Corporation, 1963.

American Fabrics Encyclopedia of Textiles, 2d ed. New York: Prentice-Hall, Inc., 1972.

Analytic Methods for a Textile Laboratory, J. W. Weaver, ed. Research Triangle Park, N.C.: American Association of Textile Chemists and Colorists, 1968.

ASTM Standards, Part 32, "Textile Materials." Philadelphia: American Society for Testing and Materials, 1974 (published annually).

ASTM Standards, Part 33, Textile Materials." Philadelphia: American Society for Testing and materials, 1974 (published annually).

Baity, Elizabeth C. *Man Is a Weaver.* New York: The Viking Press, Inc., 1949.

Bendure, Z., and G. Pfeiffer. *American Fabrics.* New York: The Macmillan Company, 1947.

Brown, H. B., and J. O. Ware. *Cotton.* New York: McGraw-Hill, Inc., 1958.

Buresh, Francis M. *Nonwoven Fabrics.* New York: Reinhold Publishing Corporation, 1962.

Carroll-Porczynski, C. Z. *Manual of Man-Made Fibers.* New York: Chemical Publishing Company, Inc., 1961.

———. *Natural Polymer Man-Made Fibers.* New York: Academic Press, Inc., 1959.

Cook, J. Gordon. *Handbook of Polyolefin Fibres.* London: Merrow Publishing Company, 1967.

———. *Handbook of Textile Fibres,* 2 Vols. London: Merrow Publishing Company, 1968.

Cotton from Field to Fabric, 5th ed. Memphis, Tenn.: National Cotton Council, 1951.

Cowan, Mary L., and Martha E. Jungerman. *Introduction to Textiles.* New York: Appleton-Century-Crofts, 1969.

Crawford, M. D. C. *The Heritage of Cotton.* New York: G. P. Putnam's Sons, 1924.

Dembeck, Adeline A. *Guidebook to Man-Made Textile Fibers*

& Textured Yarns of the World, 3d ed. New York: United Price Dye Works, 1969.

Encyclopedia of Polymer Science and Technology, H. F. Mark, N. G. Gaylord, and N. M. Bikales, eds. 15 Vols. New York: Wiley-Interscience, 1964–1971.

Grover, E. B., and D. S. Hamby, *Handbook of Textile Testing and Quality Control.* New York: Interscience Publishers, Inc., 1959.

Hall, A. J. *The Standard Handbook of Textiles.* New York: Chemical Publishing Company, Inc., 1970.

———. *Textile Finishing,* 3d ed. New York: Chemical Publishing Company, Inc., 1966.

Hamby, Dame S., ed. *The American Cotton Handbook,* 2 Vols., 3d ed. New York: Wiley-Interscience, 1965.

Handbook of Asbestos Textiles, 2d ed. Philadelphia: Asbestos Institute, 1961.

Harries & Harries. *Textiles, Decision Making for the Consumer.* New York: McGraw-Hill, 1974.

Harris, J. C. *Detergency Evaluation and Testing.* New York: Interscience Publishers, Inc., 1954.

Harris, Milton, ed. *Handbook of Textile Fibers.* New York: Textile Book Publishers, Inc., 1954.

Hathorne, Berkeley L. *Woven, Stretch, and Textured Fabrics.* New York: John Wiley & Sons, Inc., 1964.

Hess, Katherine P. *Textile Fibers and Their Uses,* 6th ed. Philadelphia: J. B. Lippincott Co., 1958.

Hollen, M., and J. Saddler. *Modern Textiles,* 4th ed. New York: The Macmillan Company, 1973.

Hoye, John. *Staple Cotton Fabrics.* New York: McGraw-Hill, Inc., 1942.

Joseph, Marjory L. *Introductory Textile Science,* 2d ed. New York: Holt, Rinehart & Winston, 1972.

Kaswell, E. R. *Handbook of Industrial Textiles.* New York: Wellington Sears, 1964.

———. *Textile Fibers, Yarns, and Fabrics.* New York: Reinhold Publishing Corporation, 1953.

Klapper, Marvin. *Fabric Almanac.* New York: Fairchild Publications, Inc., 1966.

Kornreich, E. *Introduction to Fibres and Fabrics.* New York: American Elsevier Publishing Company, Inc., 1966.

Krcma, Radko. *Nonwoven Textiles.* Manchester: Textile Trade Press, 1967.

LaBarthe, Jules. *Textiles: Origins to Usage.* New York: The Macmillan Company, 1964.

Lancashire, J. B. *Jacquard Design and Knitting.* New York: National Knitted Outerwear Association, 1969.

Leggett, W. F. *Story of Linen.* New York: Chemical Publishing Company, Inc., 1945.

———. *Story of Wool.* New York: Chemical Publishing Company, Inc., 1947.

Linton, G. E. *Applied Basic Textiles.* New York: Duell, Sloane & Pearce-Meredith Press, 1966.

———. *The Modern Textile and Apparel Dictionary,* 4th ed. New York: Textile Book Service, 1973.

———. *Natural and Manmade Textile Fibers.* New York: Duell, Sloane & Pearce-Meredith Press, 1966.

Linton, G. E., and H. Cohen. *Chemistry and Textiles for the Laundry Industry.* New York: Textile Book Publishers, 1959.

Lynn, J. E., and J. J. Press. *Advances in Textile Processing.* New York: Textile Book Publishers, 1961.

Lyons, John W. *The Chemistry and Uses of Fire Retardants.* New York: Wiley-Interscience, 1970.

Man-Made Textile Encyclopedia. J. J. Press, ed. New York: Textile Book Publishers, Inc., 1959.

Mark, H. F., S. M. Atlas, and E. Cernia. *Made-Made Fibers,* 3 Vols. New York: Interscience Publishers, Inc., 1968.

Marsh, J. T. *Textile Finishing,* 2d ed. Metuchen, N.J.: Textile Book Service, 1966.

Matthews, J. M., and H. R. Mauersberger. *Textile Fibers,* 6th ed. New York: John Wiley & Sons, Inc., 1954.

Moncrieff, R. W. *Man-Made Fibers,* 6th ed. New York: John Wiley & Sons, Inc., 1975.

Morton, Maurice. *Introduction to Rubber Technology.* New York: Reinhold Publishing Corporation, 1959.

Moss, A. J. Ernest. *Textiles and Fabrics.* New York: Chemical Publishing Company, Inc., 1961.

Pizzuto, J. J. *101 Weaves in 101 Fabrics.* New York: Textile Press, 1961.

Pizzuto, J. J., and P. L. D'Alessandro. *101 Fabrics.* New York: Textile Press, 1952.

Potter, M. D., and B. P. Corbman. *Textiles: Fiber to Fabric,* 5th ed. New York: McGraw-Hill, Inc., 1975.

Reichman, Charles. *Double Knit Fabric Manual.* New York: National Knitted Outerwear Association, 1961.

———. *Knitted Stretch Technology.* New York: National Knitted Outerwear Association, 1965.

———. *Knitting Dictionary.* New York: National Knitted Outerwear Association, 1966.

Reichman, Charles, J. B. Lancashire, and K. D. Darlington. *Knitted Fabric Primer.* New York: National Knitted Outerwear Association, 1967.

Reisfeld, A. *Warp Knit Engineering.* New York: National Knitted Outerwear Association, 1966.

Silk. New York: Japan Silk Institute, 1962.

Skinkle, J. H. *Textile Testing, Physical, Chemical, Microscopial,* 2d ed. New York: Chemical Publishing Company, Inc., 1949.

Stout, Evelyn E. *Introduction to Textiles,* 3d ed. New York: John Wiley & Sons, Inc., 1970.

Swirles, Frank M. *Handbook of Basic Fabrics, 2d ed.* Los Angeles: Swirles & Co., 1962.

Technology of Synthetic Fibers, Samuel B. MacFarlane, ed. New York: Fairchild Publications, Inc., 1953.

Textile Fibers and Their Properties. Greensboro, N.C.: Burlington Industries, 1972.

Textile Handbook, 5th ed. Washington, D.C.: American Home Economics Association, 1975.

Textiles, A Visual Experience. Springs Mills, Inc., Fort Mill, S.C.: 1974. (6 sequences)

Trotman, E. R. *Dyeing & Chemical Technology of Textile Fibers,* 4th ed. Metuchen, N.J.: Textile Book Services, 1970.

Von Bergen, Werner. *Wool Handbook,* Vol. 1, 3d ed. New York: Wiley-Interscience, 1963.

————. *Wool Handbook,* Vol. 2, Part 1, 3d ed. New York: Wiley-Interscience, 1969.

————. *Wool Handbook,* Vol. 2, Part 2, 3d ed. New York: Wiley-Interscience, 1970.

Walton, Perry. *The Story of Textiles.* New York: Tudor Publishing Co., 1936.

Ward, D. T. *Tufting: An Introduction.* London: Textile Business Press, 1969.

Wingate, Isabel. *Dictionary of Textiles.* New York: Fairchild Publications, Inc., 1967.

————. *Textile Fabrics,* 6th ed. Englewood Cliffs, N.J.: Prentice-Hall, Inc., 1970.

Recommended Periodicals

This list is not comprehensive but includes those periodicals that are of particular interest to the textile student.

American Dyestuff Reporter
American Fabrics Magazine
America's Textile Reporter
Ciba Review
Journal of the Society of Dyers and Colourists
Journal of the Textile Institute
Knitting Times
Modern Textiles
Textile Bulletin
Textile Chemist and Colorist
Textile Industries
Textile Month
Textile Organon
Textile Research Journal
Textile World

Index